"新视界"职业教育
旅游文化系列教程

总主编
总主审

Potential Guests from Afar:
A Survey of Major
Tourist Resource Countries

客源国概况

主 编 朱 英 聂 红
副主编 杨 君 王 榛 黄东梅
编 者
Adam Lane McLemore（美） 于 浣
王一冰 王 榛 朱 英 李政佐 陈 静
杨 君 杨春秀 钟 敏 黄东梅 聂 红
殷 琪 骆吉锟 谢 林

重庆大学出版社

图书在版编目（CIP）数据

客源国概况：汉、英 / 朱英, 聂红主编. -- 重庆：
重庆大学出版社, 2021.8

"新视界"职业教育旅游文化系列教程

ISBN 978-7-5689-2812-0

Ⅰ.①客… Ⅱ.①朱…②聂… Ⅲ.①旅游客源—中
国—教材—汉、英 Ⅳ.①F592.6

中国版本图书馆CIP数据核字（2021）第121441号

"新视界"职业教育旅游文化系列教程

客源国概况

主 编 朱 英 聂 红

责任编辑：陈 亮　　版式设计：陈 亮

责任校对：夏 宇　　责任印制：赵 晟

*

重庆大学出版社出版发行

出版人：饶帮华

社址：重庆市沙坪坝区大学城西路21号

邮编：401331

电话：（023）88617190　88617185（中小学）

传真：（023）88617186　88617166

网址：http://www.cqup.com.cn

邮箱：fxk@cqup.com.cn（营销中心）

全国新华书店经销

重庆共创印务有限公司印刷

*

开本：787mm×1092mm　1/16　印张：17.75　字数：551千

2021年8月第1版　2021年8月第1次印刷

ISBN 978-7-5689-2812-0　定价：52.00元

本书如有印刷、装订等质量问题，本社负责调换

总　序

当前，提高教育教学质量已成为我国高等职业教育的核心问题，而教育教学质量的提高与职业院校内部的诸多因素有关，如办学理念、师资水平、课程体系、实践条件、生源质量以及教育质量监控与评价机制等。在这些因素中，不管从教育学理论还是从教育实践来看，课程体系都是一个非常重要的因素，而教材作为课程教学的基础载体，是"三教"改革的重要组成部分，是职业教育改革的基础。

2019年《国家职业教育改革实施方案》的颁布以及2020年"中国特色高水平高职学校和专业建设计划"的启动，标志着我国职业教育进入了新一轮的改革与发展阶段，课程建设与教学改革再次成为高职院校建设和发展的核心工作。职业教育教材作为课程建设与教学改革的重要组成部分，不但对学生的培养质量起着关键作用，也决定着学校的核心竞争力和可持续发展能力。

2020年10月，由重庆青年职业技术学院和绵阳职业技术学院牵头成立了"成渝地区双城经济圈文化和旅游产教联盟"（以下简称"联盟"），旨在切实提高成渝地区旅游类专业人才培养质量，推动成渝地区文化和旅游产业协同发展，共同为职业教育添彩，为文化旅游赋能。

联盟与重庆大学出版社组织策划和出版的"'新视界'职业教育旅游文化系列教程"（以下简称"系列教程"），以多所职业院校的课程改革成果为基础，具有以下特点：

一、强调校企"双元"合作开发，注重学生职业核心能力培育

系列教程紧跟旅游产业发展趋势和行业人才需求，以典型岗位（群）的职业技能要求为目标，以"掌握基础、深化内容、理实结合、培养能力"为宗旨；关注旅游行业新业态、新模式，实时对接产业发展"新工艺、新技术、新规范"的要求；吸收旅游行业企业管理者深度参与，实现校企合作，强化学生专业技艺培养。

二、遵循学生职业能力培养的基本规律，增强学生就业竞争力

系列教程紧密结合岗位（群）技能对职业素质的要求，突出针对性和实用性，综合各位职教专家和老师提出的宝贵意见，教学设计中有机融入创新精神和自主学习内容，培养学生思辨、实践的能力。

三、坚持以立德树人为根本任务，思政教育贯穿教材编写

系列教程始终注重知识传授与价值引领相结合，始终将思政教育置于课程教学目标首位，有意、有机、有效地融入思政元素。根据课程特点、教学内容，梳理各自蕴含的思政点，以文本、视频、实践、心得书写等方式嵌入教材中，实现专业课程教育与思政教育同向同行。

四、建立普适性多媒体教学资源，以学生喜闻乐见的形式凸显理论和实践任务

系列教程强化"学习资料"功能，弱化"教学材料"属性。根据每门课程的内容特点，配套数字化教学资源库，提供电子教学课件、教学素材资源、教学网站支持等；注重活页式、工作手册式新型教材开发，实现教材立体化、多功能作用，为学生即时学习和个性化学习提供支撑。

随着职业教育发展的不断深入，创新型教材建设是一项长期而艰巨的任务。本系列教程的编写，除了相关职业院校老师们辛勤的耕耘奉献，也得到了联盟成员中诸多旅游企业的积极参与和大力支持，在此致以诚挚的谢意！

由于水平所限，不足之处在所难免，教程编写委员会殷切期望各位同行和使用者提出宝贵意见，让我们一起为职业教育的蓬勃发展贡献力量。

"'新视界'职业教育旅游文化系列教程"编写委员会
2021年7月

前　言

　　《客源国概况》由"全国首批国家示范性高等职业院校""中国特色高水平高职学校建设单位"四川工程职业技术学院和南充文化旅游职业学院外语系和旅游管理系一线教师编写。教材紧扣《导游服务规范（2011年版）》《现代酒店服务质量管理职业技能等级标准（2021年版）》和教育部《高等职业教育专科英语课程标准（2021年版）》，结合高职学生英语实际水平及未来职业岗位需求，基于编写团队多年从事高职英语教学实践的经验，以及对职业教育旅游类专业新趋势、新内涵的新思考，力图既讲清国家知识，又贴近学生旅游专业和提升学生在旅游各环节运用英语的实际能力。

　　旅游业是全球经济增长的重要引擎。据世界旅游理事会 (WTTC)发布的《2019各国旅游业对经济的影响和趋势》的报告显示，2018年，旅游业为全球经济贡献8.8万亿美元，相当于全球GDP的10.4%。世界各地有超3.19亿人口的工作是依赖旅游业提供的，占所有就业人口的10.0%。2014~2018年，旅游行业为全球新增就业数量贡献了1/5。预测显示，未来10年全球旅游行业将新增1亿个就业岗位。这意味着在未来十年内，旅游行业将创造1/4的新就业机会。而入境旅游一直都在习近平总书记和党中央的战略视野中，从亚洲文明对话大会、"一带一路"国际合作高峰论坛、亚太经济合作组织、上海合作组织等多边框架，到中国与俄罗斯、欧盟、东盟、新西兰等双边旅游年，再到中日高级别人文交流磋商机制，入境旅游推广和国际旅游合作一直都是中央政府关注的话题。旅游是构架不同文明交流互鉴和发展的桥梁，旅游从业者要当好桥梁守护人；引导学生认识文明的多样性，对多元文化进行辨析鉴赏；帮助学生树立"旅行天下，游贯古今"的豪迈志向，同时又具备用英语这种世界语言，表达中国话语，讲好中国故事的能力。基于以上情况，教材精心策划，在充分结合国家知识、英语和旅游专业的基础上，在内容、编排和细节上体现模块化、任务化、多元化、风格化的编写特色。

一、编写特色

1. 模块化

　　教材突破传统的国家地理、气候、经济、政治、历史、文化、民俗和旅游景点等内容，将每个国家的相应内容进行有机融合，形成"基本国情""特色国情""文化互鉴"和"专业任务"模块。"基本国情"和"特色国情"模块涵盖国家知识，"文化互鉴"模块在国家知识基础上进行延伸，培养学生思辨能力和坚定"四个自信"，"专业任务"模块将学生的国家知识、语言能力和旅游服务能力"三合一"进行综合训练，培养个性化、定制化服务意识和能力。各模块以"5C"为主线，从国家内容（Content）知识入手，分析文化

（Culture）异同，认识到不同文化因交流（Communication）而互鉴发展，对待不同的文化需要有思辨能力（Critical Thinking），在思辨过程中树立对中国道路、理论、制度、文化的自信（Confidence）。

2.任务化

教材按照旅游的吃、住、行、游、购、娱环节，在和企业进行充分研讨的情况下将专业任务模块划分为"送机—前台接待—客房服务—餐厅就餐—导游词—特色购物—机场送机"7个任务，每7个国家形成一个任务闭环，共3组任务闭环，每一闭环中相同任务在不同组别中各有侧重，让学生在各个环节的能力呈螺旋上升式发展。

3.多元化

考虑到高职学生的英语水平和学习习惯，教材在呈现方式和学习方法引导上尽量给学生提供多元方式。国家开篇热身练习以慕课、音频、视频等多种形式导入，既能帮助学生了解国家知识，又能练习听力。在国家知识部分，先以中文介绍引入，再以英文简表形式概述，最后以英文的"基本国情""特色国情"和"文化互鉴"部分展开和深入，中间辅以二维码提供丰富信息，以多元的呈现方式让学生全方位了解各国，并进行深入思考。同时，思维导图和"KWL（Know-Wonder-Learned）"表格让老师和学生在课前和课后都能方便使用，满足多元教学和学习需求。

4.风格化

教材编写过程中，编写团队在介绍各个国家的每一个环节都力求细致，让学生在不知不觉中能感受到旅游的小知识。各个国家开篇从各个大城市或世界知名大城市到该国的航班飞行时长告诉学生该国和中国以及其他国家的空间距离，在"基本国情"语言部分，每个国家都提供了用当地语言打招呼的方式方法，既有趣也能让学生在今后旅游服务工作中有意识地应用。在"特色国情"部分，教材不仅提炼了每个国家最具特色的内容，且在文末附上了该国旅游官方图标，让学生在不知不觉中感受旅游宣传的魅力。每个国家以人物结束，在人物的选择上，既有获得国家友谊勋章的外国友人，也有在历史上对文化交流互鉴做出巨大贡献的人物，还有如今在体育、经济等领域有重要影响的人物，通过该国人物篇的引领，让读者感受到文化的美人其美，美美与共的魅力，而旅游就是一座架起不同文化互鉴交流的魅力桥梁。

二、教材内容

全书共7章，第一章系统阐述旅游业和中国入境游市场，第二章至第七章重点介绍亚洲地区、大洋洲地区、美洲地区、欧洲地区、非洲地区和中东地区，包括泰国、新加坡、印度尼西亚、马来西亚、越南、韩国、日本、印度、新西兰、澳大利亚、美国、加拿大、巴西、英国、法国、德国、意大利、俄罗斯、埃及、南非、阿拉伯联合酋长国等21个国内入境游市场中的主要客源国家概况。全书内容丰富，中英文结合，适用性强。

本教材不仅适合高职旅游专业学生使用，也适合非旅游专业学生作为选修课教材使用，同时也适合旅游从业人员作为参考书使用。

《客源国概况》编写团队

2021年5月

致同学们的一封信

亲爱的同学们：

欢迎使用"新视界"职业教育旅游文化系列教程之《客源国概况》。作为长期工作在旅游英语教学一线的老师，我们希望这本教材能带着大家"一看""二感""三悟"，帮助你们打开通往世界的大门。

一从基本国情（Basic Facts）、特色国情（Unique Features）两个方面来看看世界不同旅游区主要客源国家的自然地理、历史人物、政治经济、民俗文化，比如走进"微笑之邦"泰国，了解"日不落帝国"的前世和今生，聆听美利坚合众国诞生之时的《独立宣言》，欣赏震撼人心的新西兰，掀起神秘中东世界的面纱……二从英文特色"5C"和"The Land and the World"阅读来深刻感受各客源国家的特色和差异，探寻它们在历史发展长河中与中国千丝万缕的联系，在比较和联系中感受到中华文化的博大精深、源远流长以及其对世界各国的影响。三从旅游专业角度悟出如何结合各个客源国情况更好地设计专业任务，服务好目标客人群体，并在服务过程中始终立足于中国，做好中国旅游人，架好中国与世界交往的桥梁，让更多客源国客人了解中国，乐游中国，爱上中国。

这本教材既涵盖客源国知识内容的学习，也夯实英语语言能力，还提升旅游专业技能，可谓集"知识内容""语言能力"和"专业技能"于一体，希望大家能充分利用每个国家的"Mind-map"，用英语厘清其内容知识，用"KWL"表格帮助自己形成更为清晰的学习目标，让你的学习事半功倍。

同学们，世界是大家的，中国是我们的。作为新一代大学生，我们需要有走出去的开放姿态，也要有责任和义务去坚守我们的荣耀。学习客源国知识，是为了更好地服务客源国客人，但更为重要的是让我们泱泱五千年的华夏古老之国以仪态万方的步伐迈向世界。

《客源国概况》编写团队

CONTENTS

Chapter 1　Tourism Industry and China Inbound Tourism

Learning Objectives

After this chapter, you will be able to:

★ describe history of tourism.

★ know the major reasons of a better tourism industry.

★ analyze the current development of China inbound tourism.

★ build confidence in China inbound tourism industry.

世界旅游业

　　旅游业是世界经济中持续高速稳定增长的重要战略性、支柱性、综合性产业。旅游活动作为一种有组织、大规模的社会性活动，是世界经济文化交流的一个重要领域，作为人类文明生活方式的一个重要组成部分，是随着世界市场经济的发展和世界政治经济文化体系的形成而逐步产生并不断发展起来的。

　　虽然古希腊人和古罗马人在很早以前就开始了长距离的贸易活动，但是真正意义上的旅游活动是近百年才出现的事情。近代旅游业发端于19世纪中叶的西欧和北美，伴随着火车和轮船的出现，19世纪六七十年代，西欧和北美出现了专门组织国内和跨国旅游的旅行社。从19世纪后期起，旅游活动的主体从少数的贵族、僧侣、商贾、政要、探险家、科学家扩大到以观光休闲和商务活动为主要目的的富裕市民，旅游的范围从国内向跨国、跨洲发展。

　　据世界旅游理事会 (WTTC)发布的《2019各国旅游业对经济的影响和趋势》的报告显示，2018年，旅游业为全球经济贡献8.8万亿美元，相当于全球GDP的10.4%。世界各地有超3.19亿人口的工作是依赖旅游业提供的，占所有就业人口的10.0%。2014~2018年，旅游行业为全球新增就业数量贡献了1/5。预测显示，未来10年全球旅游行业将新增1亿个就业岗位。这意味着在未来十年内，旅游行业将创造1/4的新就业机会。尽管2020年新冠肺炎疫情对旅游业带来了巨大冲击，但随着疫情得到进一步控制，旅游业必将成为带动全球经济复苏的重要引擎。作为全球公认的朝阳产业，旅行与旅游业孕育着蓬勃的发展生机。

World Tourism Organizations

UNWTO: United Nations World Tourism Organization (联合国世界旅游组织)
- **Formation**: November 1, 1974
- **Headquarters**: Madrid, Spain
- **Head**: Secretary-General Zurab Pololikashvili

WTTC: World Travel and Tourism Council (世界旅游理事会)
- **Formation**: 1990
- **Headquarters**: London, United Kingdom
- **Key People**: Christopher J Nassetta, Chairman
  Gloria Guevara, President, CEO

PART I   Overview of World Tourism

Tourism is travel for pleasure or business; also the theory and practice of touring, the business of attracting, accommodating (住宿), and entertaining tourists, and the business of operating tours. The United Nations World Tourism Organization (UNWTO) defines tourism more generally, in terms which go "beyond the common perception of tourism as being limited to holiday activity only", as people "traveling to and staying in places outside their usual environment for not more than one consecutive year for leisure and not less than 24 hours, business and other purposes". It boosts the revenue of the economy, creates thousands of jobs, develops the infrastructures of a country, and plants a sense of cultural exchange between foreigners and citizens. Generally, there are three basic forms of tourism: domestic tourism, inbound (入境的) tourism, and outbound (出境的) tourism.

• The History of Tourism and Travel

Travel dates back to antiquity where wealthy Greeks and Romans would travel for leisure to their summer homes and villas in cities such as Pompeii (庞培) and Baiae (巴亚). While early travel tended to be slower, more dangerous, and more dominated by trade and migration.

Travel in the Middle Ages offered hardships and challenges. However, it was important to the economy and to society. Pilgrimages were common in both the Europe and Islamic world and involved streams of travelers both locally and internationally.

In the late 16th century it became fashionable for young European aristocrats and wealthy upper-class men to travel to significant European cities as part of their education in the arts and literature. This was known as the Grand Tour. It included cities such as London, Paris, Venice, Florence, and Rome. However, The French Revolution brought with it the end of the Grand Tour.

Modern tourism originated in the middle of the 19th century in Western Europe and North America. Thanks to the advent of the train and the steamboat, the 1860s and 1870s saw the emergence of travel agencies in Western Europe and North America that specialized in organizing domestic and international tours. Starting in the late 19th century, the main body of tourism expanded from a few nobles, merchants, monks, politicians, scientists and explorers to the common people. But the really big international tourism came after World War Ⅱ.

After World War Ⅱ, the theme of the world shifted from war and revolution to peace and development, and western countries vigorously developed their economy. The rapid development of economy brings with it the improvement of living standard, the development of transportation and the generation and development of paid vacation, which makes people's demand for tourism increasingly enhanced. In addition, tourism with the purpose of sightseeing and business investigation has become the new main body of tourism activities, and the scope of tourism has also developed from local areas to transnational and trans-state.

· *The Importance of Travel and Tourism*

Travel and tourism is vital for many countries. It enriches communities at a faster rate than the overall economy. For example, between 2011 and 2019, Southeast Asia recorded the fastest annual growth rate in travel and tourism GDP per capita at 6.7 percent compared to the region's 3.7 percent overall economic growth. The Middle East saw 3 percent travel and tourism GDP per capita growth compared to just 0.3 percent for the overall region's economy.

A booming tourism industry helps to build infrastructure such as roads, parks, hospitals, schools and community areas. It also helps to preserve heritage sites, natural wonders, and precious cultures, by creating space for people to showcase their cultural traditions and protect sacred areas.

· *World Travel and Tourism Figures*

Figure 1   Direct and Total Contributions of Travel and Tourism to GDP from 2006 to 2019

Year	Direct Contribution (in Billion US Dollars)	Total Contribution (in Billion US Dollars)
2006	1,629.02	5,160.35
2007	1,809.37	5,765.03
2008	1,928.47	6,259.57
2009	1,794.88	5,803.03
2010	1,911.51	6,108.56
2011	2,157.06	6,925.29
2012	2,207.37	7,094.29
2013	2,304.81	7,432.19
2014	2,388.31	7,674.79
2015	2,320.93	7,444.04
2016	2,381.10	7,650.17
2017	2,567.88	8,240.74
2018	2,750.65	8,810.96
2019	2,892.94	9,258.29

Source: From Statista

Figure 2   Direct Contribution of Travel and Tourism to GDP in Leading Countries in 2019
（in Billion US Dollars）

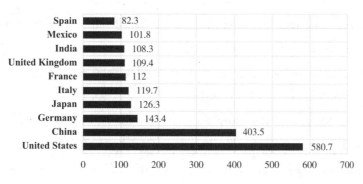

Source: From Statista

Figure 3   Outbound Travel and Tourism Expenditure in Leading Countries in 2019
（in Billion US Dollars）

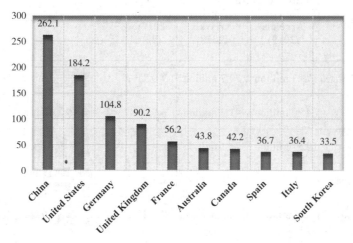

Source: From Statista

Figure 4   Countries with the Highest Employment in Travel and Tourism Industry in 2019
（in Thousand Persons）

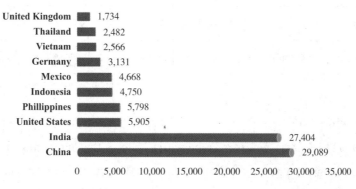

Source: From Statista

• *Overview of World Tourist Areas*

Americas

Although the American continent holds only third rank in world tourist destinations, after Europe and the Asia-Pacific region, tourism in the Americas is nevertheless an important phenomenon, with 210.9 million international arrivals for 2017, representing 16 percent of world tourist arrivals according to UNWTO in 2018.

However, on the scale of the entire continent, the tourist development of areas is, for geo-historical, cultural, economic and political reasons, a patchy (分布不均的), unequal process. The majority of tourist arrivals is concentrated in North America, with 137 million arrivals for 2017, whereas, for the same period, there were only 36.7 million in South America, 26 million in the Caribbean and 11.2 million in Central America.

Figure 5　The Top 10 Destinations in Americas

Rank	Destination	International Tourist Arrivals (2019)	International Tourist Arrivals (2018)	Change (2018 to 2019) (%)	Rank	Region	International Tourism Receipts (2019) (in Million US Dollar)
1	United States	79.3 million	79.7 million	▼0.5	1	United States	214,134
2	Mexico	45.0 million	41.3 million	▲9.0	2	Canada	28,012
3	Canada	22.1 million	21.1 million	▲4.7	3	Mexico	24,573
4	Argentina	7.4 million	6.9 million	▲7.2	4	Dominican Republic	7,468
5	Dominican Republic	6.4 million	6.6 million	▼3.2	5	Brazil	5,995
6	Brazil	6.3 million	6.6 million	▼4.1	6	Colombia	5,652
7	Chile	4.5 million	5.7 million	▼17.5	7	Argentina	5,241
8	Peru	4.35 million	4.4 million	▼1.1	8	Panama	4,521
9	Cuba	4.3 million	4.7 million	▼8.5	9	Bahamas	4,126
10	Colombia	4.2 million	4.0 million	▲0.3	10	Costa Rica	4,010

Source: From United Nations World Tourism Organization

Asia and the Pacific

"UNWTO/GTERC Asia Tourism Trends-2018" shows that international tourist arrivals in Asia and the Pacific grew 6 percent in 2017 to reach 323 million, around a quarter of the world's total. Of all world regions, Asia and the Pacific, the second-most visited after Europe, has grown the fastest in international tourist arrivals since 2005. Arrivals increased an average of 6 percent per year, above the world average of 4 percent.

Asia and the Pacific plays a vital role as a source market, fueling much growth in both regional and long-haul destinations. The region produced 335 million international travelers spending US$ 502 billion in 2017, 37 percent of the world total. Around 80 percent of these visits were concentrated in Asia destinations.

Figure 6　The Top 10 Destinations in Asia and the Pacific

Rank	Destination	International Tourist Arrivals (2019)	International Tourist Arrivals (2018)	Change (2018 to 2019) (%)	Rank	Region	International Tourism Receipts (2019) (in Million US Dollar)
1	China	65.7 million	62.9 million	▲4.5	1	Thailand	60,521
2	Thailand	39.8 million	38.2 million	▲4.2	2	Japan	46,054
3	Japan	32.2 million	31.2 million	▲3.2	3	Australia	45,709
4	Malaysia	26.1 million	25.8 million	▲1.2	4	Macau, China	40,060
5	Hong Kong, China	23.8 million	29.3 million	▼18.8	5	China	35,832
6	Macau, China	18.6 million	18.5 million	▲0.5	6	India	30,720
7	Vietnam	18.0 million	15.5 million	▲16.1	7	Hong Kong, China	29,043
8	India	17.9 million	17.4 million	▲2.9	8	South Korea	21,628
9	South Korea	17.5 million	15.3 million	▲14.4	9	Singapore	20,052
10	Indonesia	15.5 million	13.4 million	▲15.7	10	Malaysia	19,823

Source: From United Nations World Tourism Organization

Europe

The outstanding growth industry of tourism—supplementing business, professional, and student travel—brings employment and foreign exchange to many Europeans, especially in the Mediterranean countries, with their combination of sunshine, beaches, scenery, and historical monuments. The world-renowned cities of Europe attract large numbers of tourists as well. In fact, European countries are consistently among the top tourist destinations of the world; they draw visitors from within Europe as well as from other continents. Regardless, the travel and tourism sector has had a positive impact on the European economy, directly contributing an estimated 782 billion euros to GDP in 2018.

Figure 7   The Top 10 Destinations in Europe

Rank	Destination	International Tourist Arrivals (2019)	International Tourist Arrivals (2018)	Change (2018 to 2019) (%)	Rank	Region	International Tourism Receipts (2019) (in Million US Dollar)
1	France	—	89.4 million	—	1	Spain	79,714
2	Spain	83.7 million	82.8 million	▲1.1	2	France	63,801
3	Italy	64.5 million	61.6 million	▲4.7	3	United Kingdom	50,437
4	Turkey	51.2 million	45.8 million	▲11.8	4	Italy	49,596
5	Germany	39.6 million	38.9 million	▲18.8	5	Germany	41,638
6	United Kingdom	39.4 million	38.7 million	▲1.8	6	Turkey	29,829
7	Austria	31.9 million	30.8 million	▲3.6	7	Austria	22,942
8	Greece	31.3 million	30.1 million	▲4.0	8	Portugal	20,351
9	Portugal	24.6 million	22.8 million	▲7.9	9	Greece	20,351
10	Russia	24.4 million	24.6 million	▼0.8	10	Netherlands	18,487

Source: From United Nations World Tourism Organization

Africa

Tourism is one of the largest industries worldwide and provides 7 percent of Africa's GDP. It indirectly employs 24.6 million people across the continent (6.8 percent of total employment). International visitors show more interest in tourism beyond safaris (陆路旅行). Airbnb was rapidly expanding in Africa and the first Airbnb Africa Travel Summit was held in the Cape Town (开普敦) township of Langa in 2018. Ethiopian Airlines had been offering new routes to develop pan-African travel and helped make Addis Ababa (亚的斯亚贝巴，埃塞俄比亚首都), a key tourist gateway for all of Africa.

Figure 8   The Top 10 Destinations in Africa

Rank	Destination	International Tourist Arrivals (2019)	International Tourist Arrivals (2018)	Change (2018 to 2019) (%)	Rank	Region	International Tourism Receipts (2019) (in Million US Dollar)
1	Egypt*	13.0 million	11.3 million	▲15.0	1	Egypt	13,030
2	Morocco	12.9 million	12.3 million	▲4.9	2	South Africa	8,384

Continued

Rank	Destination	International Tourist Arrivals (2019)	International Tourist Arrivals (2018)	Change (2018 to 2019) (%)	Rank	Region	International Tourism Receipts (2019) (in Million US Dollar)
3	South Africa	10.2 million	10.5 million	▼2.9	3	Morocco	8,179
4	Tunisia	9.4 million	8.3 million	▲13.3	4	Tanzania	2,605
5	Algeria	2.4 million	2.7 million	▼11.1	5	Tunisia	2,116
6	Zimbabwe	2.3 million	2.6 million	▼11.5	6	Mauritius	1,779
7	Mozambique	2.0 million	2.7 million	▲25.9	7	Uganda	1,463
8	Ivory Coast	—	2.0 million	—	8	Nigeria	1,449
9	Kenya	—	1.9 million	—	9	Ghana	1,425
10	Botswana	—	1.7 million	—	10	Kenya*	1,072
Note: Egypt is classified under "Middle East" in the UNWTO.					Note: Number for Kenya is for 2018.		

Source: From United Nations World Tourism Organization

Middle East

Over the past decade, the Middle East has developed into a global hub for tourism and leisure. Visitors are attracted to the region's retail offerings, hotels, beaches, and unique experiences such as a trip to the top of Burj Khalifa (哈利法塔), Sheikh Zayed Grand Mosque (谢赫扎伊德教堂) in the UAE, Museum of Islamic Art in Qatar (卡塔尔) and the old-fashioned souks (露天市场) in Oman.

According to the latest Travel and Tourism Competitiveness Index (旅游竞争力指数) elaborated by the World Economic Forum (世界经济论坛), the Middle East outperforms other regions mainly in indicators related to business environment and price competitiveness. The Middle East was the second-best performer in travel and tourism showing an annual growth rate of 5.3 percent in 2019. In terms of nations, Oman showed the best improvement in aspects like international openness and environmental sustainability. Meanwhile, the United Arab Emirate lead in air transport and tourist service infrastructure. In the same way, Saudi Arabia achieved the best overall performance from the region in all the travel and tourism indicators of the report.

Figure 9　The Top 10 Destinations in the Middle East

Rank	Destination	International Tourist Arrivals (2019)	International Tourist Arrivals (2018)	Change (2018 to 2019) (%)	Rank	Region	International Tourism Receipts (2019) (in Million US Dollar)
1	Saudi Arabia	17.5 million	15.5 million	▲12.9	1	United Arab Emirates	21,800
2	United Arab Emirates	16.7 million	15.9 million	▲5.0	2	Saudi Arabia	16,382
3	Egypt	13.0 million	11.3 million	▲15.0	3	Egypt	13,030
4	Iran	9.1 million	7.3 million	▲24.7	4	Lebanon	8,593
5	Israel	4.6 million	4.1 million	▲12.2	5	Israel	7,600
6	Jordan	4.5 million	4.2 million	▲7.1	6	Jordan	5,786
7	Bahrain	3.8 million	4.4 million	▼13.6	7	Qatar	5,442
8	Oman	2.5 million	2.3 million	▲8.7	8	Iran	4,402
9	Qatar	2.1 million	1.8 million	▲16.7	9	Bahrain	3,681
10	Lebanon	1.9 million	2.0 million	▼5.0	10	Iraq	3,593

Source: From United Nations World Tourism Organization

PART II　Tourism Industry in China

Tourism has become an essential contributor to China's domestic economy since the beginning of reform and opening-up in the early eighties. The emergence of an affluent middle class and the development of the infrastructure are both supporting this travel boom. The Chinese tourism market has transformed into one of the world's most-watched inbound and outbound tourist markets. The number of domestic trips reached six billion in 2019, indicating an exponential increase compared to the number of trips made in China ten years ago.

· *China's Inbound and Outbound Tourism*

In recent years, China has witnessed unprecedented development in its tourism industry thanks to the implementation of the reform and opening-up policy.

Inbound tourism is a basic indicator for measuring the comprehensive strength of a country's tourism industry and the level of international competition.

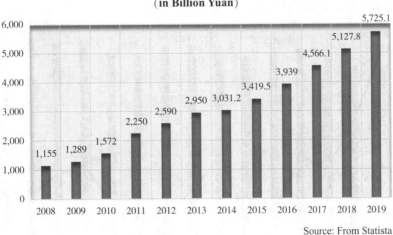

Figure 10　China's Revenue from Tourism from 2008 to 2019
（in Billion Yuan）

Source: From Statista

Among global destinations, China ranks in the top 10 in terms of total inbound tourists. The following ranking by Forbes lists China at No. 4.

Figure 11　The Top 10 Inbound Tourism Countries in 2017　（in Million Persons）

No. 1	France: 86.9	No. 6	Mexico: 39.3
No. 2	Spain: 81.8	No. 7	United Kingdom: 37.7
No. 3	United States: 75.9	No. 8	Turkey: 37.6
No. 4	China: 60.7	No. 9	Germany: 37.5
No. 5	Italy: 58.3	No. 10	Thailand: 35.4

Source: From Forbes

Looking back over the 40-year progress, China's inbound tourism has played a significant role in promoting the national tourism system and establishing the international image. Its outbound tourism has also contributed greatly to the world's economy and well-being.

Since China carried out the reform and opening-up policy in 1978, the number of inbound tourists has increased dramatically. According to data from the China Tourism Academy (CTA), a think tank under the Ministry of Culture and Tourism, and China's National Bureau of Statistics (NBS), the number of inbound tourists reached 139.48 million in 2017, compared with an estimated 1.8 million tourists entering the Chinese mainland in 1978, though there are some drops in the number of tourists during some years.

Still, inbound arrivals to the Chinese mainland reached 29.1 million in 2017, up 3.6 percent on the previous year, bringing in 69.5 billion US dollars of revenue, up 4.1 percent on the previous year, according to CTA's reports.

In particular, the CTA noted that in 2017, an increasing number of inbound tourists were from the Belt and Road countries, meaning that China's Belt and Road Initiative has a great impact on the aforementioned countries.

Figure 12   Inbound Tourist Arrivals and Growth Rate

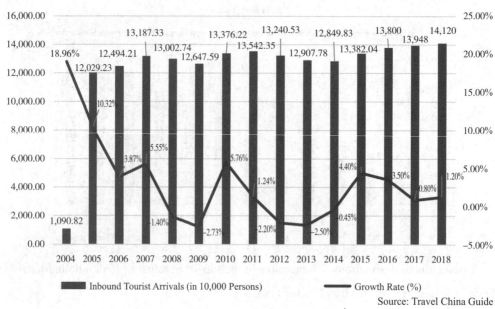

Source: Travel China Guide

Figure 13   China's Outbound and Inbound Tourists

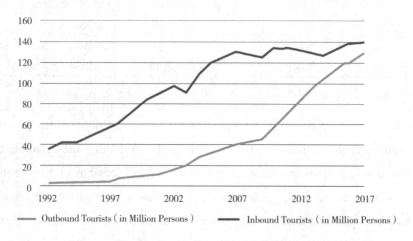

Source: China Tourism Academy, China's National Bureau of Statistics

With regards to the number of China's outbound tourists, as shown in the above info-graphic, the number of outbound tourists has continued to grow steadily since 1992 and is expected to increase in the coming years as it can be forecast from the info-graphic.

In addition, the reports released by the CTA show that outbound tourists spent 115.29 billion US dollars on their trips in 2017 and China's outbound tourism market is estimated to increase by five percent annually on average in the coming years, evidencing that China's outbound tourism has made great contribution to the tourism and economy industries around the globe.

According to the data from the NBS, tourists from Myanmar, Vietnam, Japan, South Korea, the United States and Russia account for the top six foreign visitors to China from 1990 to 2017. For overseas tourists, Hong Kong, Shanghai, Beijing, Macao and Guangzhou are the top five China travel destinations, Travel China Guide reported.

· *China's Tourism Facts and Figures*

Figure 14   China's Tourism Statistics

	Statistics in 2017	**Statistics in 2018**	**Statistics in 2019**
Inbound Tourism	139.48 million trips	141.2 million trips	143 million trips
Inbound Tourism Revenue	USD 123.4 billion	USD 127.1 billion	USD 129.6 billion
Outbound Tourism	130 million trips	149.72 million trips	166 million trips
Domestic Tourism	5001 million trips	5539 million trips	6060 million trips
Domestic Tourism Revenue	CNY 4.57 trillion	CNY 5.13 trillion	CNY 5.6 trillion

Source: From Travel China Guide

Figure 15   Numbers of Tourist Arrivals

	Number of Tourist Arrivals in 2016 (in Million Persons)	**Number of Tourist Arrivals in 2017 (in Million Persons)**	**Number of Tourist Arrivals in 2018 (in Million Persons)**
Total Tourist Arrivals	138	139.48	141.2
Foreign Tourists	28.15	29.17	30.54
Visitors from Hong Kong, China	81.06	79.80	79.37
Visitors from Macau, China	23.50	24.65	25.15
Visitors from Taiwan, China	5.73	5.87	6.14

Source: From Travel China Guide

Figure 16   Top 10 China's Inbound Tourism Destinations in 2018

Order	City	**Number of Tourist Arrivals in 2018 (in Million Persons)**
1	Shenzhen	12.07
2	Guangzhou	9.00
3	Shanghai	8.73
4	Hangzhou	4.02
5	Beijing	3.93
6	Xiamen	3.86
7	Chongqing	3.58
8	Tianjin	3.45
9	Chengdu	3.01
10	Wuhan	2.50

Source: From Travel China Guide

Figure 17   Travel Purpose (2018)

Travel Purpose	Percentage (%)
Sightseeing and leisure	33.5
Working staff	15.5
Meeting/ Business	12.8
Visiting relatives and friends	2.8
Others	35.3

Source: From Travel China Guide

Figure 18   Inbound Tourist Age Group (2018)

Age	Percentage (%)
Under 15	3.4
15-24	13.7
25-44	49.9
45-64	28.4
Over 64	4.6

Source: From Travel China Guide

Task: Draw your mind-map on the "Tourism in My Eyes" page based on the facts of Tourism Industry and China Inbound Tourism and then share with your peers by using your mind-map.

Mind-map: Tourism in My Eyes

Name: _____　　Date: _____

KWL Chart

Topic: _____   Name: _____   Date: _____

Know	Wonder	Learned
What do you think you already know about tourism?	What do you wonder about world tourism market? Write your questions below.	Write what you've learned about tourism.

裁

切

线

Chapter 2 Southeast Asia

Section 1 Thailand

Learning Objectives

A flight to Bangkok is 3 hours from Chongqing, 3.5 hours from Singapore, 7 hours from London and 8.5-13.5 hours from New York depending on the flight connections.

After this section, you will be able to:

★ know the basic facts of Thailand, especially the geographical features, festivals, religion and etiquette.

★ list the typical landmarks and attractions in Thailand.

★ apply Thai social norms, taboos and unique features to serving inbound Thai tourists, making them feel at home.

★ promote the image of Chinese tourism by relating China and Thailand from history, people, culture or etiquette.

"泰"爱微笑之泰国

泰国，素有"黄袍佛国""千佛之国""微笑之国"的美誉，是一个具有两千多年佛教史的文明古国。泰国位于亚洲中南半岛中南部，与柬埔寨、老挝、缅甸、马来西亚接壤，东南临泰国湾（太平洋），西南濒临安达曼海（印度洋），国土面积51.3万平方千米，在东南亚国家中居第三位。

全国共有30多个民族，6900万人口（2020年），泰族为主要民族，占人口总数的40%，通用泰语，90%以上的民众信奉佛教。全国分中部、南部、东部、北部和东北部五个地区，现有77个府。曼谷是泰国的首都和最大城市，为泰国政治、经济、贸易、交通、文化、科技、教育和宗教中心。泰国旅游业开发较早，已经成为该国主要经济来源。"Amazing Thailand Always Amazes You"是泰国旅游对外宣传标语。其旅游资源丰富，基础设施完善，旅游服务也非常周到。主要旅游城市和旅游区有"天使之城"曼谷、"泰北玫瑰"清迈、"东方夏威夷"芭提雅、"泰国明珠"普吉岛、"椰林海岛"苏梅岛和"金汤城池"大城等。别具风味的泰国菜、热带岛屿、泰式传统按摩、古老神秘的寺庙和小清新旅游等都广受欢迎。2017年赴泰中国游客数量超980万人次，泰国已成为许多中国游客出境游首选目的地，可以说是国人出国旅行的"启蒙课堂"。

据统计，1979年泰国来华旅游0.97万人次，发展数十年，到2017年达77.57万人次，2018年达83.3万人次。在影响泰国游客来中国旅游的因素中，中国的悠久历史占比最高，其次是优美的自然风光。那么，面对旅游业非常成熟的泰国潜在客源市场，如何借鉴泰国发达旅游业经验，提供优质上乘服务、体现友善和谐之美、弘扬优秀的中国传统文化等都是值得思考的问题。

Thailand Facts

• **Name**: The Kingdom of Thailand; Thailand

• **Capital**: Bangkok

• **Government**: Constitutional Monarchy

• **The King of Thailand**: Maha Vajiralongkorn, Rama Ⅹ (October, 2016-   )

• **Official Language**: Thai

• **Population**: 69 Million (2020)

• **Currency**: THB 100 ≈ CNY 21.18 (2021)

• **National Symbols**: Elephant, Trollflower

• **Thai New Year**: Songkran (宋干节) (April 13-April 15)

PART I   Let's Go

★ First Glance

Watch the video, and then answer the following questions.

> 1. What is your impression on Thailand?
>
> 2. What attracts you most after watching this video?
>
> 3. Where would you like to visit most in Thailand? Why?

★ Viewing and Listening

Watch the video again and fill in the blanks with the words you have heard.

> It's been a period of reckoning. We all feel the changes. The distance we now have to keep, the new norms we now have to practice. Traveling in Thailand will not be the same. We still have _____ on when out and about. And also when diving down and greeting these underwater wonders, all renewed and thriving. _____, can be done on a beach that's never been more beautiful. Washing hands thoroughly at a living creek as long as you wish. Social _____ at the top of a mountain will be more invigorating than ever. But then, nothing beats human _____ at a real marketplace. Delicious and hygienic food delivery here is packed with friendship and big, _____ smiles. Conference calls can now be made with a _____ scenic background. No download needed. You can be a chef, a dancer, whoever you want to be. A lot of things might have changed, but traveling Thailand will still bring you the same _____, or even more. Because Thailand is now work from heart, renewing, restoring, taking care of ourselves, to welcome you back the best we can.

PART II Explore the Land

• *Geography*

Located in the center of mainland Southeast Asia, Thailand consists of two broad geographic areas: a larger main section in the north and a smaller peninsular extension in the south. The main body of the country is surrounded by Myanmar (缅甸) to the west, Laos to the north and east, Cambodia (柬埔寨) to the southeast, and the Gulf of Thailand to the south.

Thailand weather consists of six months of rainfalls during the wet season, three months of dry and cooling breezes during the winter, and three months of heat during the summer. The average temperature of Thailand ranges from 18℃ to 38℃.

Bangkok is the capital and by far the largest city. Chiang Mai, Chiang Rai, Phuket, Pattaya and Koh Samui (苏梅岛) are the most popular tourist destinations in Thailand.

• *People*

The people of Thailand are called Thais, which can refer both to the citizens of Thailand and ethnic Thais. There are 69 million people in Thailand. About 40 percent of the population are Thai. Other ethnic groups include citizens of Lao, Chinese, Malay, Khmer, Karen, and Indian descent.

Thais mainly announce themselves Buddhists. The modern Thai are mainly Theravada Buddhist (小乘佛教徒) and strongly identify their ethnic identity with their religious practices that include aspects of ancestor worship, among other beliefs of the ancient folk legend of Thailand.

• *Language*

Thai or Central Thai, also known as Siamese, is the national and official language of Thailand and spoken by about 68 million people worldwide. English is widely used in Thailand for commercial and many official purposes.

The relationship between spelling and sound is fairly complicated and Thai spelling is a hassle because there are 44 consonants, 32 vowels, and five tones. Thai pronouns are selected according to the gender and relative status of speaker and audience. "ka" and "krab" are placed at the end of the sentence to represent female and male respectively.

The most common ways to greet someone in Thailand are:

Sa wat dee ka! (Hello!)

Yin dee tee dai roo juk ka. (Nice to meet you.)

Sa bai dee mai? (How are you?)

• *Attractions*

Bangkok

Bangkok is the capital and largest city of Thailand. It is also known as the "City of Angels" and the "Capital of Buddhism", located on the east bank of the Chao Phraya River (湄南河). The administrative region of Bangkok is divided into 38 areas, consisting of over 24 counties and 150 districts.

The Greater Bangkok Metropolitan Area was formed in 1972. Besides its famous shopping and infamous nightlife, Bangkok is also a place with plenty else to see and do. Among Bangkok's well-known sights are the Grand Palace (大皇宫) and major Buddhist temples. The Grand Palace is a complex of buildings at the heart of Bangkok. It has been the official residence of the Kings of Siam since 1782. The Erawan Shrine (四面佛) demonstrates Buddhism's deep-rooted influence in Thai culture.

Chiang Mai

Chiang Mai, known as the "Rose of Northern Thailand", the largest city in northern Thailand, is the capital of Chiang Mai Province and was a former capital of the Kingdom of Lan Na (1296-1768). It is 700 kilometers north of Bangkok and has over 300 Buddhist temples. It hosts many Thai festivals, including Songkran Festival and Chiang Mai Flower Festival.

The temple Wat PhraThat Doi Suthep (双龙寺) is Chiang Mai's most famous and sacred temple in northern Thailand. It's also known simply as Doi Suthep, after the mountain on which it stands. It lies at the height of about 1,060 meters and boasts a stunning view of Chiang Mai. The walls surrounding the complex are decorated with gorgeous mural paintings that tell the story of the Buddha and his followers. Visitors come from all over Thailand to offer lotus flowers, incense, and candles. Every day, at 6:00 PM, monks come together to pray and chant, which is a wonderful experience.

Phuket Island

Located in the south of Thailand, Phuket Island is the largest and earliest developed island in

Thailand. Here people can experience snorkeling (浮潜), motorboats, surfing and water towing. As night falls, various bars will keep visitors entertained until dawn, and featured ladyboy and Muay Thai boxing will also keep tourists excited. If visitors want refreshment or recreation, they can always enjoy seafood meal and classic Thai Spa in Phuket Island.

Pattaya

Pattaya is a resort city in Thailand. It is about 100 kilometers southeast of Bangkok. Once a fishing town, Pattaya first boomed as an R&R (Rest and Recuperation) destination during the Vietnam War. Famous for its sunshine, beach, seafood, floating market and Coral Island, Pattaya is known as the Oriental Hawaii.

Chiang Rai

Chiang Rai is the northernmost province of Thailand. The famous attractions include Golden Triangle, White Temple, Doi Tung Royal Villa (王太后行宫) and Mae Sai (美赛), which is located on the border between Myanmar and Thailand, 720 kilometers away from Bangkok.

Koh Samui Island

When it comes to the most romantic honeymoon island in Thailand, it has to be Koh Samui. It is the third largest island in Thailand. "Coconut Island" is Koh Samui's nickname because of the tens of thousands of coconut trees on the island. Cultivation of tropical plants was once an important source of income for the island.

· *Thai Food*

Thai food is known for its enthusiastic use of fresh herbs and spices. Common flavors in Thai food come from garlic, galangal, lemon grass, green onion, pepper, kaffir lime (green lemon) leaves, shrimp paste, fish sauce, and chilies. Thai meals typically consist of rice (khao in Thai) with many complementary dishes shared by all.

Popular Thai food:

• **Tom Yam Goong**: Hot and sour shrimp soup.

• **Pad Thai** (泰式炒河粉): Thai-style stir-fried rice noodles.

• **Som Tam** (青木瓜沙拉): Crunchy shredded raw green papaya mixed with garlic, chili, fish sauce, peanuts, lime juice, and dried shrimp.

• **Mango Sticky Rice**: A combination of mango and sticky rice topped with coconut milk.

• **Thai Curry**: Coconut milk-based curry made with a spice paste, meat or seafood.

· *Unique Thailand*

Buddhism and Temple

Thailand is unique in that it's the most Buddhist nation on the earth, with around 90% of the population identifying as practicing Theravada Buddhists. Monks are highly respected and there are an estimated 40,000 Buddhist temples in Thailand. Many temples are open to tourists.

The six iconic temples are worth the visit:

Bangkok: Wat Phra Kaeo (玉佛寺), Erawan Shrine, Wat Arun (郑王庙);

Chiang Mai: Doi Suthep, Wat Chedi Luang (契迪龙寺);

Chiang Rai: Wat Rong Khun (White Temple).

Namaste

Namaste (合十礼) is a daily etiquette in Thailand. Age and social status determine the order of the Namaste, that is, the junior salutes first to the elder, the commoner salutes first to the royal monk, and the royal first to the monk. When one salutes, the higher his/her hands are, the more respect he/she shows to the other person. But only when worshiping the Buddha can one hold his/her hands together high above his/her head.

Muay Thai

Muay Thai, known as Thai boxing, is one of the most popular sports in Thailand. The sport is also known as the art of the eight limbs (八肢艺术) because athletes use different parts of their body to fight. Thai boxing originated in Thailand, and has become a popular fighting sport worldwide. Many tourists travel to Thailand specifically to watch traditional Thai boxing.

Floating Market

Tourists might feel as though they are entering a different world upon visiting a Thai floating market. While some countries in Asia have their own floating markets, none compare to Thailand's. The most popular one in Bangkok is the Damnoen Saduak Floating Market, which is usually bursting with tourists. Amphawa Floating Market is Bangkok's second most popular floating market for its seafood. Most people who visit this market are Thai, making it much more authentic.

Thai Massage

"Thai massage" or "Thai yoga massage" is one of the main attractions for tourists. It is an ancient healing system combining acupressure (指压法), Indian Ayurvedic (印度草药按摩) principles, and assisted yoga postures.

Ladyboy

Ladyboy, is mainly concentrated in Bangkok and Pattaya, with Pattaya being the most prevalent. In Thailand, ladyboys have developed into a tourism culture. Tiffany's Show Pattaya has become one of Pattaya's top attractions to visit.

Task: Draw your mind-map on the "Thailand in My Eyes" page based on the facts of Thailand and then introduce Thailand to your peers by using your mind-map.

★ 5C Reading on Thailand

A. Read the following passage and underline the reason why Thailand is called the land of smiles.

The Land of Smiles

"Fly all over Thailand, worry less with Thai smile" is the official slogan of Thai Airways. Thailand is known as the land of smiles. The nickname was first dubbed in a promotional sense, hoping to attract visitors in with its promise of white sand beaches, affordable travel costs, and the extreme hospitality of the locals. The coastlines of southern Thailand are some of the most stunning in the world. The cost of accommodation and food remain extremely low in comparison to Western countries and even those surrounding the land of smiles. Last but not least, the locals are, for the most part, helpful, courteous, and kind. Another reason why the country may have been gained this nickname is because Thais really do smile, or a lot, even in situations where a smile is not always needed. Although Thailand is famously known as the land of smiles, and for good reason, Thai smile does not automatically mean that the person is happy. This can lead to misunderstandings between Westerners and Thais. Saving face is important to many Thais. Instead of showing an emotion like anger or anxiety, for example, some locals will simply slap on a smile and act as if all is well.

Very often though, the Thai smile is a welcoming one. There is a definite attitude in Thailand that life should be enjoyed. Being too serious is unhealthy and causes stress and illness. Thai people advise tourists, don't think too much, and be happy. It's good advice.

> 你认为微笑对旅游业发展有什么重要作用?

B. Discuss the following questions based on the above reading material.

1. Why is Thailand called the land of smiles?

2. How does the tourism image of Thailand promote the development of its tourism?

PART III Welcome Guests from the Land

★ Project—Preparations for Airport Pick-up

You are a tour guide for a group of Thai international students who will arrive in Chengdu by air next week. You are going to make preparations for the airport pick-up. Please discuss with your peers and list 5 things to do for the preparations. Also, you need to take Thai culture and custom into consideration.

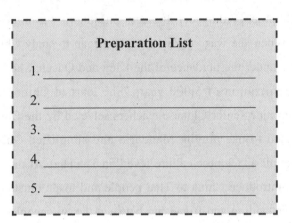

Preparation List

1. _____
2. _____
3. _____
4. _____
5. _____

Your Goals
1. Make the Thai students happy.
2. Make more international students know about China.

• Tasks

A. Tell your partner the reason why you choose these five things.

B. State your airport pick-up preparations briefly.

Reference Process of Airport Pick-up

1. Confirm flight and tourists' information.

2. Be ready for information communication and airport pick-up.

3. Make sure the vehicle is in good condition, clean and sanitary.

4. Check flight information, confirm arrival time, and get to the airport early.

5. Contact and greet visitors proactively.

6. Offer careful service and guide visitors to the bus.

7. Deliver a welcome speech on the bus and introduce travel-related matters.

8. Before arriving at the hotel, explain the arrival arrangements and remind guests to take their luggage and valuables.

★ *The Land and the World*

Thai Princess Maha Chakri Sirindhorn—True Friend of China

Princess Sirindhorn (诗琳通公主) , born on April 2, 1955, is the second daughter of King Bhumibol Adulyadej. Princess Sirindhorn was intelligent and eager to learn. When she was very young, she began to study Chinese history and literature under the guidance of the King and Queen. She loved China's splendid civilization of 5,000 years. She learned Chinese and Chinese culture from nine senior Chinese teachers selected by the Chinese Embassy. She learned to use pinyin, Mandarin and simplified Chinese characters, which set off a "Chinese culture fever" in Thailand. At the same time, Princess Sirindhorn wrote a book to introduce China to Thai people and made outstanding contributions to enhancing the mutual understanding and friendship between the two peoples. She has become a worthy envoy of China-Thailand friendship. In recognition of her contribution in spreading Chinese culture, Princess Sirindhorn was awarded the Chinese Language and Culture Friendship Award (中国语言文化友谊奖) by China's Ministry of Education.

Princess Maha Chakri Sirindhorn has been awarded the Medal of Friendship from the People's Republic of China in 2019, which is the highest medal offered to foreigners by China.

On behalf of those awarded the Medal of Friendship, Princess Maha Chakri Sirindhorn said all six foreign awardees are "indeed friends of China" who would like to contribute to friendship between their countries and China. "Distance cannot separate true friends, who remain close even when thousands of miles apart," she said, citing the words of Zhang Jiuling, a renowned poet of Tang Dynasty.

Mind-map: Thailand in My Eyes

Name: _____   Date: _____

KWL Chart

Topic: _____   Name: _____   Date: _____

Know	Wonder	Learned
What do you think you already know about Thailand?	What do you wonder about Thailand? Write your questions below.	Write what you've learned about Thailand.

裁切线

Section 2　Singapore

Learning Objectives

A flight to Singapore is 4.5 hours from Chengdu, 8 hours from Tokyo, 13 hours from London and 12.5 hours from New York.

After this section, you will be able to:

★ know the geographical features and importance of Singapore.

★ understand the multi-lingual and multi-cultural Singapore.

★ list the major theme parks and landmarks in Singapore.

★ apply Singaporean social norms, taboos and unique features to serving inbound Singaporean tourists, making them feel at home.

★ know the influence of Chinese festivals, language and social norms on Singaporean ones.

心想"狮城"之新加坡

新加坡共和国位于马六甲海峡北岸、马来半岛南端，是一个城市岛国，总面积724.4平方千米，由新加坡岛及附近63个小岛组成，其中主岛新加坡岛占全国面积的88.5%。新加坡地处太平洋与印度洋之间的航运要冲，为马六甲海峡出入口的咽喉要地，是亚、非、欧和大洋洲的重要国际海、空航线的枢纽。属热带海洋性气候，常年高温潮湿多雨，年平均气温24~32℃。新加坡是一个多元种族的社会，主要是来自马来半岛、中国、印度和斯里兰卡的移民后裔。总人口约为570万 (2019年)，公民和永久居民约为403万，华人占74%左右，其余为马来人、印度人和其他种族。马来语为国语，英语、华语、马来语和泰米尔语为官方语言，英语为行政用语。

新加坡是城市国家，整个城市就是旅游的目的地，被誉为"花园城市"，主要游览景点有圣淘沙名胜世界、裕华园、晚晴园、野生动物园、植物园、国家博物馆等。多元文化的都市旅游是新加坡旅游的重要特点。都市旅游、购物美食、娱乐休闲、主题公园、邮轮度假和商务会展等形式多样。新加坡是个自由港贸易中心，来自世界各地的货物品种齐全、价格便宜，购物成为新加坡吸引游客的一个重要内容。新加坡连续22年被国际协会联盟评选为"亚洲最佳会议城市"，连续5年被著名《亚太商旅杂志》的读者评选为"最佳商务城市"。新加坡每年接待会议客人150万人次。新加坡曾使用以下旅游宣传口号——新加坡：无限惊喜新加坡；新加坡：发现，发现，处处有发现；新加坡：说得完，游不完；新加坡：三天还不够。

旅游业是新加坡支柱产业之一，旅游业对新加坡GDP贡献率达到10%。新加坡是亚洲的主要客源产出国之一，2017年出境旅游988.9万人次。新加坡出境旅游者主要目的地在亚太地区，前五位出境旅游目的地为马来西亚、印度尼西亚、泰国、中国内地以及中国香港。自20世纪80年代以来，新加坡来华旅游人数不断增加，1979年来华游客仅1.3万人次，2015年90.53万人次，2017年94.02万人次，2018年97.8万人次。

Singapore Facts

- **Name**: Republic of Singapore
- **Capital**: Singapore
- **Government**: Parliamentary Republic
- **Languages**: English, Mandarin, Tamil, Malay

- **Population**: 5.7 Million (2019)
- **Life Expectancy**: 83.1 Years (2019)
- **Currency**: SGD 100 ≈ CNY 477.15 (2021)
- **National Symbol**: The Merlion
- **National Day**: August 9

PART I   Let's Go

★ *First Glance*

Listen to the audio, and then answer the following questions.

1. Which of the five unique aspects impresses you most? And why?

2. What do you want to learn about Singapore after this audio? Write down your thoughts in the KWL chart.

★ *Listening*

Listen to the audio again and write down the corresponding aspect of each picture.

_____

_____

PART II *Explore the Land*

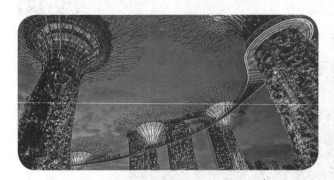

• *Geography*

Singapore is an island country off the southern tip of the Malay Peninsula in Southeast Asia. It is separated from Malaysia by the Straits of Johor, and from Indonesia's Riau Islands by the Singapore Strait. Singapore has a strategic location for Southeast Asian sea routes.

Singapore is not only one island. 63 islands belong to the city state and are dotted around the Singapore coastline, and most of these islands are inhabited. The largest island, after the main island, is Sentosa in the south of the main island.

• *People*

According to the most recent census, nearly 23% of Singaporean residents were foreign-born. The same census also reports that about 74% of residents were of Chinese descent.

Famous Singaporeans are:

• Lee Kuan Yew, founding father of modern Singapore (1923-2015);

• Ashley Islam, much celebrated fashion designer;

• Dick Lee, musician and Singapore's idol judge;

• Fann Wong, Hollywood actress, played in "Shanghai Nights";

• Joseph Schooling, 21-year-old swimmer who won the first-ever Olympic gold medal for Singapore in the 2016 Olympics.

• *Language*

The official languages in Singapore are English, Mandarin Chinese, Tamil and Malay. The national anthem's lyrics are written in Malay. Almost all Singaporeans are bilingual, that means they speak English and another home language such as Malay or Mandarin or a Chinese dialect such as Hokkien (闽南话).

The Singaporeans speak English with a local twist: "Singlish" adds often a "lah"or "leh" at the end of a word.

Just try it out:

"Can lah" means "Yes, it's possible".

"Can can" means "Yes, of course, let's do this".

"I don know leh" means "Somehow I do not know".

"I don need lah" means "I really don't need this".

• *Attractions*

Marina Bay

Marina Bay (滨海湾) represents all things modern and super-stylish, from trendy dining destinations to exciting leisure spots. The Marina Bay area is home to some of the city's most distinctive architectural icons, including the soaring structure of Marina Bay Sands and the charmingly durian-shaped Esplanade. The statue of the Merlion—Singapore's national icon—once occupied the mouth of the Singapore River, and was moved to its current location overlooking Marina Bay in 2002.

Gardens by the Bay

A national garden and premier horticultural attraction for local and international visitors, Gardens by the Bay (滨海花园) is a showpiece of horticulture and garden artistry that presents the plant kingdom in a whole new way, entertaining while educating visitors with plants seldom seen in this part of the world. Nature's beauty is unveiled with Gardens by the Bay's surreal sights, paradise-like spaces and lush greenery. The Supertree Grove is home to Gardens by the Bay's most iconic structures and a great location for unforgettable vistas. People are able to spend an entire day discovering the wonders of nature with family at Gardens by the Bay.

Sentosa Island

Before it was known as Sentosa (圣淘沙), this island just off Singapore's southern coast was a British military fortress. After the Japanese defeat in World War Ⅱ, Singapore returned to British rule, and the island was renamed "Sentosa" which translates to "peace and tranquility".

Over the course of its remarkable history, Sentosa has transformed into a beloved island resort, best known for its tropical beaches, luxurious hotels and thrilling attractions. Sentosa Island has many resorts and family entertainment centers such as the Universal Studios (环球影城), Waterworld.

People can get to Sentosa by taking the monorail or riding a cable car, but the pedestrian boardwalk is a great option as well if visitors fancy a stroll.

Botanic Gardens

Founded in 1859, the Singapore Botanic Gardens (植物园) showcases the best and most spectacular of tropical flora set in stunning verdant landscape. The Gardens is the first and only tropical botanic garden on the UNESCO's World Heritage List. Botanic Gardens devote their resources to the study and conservation of plants, as well as making the world's plant species diversity known to the public. These gardens also play a central role in meeting human needs and providing well-being.

Orchard Road

Orchard Road (乌节路) is every shopper's paradise. From luxury retail to world-class international cuisines, Singapore's most famous shopping area is home to a wealth of experiences. People will be spoilt for choice at Orchard Road, where luxury hotels, world-class malls and fine dining await them at every turn.

Singapore Zoo

Singapore Zoo is listed as one of the world's best zoo not for nothing. It has all the traditional zoo animals like elephants, tigers, lions, monkeys, and crocodiles, but also features amazingly diverse shows.

Set in a rainforest environment, Singapore Zoo is home to over 2,800 animals from over 300 species of mammals, birds and reptiles. Delight in an exciting outdoor feast at Jungle Breakfast with Wildlife, an internationally popular, award-winning program that offers amazing experience with orangutans (猩猩). The fun is endless with interesting animal presentations, photography with animals and more.

• *Singapore Food*

Singaporeans love to eat rice and rice noodle dishes. The Singaporean staple diet does not include dairy-based dishes.

Singaporeans love to eat out and there are many food courts (食阁) or food centers all over the city. Here people come to eat breakfast, lunch or dinner or just visit for a snack during the day. Food courts are called hawker centers.

Here are popular Singapore food:

• **Satay** (沙嗲烤肉): Grilled chicken or beef cubes on a stick served with peanut sauce available at many street stalls and hawker centers.

• **Kaya Toast** (咖椰烤面包): Popular snack or breakfast. Toast with coconut egg jam and sweet sugary topping.

• **Singapore Chili Crab** (新加坡辣椒蟹): Crab in very spicy chili sauce.

• **Yu Shen Prosperity Noodles** (捞鱼生): Singaporean traditional dish to celebrate Chinese New Year.

• *Unique Singapore*

Changi Airport

The pride and joy of Singaporeans, Changi (新加坡樟宜机场) is famous for its high level of efficiency and extensive range of amenities.

Passengers can expect to be home within an hour of landing in the city-state, while those in transit have access to everything from free movie theaters and gaming centers to shower facilities, leg massage stations and sleeping lounges.

Skytrax voted the airport famous for its butterfly garden, movie theater, and swimming pool the best in the world in its annual World Airport Awards for the seventh year in a row.

Gum Control

Chewing gum is a tightly controlled commodity in the city state.

The government outlawed the sale of gum in 1992 in an effort to keep public areas clean. But the ban, which grabbed global attention when it was first announced, has since been eased. Just over a decade ago, pharmacies and dentists were granted permission to sell so-called therapeutic gum used for medicinal or dental purposes, such as nicotine and sugar-free gum.

While the restrictions continue to be perceived as overbearing by some, their value is quickly apparent in Singapore's clean streets.

Ice Cream Sandwich Carts

Singaporeans love their ice cream between two slices of bread. The native snack, sold by street vendors across the island, is the perfect way to cool down under the sweltering Singapore sun.

Bag Drinks

From morning kopi-o (咖啡乌，咖啡名) to afternoon teh tarik (拉茶), hot and cold beverages purchased from hawker centers are often served in plastic drawstring bags with a straw because it's cheap and convenient.

Chopping

Kleenex (舒洁面巾纸) packets serve a dual function here in Singapore. Apart the obvious, they are also used to reserve tables at food courts or public eating areas-a common practice called "chopping (占位置)".

The more daring "choppers" use their staff IDs, keys and even mobile phones to reserve their seats while they are off purchasing food. This is also a showcase of how safe the city is.

Task: Draw your mind-map on the "Singapore in My Eyes" page based on the facts of Singapore and then introduce Singapore to your peers by using your mind-map.

★ 5C Reading on Singapore

A. Read the following passage on Singaporean festivals and languages.

The Singaporeans celebrate many festivals. Among the most popular are: Chinese New Year, Mid-autumn or Moon Festival, Christmas. For these celebrations, people will see everywhere thousands and thousands of lanterns and light decorations. Chinese New Year is usually celebrated in February according

to Chinese lunar new year. Here is an image with one of the 2021 decorations in the city. According to the Chinese lunar calendar, 2021 is the "Year of the Ox", so this is why people decorated the street crossing with huge oxen.

The national language of Singapore is Malay while English, Malay, Mandarin Chinese, and Tamil are the four official languages in Singapore. English is the most widely spoken language, and the medium of instructions in school. English is also the language of business and government in Singapore, based on British English. A unique and widely spoken language in Singapore is the Singlish. It is primarily the colloquial form of English, having a distinct accent, and ignoring the basic standards of English grammar. All the schools in the city teach the language of the child's parentage, along with English, to ensure the child stay in touch with the traditional roots.

Language	Percentage (%)
English	37
Mandarin	35
Chinese Dialects	13
Malay	10
Tamil	3
Others	2

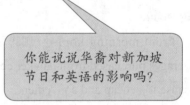

你能说说华裔对新加坡节日和英语的影响吗？

B. Discuss the following questions based on the above reading material.

1. Do you know Singaporeans celebrate Chinese New Year before you read it? How does this reshape your understanding on Singapore and its people?

2. Why are there similarities between Singaporean and Chinese festivals?

3. Discuss the meaning of the following Singlish sentences.

a) One Chicken Rice da bao.	b) OK lah.
c) I wan go Orchard MRT.	d) Tomorrow dun need camera.
e) Corright.	f) I fly SQ lah.
g) Repeat again or Ha?	h) How can lah?

PART III   Welcome Guests from the Land

★ *Project—Bellman Reception*

You are a bellman at a five-star hotel. A Singaporean family arrive, and you're supposed to welcome them and deliver the luggage to their room after check-in. Make sure you behave professionally, gracefully and impressively. Discuss with your partners how you would structure the dialogue.

My Top 3 Concerns

1. _____

2. _____

3. _____

Bellman Job Description

Handling guests' luggage is one of the main duties of a bellman. At luxury hotels, bell service staff are typically responsible for unloading luggage at curbside upon a guest's arrival, as well as delivering the luggage to a guest's room after check-in. Bellmen may also assist guests with laundry service.

· *Tasks*

   A. *Tell your partner the reason why you are concerned about the above three things.*

   B. *Make a dialogue to greet the guests and help them with luggage. You can use the sample dialogue as reference.*

Sample Dialogue

Bellman (B)   Guest (G)

B: Good morning, Madam. Welcome to InterContinental Hotel. Do you have any luggage with you?

G: Yes, in the trunk.

B: Excuse me. I would check your luggage. I have three pieces of luggage. Is that correct?

G: Yes, that's right.

B: Would you like to follow me to the lobby, please?

G: Sure, thank you.

B: You're welcome. Mind your step, please.

G: Thank you.

B: You're welcome. I will come later when you finish your registration.

(A moment later.)

B: Are you ready to go to your room now, Mrs. Johnson?

G: Yes, certainly.

B: Mrs. Johnson, this is your room. Hope you enjoy your stay. The weather in December is quite different from Singapore. If you need anything, please let us know.

★ *The Land and the World*

Sia Yong—Friendship Ambassador

Sia Yong (谢镛), former President of Sino-Singa Friendship Association (later China Singapore Friendship Association). Born in Fujian in southeast China, he left China at age eight with his father.

He worked as, among other things, a mechanic, egg seller and sailor before becoming a reporter after the war in 1945 at the now-defunct Nanyang Siang Pau newspaper.

He founded the Sino-Singa Friendship Association in 1993 and was its president till he stepped down in 2006. The Association has played an important role in bringing the people of both countries together through various activities and exchanges, thus strengthening mutual understanding and friendship. This has contributed significantly to the warm and multifaceted relations China and Singapore enjoy today. Sia Yong was awarded Friendship Ambassador in 2004 by the Chinese People's Association for Friendship with Foreign Countries (中国人民对外友好协会).

✂

裁

切

线

Mind-map: Singapore in My Eyes

Name: _____   Date: _____

KWL Chart

Topic: _____　　Name: _____　　Date: _____

Know What do you think you already know about Singapore?	**Wonder** What do you wonder about Singapore? Write your questions below.	**Learned** Write what you've learned about Singapore.

裁

切

线

Section 3   Indonesia

Learning Objectives

A flight to Jakarta is about 6.4 hours from Shanghai, 7.5 hours from Tokyo, 7 hours from Sydney, and 20 hours from Los Angeles.

After this section, you will be able to:

★ know the geographical features of Indonesia, especially its maritime economy and tourism.

★ list typical attractions in Indonesia.

★ apply Indonesian social taboos and unique features to serving inbound Indonesian tourists, making them feel at home.

★ promote the image of Chinese tourism by relating China and Indonesia from history, people and maritime economy.

蔚蓝"印"象之印度尼西亚

　　印度尼西亚共和国（以下简称"印尼"）由17508个岛屿组成，是全世界最大的群岛国家，被誉为"千岛之国"。疆域横跨亚洲及大洋洲，濒临印度洋和太平洋，是连接两大洲和两大洋的海上枢纽，具有重要的战略地位。

　　印尼地理结构复杂，旅游资源丰富。旅游业是印尼政府五大优先发展的支柱产业之一，也是印尼的重要创汇来源。印尼国家旅游部推出各种战略手段，对国家品牌重新定位，将"访问印度尼西亚年(Visit Indonesia Year)"变成"精彩印度尼西亚(Wonderful Indonesia)"，以提升印尼旅游业的形象和竞争力。印尼旅游部数据显示，2018年国际游客数量达580万人次，中国在2016 年和 2017年连续两年成为印尼最大的国际客源国。

　　2013年习近平主席访问印尼时提出建设"21世纪海上丝绸之路 (21st Century Maritime Silk Road)"倡议，印尼地处"丝绸之路经济带"的要津，2014年，印尼总统佐科·维多多(Joko Widodo)提出"全球海上支点 (Global Maritime Fulcrum)"战略，两国政府积极推进印尼海洋强国战略与共建21 世纪海上丝绸之路倡议的对接。2020年为中国印尼建交70周年，在两国携手抗疫的特殊时刻，为促进印尼与中国疫情后的旅游合作，12月18日在印尼以线上线下联动的方式举行了中印尼旅游与投资论坛。双方形成旅游开发和投资等方面的合作共识：中印尼旅游资源丰富，出境游市场潜力巨大，发展前景光明。印尼华人约占总人口的5%，年轻人比例高，是中国"Top 15"的客源国，近年来川渝游客人数增长势头明显。作为我国未来需开发的客源市场，存在着不可低估的发展潜力。

Indonesia Facts

- **Official Name**: Republic of Indonesia
- **Capital**: Jakarta
- **Government**: Federal Republic
- **Language**: Bahasa Indonesia
- **Population**: 268 Million (2020)

- **Life Expectancy**: 69.1 Years (2019)
- **Currency**: IDR 100 ≈ CNY 0.05 (2021)
- **National Symbols**: Garuda, Moon Orchid
- **Independence Day**: August 17

PART I   Let's Go

★ *First Glance*

Watch the video, and then answer the following questions.

1. Is it different from what you know about Indonesia?

2. What impresses you most after seeing the video?

3. What is the title of the song and why is it chosen for the video?

★ *Viewing and Listening*

Watch the video again and fill in the blanks with the words you have heard.

I see trees of green, _____ too.

I see them _____ for me and you.

And I think to myself what a wonderful world.

I see _____ of blue and clouds of white.

The bright blessed day, the dark sacred night.

And I think to myself what a wonderful world.

The colors of the _____ so pretty in the sky.

Are also on the faces of people going by.

I see friends shaking hands saying how do you do.

They're really saying I love you.

I hear _____ cry; I watch them grow.

They'll learn much more than I'll never know.

And I think to myself what a wonderful world.

Yes I think to myself what a wonderful world.

PART II Explore the Land

· *Geography*

Indonesia, officially the Republic of Indonesia, is a country with a strategic position in Southeast Asia and Oceania, between the Indian and Pacific oceans, located astride the equator in the humid tropics and extends some 3,700 kilometers eastwest.

It consists of more than seventeen thousand islands, including Sumatra, Java, Bali, Borneo, Sulawesi and New Guinea. Indonesia is the world's largest island country and the 14th-largest country by land area, at 1,913,579 square kilometers.

The location has played a profound role in economic, political, cultural, and religious developments there. Control of the Malacca Straits between Sumatra and Malayan peninsula, the Suanda Strait separating Sumatra and Java, the Palawan passage between Borneo and the southern Philippines, enabled powerful and wealthy maritime kingdom to emerge. For more than two thousand years, trading ships sailed between the great civilizations of Indonesia and China via the waters and islands.

· *People*

Indonesia is the world's 4th-most populous country, only after China, India and America. People in Indonesia are called Indonesians. People of Malay descent make up a large portion of the population in Indonesia.

There are more than three hundred ethnic groups in Indonesia, each with its own culture. Among them, the Javanese are the most numerous group. The Javenese developed sophisticated language and kingdoms, their culture still visible in the courts of Yogyakarta (日惹) and Surakarta. The largest population of Chinese are in Java, eastern Sumatra, and western Kalimantan, but they are to be found everywhere.

• *Language*

Bahasa Indonesia, "the Indonesian Language", is the national language taught in schools and spoken in all but the remotest areas. It evolved from a literary style of Malay language. The differences between standard Malay and standard Indonesian reside largely in their idioms and in certain items of vocabulary. In 1972 Indonesia and Malaysia agreed on a uniform revised spelling of the language so that communications could be improved and literature more freely exchanged between the two countries.

English is widely spoken in the main tourist areas and in business and commercial organizations. Several common used phrases in Bahasa Indonesian are:

Apa kabar? (How are you?)

Terima Kasih. (Thank you.)

Selamat tinggal! (See you.)

• *Attractions*

Jakarta

Jakarta is the largest city and capital of Indonesia. Lying on the northwest coast of Java Island, Jakarta is the country's economic, cultural and political center and the most populous city not only in Indonesia but in Southeast Asia as a whole.

Jakarta is a huge, sprawling metropolis, home to over 10 million people with diverse ethnic group backgrounds from all over Indonesia. During the day, the number of people even increases with commuters making their way to work in the city and flock out again in the evenings. With its many suburbs, Jakarta has become a megapolitan city. It is no wonder that travelers will find Jakarta as a dynamic city, with activities taking place around-the-clock throughout its populated areas.

Java

Java is an island of Indonesia, bordered by the Indian Ocean on the south and the Java Sea on the north. With a population of over 145 million, Java constitutes 56.7 percent of the Indonesian population and is the world's most-populous and the most developed island. Much of the well-known part of Indonesian history took place on Java. Java was also the center of the Indonesian struggle for independence during the 1930s and 1940s. Java dominates Indonesia politically, economically and culturally. Four of Indonesia's eight UNESCO World Heritage Sites are located in Java: Ujung Kulon National Park, Borobudur Temple, Prambanan Temple, and Sangiran Early Man Site.

Central Java is well-known for the temple of Borobudur and the two cities of Yogyakarta and Surakarta, each a center of traditional Javanese culture. The courts keep alive the ancient traditions in music, dance, and drama. Yogyakarta, with its proximity to Borodudur, is better-known, but Surakarta still retains much of the feel of the old city and royal court.

Bali

Bali is one of Indonesia's seventeen thousand islands and also a province. East of Java and west of Lombok, the province includes the island of Bali and a few smaller neighboring islands. The provincial capital, Denpasar, is the most populous city in the Lesser Sunda Islands and the second-largest, after Makassar, in eastern Indonesia. Bali is Indonesia's main tourist destination, with a significant rise in tourism since the 1980s. Tourism-related business makes up 80% of its economy.

Bali is a very well-known holiday destination for visitors from both the West and the East. Blessed with an abundance of must-visit attractions, it can be reached easily via various domestic and international flights landing at the Ngurah Rai International Airport or via ferry/boat rides from Java and Lombok. The distance by air from Jakarta to Bali is about 1,000 kilometers.

· *Indonesian Food*

Indonesia has around 5,350 traditional recipes, with 30 of which considered the most important. Many Indonesians are familiar with Western customs and tourist and business hotels provide Western-style food.

Padang Food

In Indonesia the most worth trying food may be Padang food, which is among the most popular food in Maritime Southeast Asia, known across Indonesia as Masakan Padang after the city of Padang, the capital city of West Sumatra Province. The cuisine is usually cooked once per day. After the customers are seated, they do not have to order. The waiter immediately serves the dishes directly to the table, and the table will quickly be set with dozens of small dishes filled with highly flavored foods such as beef rendang, curried fish, Soto Padang, and of course, spicy sauces common at Indonesian tables. Customers only pay for what they eat.

Other Popular Indonesian Food

About 30%-40% of the tourism revenue in Indonesia is from culinary expense. Indonesian food doesn't have the same popularity abroad as other regional cuisines, like Thai food. In an effort to change this, the Indonesian Ministry of Tourism has set five typical Indonesian dishes that are to be officially considered the nations' best foods. They are:

Soto: Classic soup with a wide variety of taste, textures, thickness, and ingredients, adopts the cultural sensibilities of many different parts of Indonesia.

Rendang (椰浆咖喱): A kind of thick sauce best served with beef. It is prepared with herbs and spices cooking for a few hours until all the liquids have been completely absorbed by the meat.

Sate or Saté (加香烤肉): Served in curry sauce and peanuts, usually a treat in the evening.

Nasi Goreng: Literally meaning "fried rice" in both the Indonesian and Malay languages, it is an Indonesian rice dish with pieces of meat and vegetables added. The best way to test the quality of a new restaurant is to order their Nasi Goreng.

Gado-Gado: The Indonesian salad that can be made up of a wide variety of vegetables, but is only complete with a thick and abundant peanut sauce dressing.

• *Unique Indonesia*

The Pancasila

The Indonesian government bases its ruling philosophy on the Pancasila or in English "the Five Principles" of the States set forth by President Sukarno in 1945. They are: the belief in the one and only God, the just and civilized humanity, the unity of Indonesia, the democracy guided by the inner wisdom in the unanimity arising out of deliberations amongst representatives, and the social justice for the whole of the people of Indonesia. The purpose of the Five Principles was to provide a broad statement of nationalist aims in a form all Indonesians could accept.

Wayang

Wayang (哇扬, 木偶戏) is a traditional form of puppet theater play originated on the Indonesian island of Java. Wayang refers to the entire dramatic show. Performances are accompanied by a gamelan (印尼民族管弦乐器) orchestra in Java, and by gender Wayang in Bali. Traditionally, a Wayang is played out in a ritualized midnight-to-dawn show by a dalang, an artist and spiritual leader. People watch the show from both sides of the screen.

Batik

Batik is an Indonesian technique of wax-resist dyeing applied to the whole cloth. This technique originated from the island of Java, Indonesia. Batik is made either by drawing dots and lines of the resist with a spouted tool called a canting, or by printing the resist with a copper stamp called a cap. The applied wax resists dyes and therefore allows the artisan to color selectively by soaking the cloth in one color, removing the wax with boiling water, and repeating if multiple colors are desired. Batik is both an art and a craft, which is becoming ever more popular and well-known among contemporary artists all over the world, as a wonderfully creative medium. The art of decorating cloth using wax and dye, has been practiced for centuries in many other parts of the world including Asia, South America and Europe.

Pinisi

Pinisi (皮尼西帆船, 木质双桅帆船), or the art of boatbuilding in south Sulawesi, refers to the rig and sail of the famed "Sulawesi schooner". The construction and deployment of such vessels stand in the thousand-year long tradition of boatbuilding and navigation that has brought forth a broad variety of sophisticated watercrafts. For both the Indonesian and the international public, Pinisi has  become the epitome of the Archipelago's indigenous sailing craft. UNESCO acknowledged "Pinisi, Art of Boatbuilding in South Sulawesi" on the list of intangible cultural heritage in 2017, following Wayang and Batik, etc.

Task: Draw your mind-map on the "Indonesia in My Eyes" page based on the facts of Indonesia and then introduce Indonesia to your peers by using your mind-map.

★ 5C Reading on Indonesia

A. Read the following passage about the 21st Century Maritime Silk Road.

On October 3, 2013, on the occasion of the 10th Anniversary of the China-ASEAN Strategic Partnership, President Xi Jinping proposed jointly building a 21st Century Maritime Silk Road in his speech to the Indonesian parliament. The initiative aims to boost China-ASEAN maritime cooperation and forge closer ties in a community of a shared future. It calls for joint efforts across the region and beyond.

The initiative has aroused great response in Indonesian government. On November 13, 2014, President Joko Widodo presented the concept of Global Maritime Fulcrum (支点), which rests on seven main pillars: maritime and human resources; maritime defense, security, law enforcement, and safety at sea; maritime governance; maritime economy and infrastructure; maritime spatial management and environmental protection; maritime culture; and maritime diplomacy and aims to exploit the potential for the ocean in order to lead to the comprehensive domestic development.

The concept of the Global Maritime Fulcrum and the China's cooperative inventive of the 21st Century Maritime Silk Road fit each other highly. The cooperation between the two countries has broad development prospects. Tourism is also an area in which China and Indonesia will reinforce their intercommunication and cooperation. Indonesia has more than 17,000 islands and a considerable potential for the development of marine tourism.

思考"一带一路"和"全球海洋支点"的契合点。

B. Discuss the following questions based on the above reading material.

1. Why has Indonesia hightlighted the "Global Maritime Fulcrum"?

2. How has "21st Maritime Silk Road" initiative significantly influenced Indonesia?

3. What benefits can we take from the "21st Maritime Silk Road" initiative and the "Global Maritime Fulcrum" strategy?

PART III   Welcome Guests from the Land

★ *Project—Choosing a Hotel for Indonesian Guests*

You are a tour guide for a group of Indonesian tourists. They will visit Chengdu and Chongqing next month. To make the trip in China unforgettable and memorable experience, they hope to stay in a hotel full of Chinese elements. Decide 3 hotels to recommend based on what you know about Indonesian people and culture. Also, you need to take local Chinese culture into consideration.

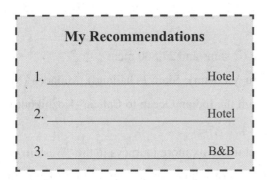

My Recommendations

1. _____ Hotel

2. _____ Hotel

3. _____ B&B

Your Goals
1. Cater for the Indonesian tourists.
2. Make more international tourists know China better.

• *Tasks*

A. Tell your partner the reasons why you choose the hotels or B&Bs (*bed-and-breakfasts*).

B. Prepare a 3-minute presentation on your recommendation.

For Your Reference

Both as bustling cities, Chengdu and Chongqing have wide varieties of hotels available for visitors to stay in: from 5-star hotels in the downtown area, with breathtaking views to some of the many hostels, suitable for young backpackers. Your recommendation may consider what your guests want to experience: luxury experience of the high-class hotels or a more local and authentic experience.

Besides, staying at a bed-and-breakfast (B&B) is also a wonderful alternative in the two cities. Many B&Bs are situated in convenient places in the cities and tend to offer all those special extra touches that can make the travel wonderful. B&Bs offer great ways to experience a destination like a local. Hosts frequently live on-site and can offer insight into local life—something guests not as likely to glean from a formal conversation with a hotel concierge. Plus, B&Bs can be found in city centers as well as in residential or rural areas.

You may do some field research and know more about hotels and B&Bs in Chengdu and Chongqing to find good accommodations for your guests.

★ *The Land and the World*

Zheng He and Indonesia

Zheng He (1371-1433) was a great Chinese explorer and fleet commander. He was selected by the emperor to be commander in chief of a series of missions to the "Western Oceans" and established Chinese trade in new areas.

Zheng He first set sail in 1405, commanding 62 ships and 27,800 men.

The fleet visited Champa (now in southern Vietnam), Siam (Thailand), Malacca (Melaka), and the island of Java (Indonesia) and then through the Indian Ocean to Calicut (Kozhikode) on the Malabar Coast of India and Ceylon (Sri Lanka).

After the first voyage, Zheng He and his fleet made six more journeys to the "Western Oceans" and each time he stopped in Indonesia. The location of Indonesia has played a profound role here. For more than two thousand years, trading ships sailed between the great civilizations of Indian and Pacific Ocean via the waters and islands.

In 1413, during his 4th voyage, Zheng He landed in Semarang, capital of Central Java Province, the third port city of Indonesia and important port of Maritime Silk Road.

In the place where Zheng He prayed daily for peace and safety, people set up a temple, and name of the city was changed to Semarang, after the nickname Sanbao of Zheng He to memorize him.

Zheng He's Enormous Treasure Ship

Zheng He Statue & Zheng He Temple

Lawang Sewu, Semarang Landmark Building

Mind-map: Indonesia in My Eyes

Name: _____   Date: _____

KWL Chart

Topic: _____   Name: _____   Date: _____

Know	Wonder	Learned
What do you think you already know about Indonesia?	What do you wonder about Indonesia? Write your questions below.	Write what you've learned about Indonesia.

裁

切

线

Section 4　Malaysia

Learning Objectives

A flight to Kuala Lumpur is around 6 hours from Beijing, 20 hours from New York, 14 hours from London and 7 hours from Tokyo.

After this section, you will be able to:

★ know the geographical features of Malaysia, especially its natural beauty.

★ have a better understanding of the uniqueness of Malaysia.

★ understand the multi-ethnic, multi-religious and multi-cultural Malaysia.

★ apply Malaysian social norms, customs, taboos and unique features to serving inbound Malaysian tourists, making them feel at home.

★ know the influence of Chinese history, culture, architecture, cuisine and immigration on Malaysia.

走"马"观化之马来西亚

马来西亚位于亚洲东南部,由马来半岛南部的马来亚和加里曼丹岛北部的沙捞越、沙巴组成,北与泰国接壤,南与新加坡隔柔佛海峡相望,东临中国南海,西濒马六甲海峡,海岸线长4192千米,面积33万平方千米。人口3275万(2021年),主要由马来人(69.1%),华人(23%),印度人(6.9%)组成,信奉伊斯兰教、佛教、印度教和基督教,国语为马来语,英语为官方语言,华语、泰米尔语使用广泛。首都吉隆坡,是全国最大的城市、政治、经济及文化中心,也是对东南亚文化、教育、体育、财政、经济、商业、金融极具影响力的国际大都会。

马来西亚阳光充足、气候宜人、海岸线绵长,高质量的海滩、奇特的海岛、密布的热带丛林、丰富的野生动植物、种类繁多的异兽珍禽、千姿百态的洞穴、古老的民俗风情、历史悠久的文化遗迹与现代都市魅力交互碰撞。马来西亚旅游资源丰富,有缤纷多元、魅力之都吉隆坡,历史古都马六甲,"亚洲美食天堂"槟城,赏鸟天堂沙巴,东南亚植物多样性中心基纳巴卢国家公园,素有"南方蒙地卡罗"之美誉的云顶高原避暑胜地等。旅游业是马来西亚第三大经济支柱,第二大外汇收入来源,2019年旅游业占GDP的15.9%,提供了23.5%的就业岗位,在2019年全球旅游业竞争力榜单中排第29位。以"亚洲魅力所在""多民族和谐共荣的亚洲旅游天堂"等作为旅游宣传口号,马来西亚将推广旅游业视为使命。

中马友好往来已有2000多年历史。赴马来西亚游客从1991年的四五万人次已增加到2018年的294万人次,中国已成为马来西亚第一大客源国。马来西亚是中国第五大客源国,2018年来华游客共计129.1万人次,客源以华人为主,主要来自吉隆坡、槟城和新山。超70%的马来西亚人有海外旅游的经历,出境到访最多的是新加坡、泰国、中国大陆、中国香港、中国台湾等国家和地区。在优质服务马来西亚客源的同时,还要学习马来西亚在国家整体发展战略层面上,以多元文化和自然遗产优势为基础,寻求保护和发展共赢的生态旅游实践道路,适度发展旅游业的成功经验,助力我国旅游资源开发和品牌的对外宣传和推广。

Malaysia Facts

- **Name**: Malaysia
- **Capital**: Kuala Lumpur
- **Government**: Constitutional Monarchy
- **Languages**: Malay, English, Mandarin, Tamil
- **Population**: 32.75 Million (2021)
- **Life Expectancy**: 75 Years (2019)
- **Currency**: MYR 100 ≈ CNY 153.14 (2021)
- **National Symbols**: Malayan Tiger, Hibiscus
- **National Day**: August 31

PART I Let's Go

★ *First Glance*

Watch the video, and then answer the following questions.

1. Are Malaysian people friendly? How do you know that?

2. What are the unique features of Malaysia?

3. What are the words you'd like to use to describe Malaysia after watching the video?

★ *Viewing and Listening*

Watch the video again and fill in the missing words of the song lyrics.

You will love Malaysia now and forever

Different _____ everywhere

The soul of Asia is surely here

This beautiful _____

You will love the _____ of Malaysia

Where the sun loves to shine

On sandy _____ and clear waters

With smiles of _____ races

This land is beautiful

It steals your _____ away

This land is _____

Only a smile away

The _____ of Asia

The essence of Asia

In this land where _____ come true

Malaysia

Malaysia is truly Asia

People _____ everywhere

Showing you how much they care

Welcome to Malaysia

PART II   Explore the Land

· *Geography*

Malaysia is located in Southeast Asia, lying just north of the equator. It is composed of two regions: Peninsular Malaysia (West Malaysia) which is on the Malay Peninsula, and East Malaysia which is on the island of Borneo. Peninsular Malaysia is bordered by Thailand and linked to Singapore by a causeway and a bridge, and East Malaysia is bordered by Brunei and Indonesia.

There are hundreds of islands along the coastline of Malaysia, and Langkawi (兰卡威) is the biggest one. The Mulu Caves in East Malaysia is one of the largest cave systems in the world. Malaysia's highest point is Mount Kinabalu, which is 4,095 meters high. There are four UNESCO World Heritage Sites in Malaysia.

· *People*

Malaysia is a multiracial country with a rich cultural heritage. Over 69.1% of the population are Malay or indigenous people. About 23% are Chinese and 6.9% are Indian. The total population is about 33 million, of which 78.4 % is urban. Almost 44% of all Malaysians are under 24 years of age.

· *Language*

The diverse Malaysian country is home to 137 living languages. Spoken by over 80% of the population, Malay is the national language and also one of the two official languages. English is one of the most common languages which is used widely as a medium of education, communication and government houses. Mandarin is spoken by quite a number of people, and Hokkien is the most popular dialect. Tamil is spoken by Indians as their native language, and there are more than five hundred Tamil medium schools spread throughout Malaysia.

Some commonly used Malay phrases are:

Hallo. (Hello.)

Apakhabar? (How are you?)

Khabarbaik. (I'm fine.)

TerimaKasih. (Thank you.)

Selamatjalan/Selamattinggal. (Goodbye.)

• *Attractions*

Kinabalu National Park

On the island of Borneo lies Kinabalu Park (京那巴鲁国家公园), Malaysia's first World Heritage Site declared by UNESCO in December 2000 for its outstanding universal values and the role as one of the most important biological sites in the world. Mount Kinabalu, standing at 4,095.2 metres tall, is the highest mountain on the island of Borneo and the 20th most prominent peak in the world.

Kinabalu Park, with four climatic zones, boasts one of the richest collections of biodiversity in the world, housing and protecting more than 4,500 species of flora and fauna—including 326 bird species, an estimated number of over 100 mammal species, over 110 land snail species. It is also one of the most popular tourist attractions in Sabah and whole of Malaysia.

Langkawi

Langkawi is a serene archipelago of 99 islands. The largest one is the Langkawi Island, which has UNESCO World Geopark status because of its richly populated wildlife conservation areas. The best way to experience these ecological wonders is from high above, on the Langkawi Sky Bridge that stretches above the rainforest.

Surrounded by sea, the interior of the main island is a mixture of picturesque paddy fields and jungle-clad hills. Nature lovers will find the island just as agreeable as the shoreline fringed by powder-fine sand and swaying coconut trees. The island is especially recognized for its excellent diving opportunities.

Archaeological Heritage of the Lenggong Valley

The Lenggong Valley (玲珑谷) has four archaeological sites dating back almost 2 million years. There are prehistoric remains from the Palaeolithic (旧石器时代的), Neolithic (新石器时代的) and Metal Ages, which includes skeletons, cave drawings, weapons and pottery.

Discoveries here have been ground-breaking. In 1987, Kota Tampan was found to have Palaeolithic tools, the earliest record of human invention. In 1991, the complete skeleton of Southeast Asia's earliest man, dubbed Perak Man (霹雳人), was uncovered. The cave sites make a remarkable place to visit, as it feels like walking through an open-air museum with prehistoric artefacts.

Kuala Lumpur

Kuala Lumpur is the capital city of Malaysia, boasting gleaming skyscrapers, colonial architecture, charming locals and a myriad of natural attractions. It is widely recognized for numerous landmarks, including the iconic Petronas Twin Towers (国油双峰塔) , Petaling Street flea market and Batu Caves.

Kuala Lumpur is packed with incredible street food stalls that even challenge some of the country's best high-end restaurants when it comes to quality. Visitors can get a taste of Malaysia and dine like the locals do at the best street food stalls. Wandering the streets of Kuala Lumpur can mean dipping in and out of an urban present into an ancient past.

Malacca

Being Malaysia's historical heart, Malacca played an important role in the development of trade between Europe and the East, especially China. It is famous for its unique blend of beautiful ancient architecture and breathtaking modern structures coexisting in a single space. Steeped in culture, history and traditions, Malacca allows its visitors a peek into the Malaysian way of life through its museums, architecture and cuisine. Malacca is truly a melting pot of cultures with a unique blend of Chinese, Portuguese, Dutch and British influences.

Penang

Located in the Strait of Malacca, Penang was an important trade route for Europe, the Middle East, India and China in the past. The influences of Asia and Europe have endowed it with a specific multicultural heritage. Being a world renowned exotic holiday destination and nicknamed the Pearl of the Orient, Penang has no shortage of cultural sights and natural scenery. The administrative capital, George Town, is a UNESCO World Heritage Site. Regarded as the food capital of Malaysia, Penang is deemed to be the top foodie destination to visit in the world by Lonely Planet in 2014.

• *Malaysian Food*

With strong influences from China, India, Singapore, and Indonesia, Malaysian cuisine is a blend of many interesting ingredients and flavors.

Here are popular Malaysian foods:

• **Nasi Lemak** (椰浆饭): Coconut rice cooked in coconut milk with boiled egg, vegetables, curried meat such as chicken or beef and sambal-chili sauce.

• **Hokkien Mee** (福建炒面): A stir-fried noodle dish popular throughout Southeast Asia with origins in China's Fujian Province.

• **Laksa** (辣味米粉汤): Spicy noodle soup with Chinese and Malaysian influences.

• **Ais Kacang** (红豆冰): A dessert originally made of only shaved ice and red beans. Today it comes in bright colors, and with different fruit cocktails and dressings.

• **Nyonya Kuih** (娘惹糕): Homemade sweets made by steaming with local ingredients like coconut, rice and pandan leaves by the Nyonya wives for celebrations and prayers.

• *Unique Malaysia*

Vibrant Multicultural Society

Malaysia is a country that celebrates its diversity. In Malaysia the various races are encouraged to keep their ethnic names and their languages, to practice their respective religions and to embrace not only their own cultures, but fellow citizens. All this has served to create a vibrant multicultural society. Malaysia is very unique in the sense of its culture. People of different religions and backgrounds mix easily together, respect and live with each other peacefully. The outcome is a spectacular mix of people, food, traditions and culture.

Rafflesia

Rafflesia (大王花) is the world's largest and heaviest flower. Rafflesia arnoldii can grow up to 1 meter in diameter and can weigh up to 10 kilograms. It is often called "the Monster Flower" as it's so big and has a foul odour that attracts insects. The huge red flower with five petals does not have a stem, leaves or even roots, but is a parasite (寄生植物) growing on a host vine. It is one of the rarest plants in the world and on the verge of extinction.

Graffiti

Graffiti (涂鸦) scene in Malaysia has been on a flourishing trend over the recent years. Ranging from simple written wordings to elaborate wall paintings, graffiti are drawings painted on a wall or other building surface. As one of the elements of hip-hop culture, Graffiti is more than just expression of social messages but display of artistic imagination using spray paint.

Every graffiti has a different story to tell and it represents the history of the place and of its citizens. One of the most well-known pieces to check out in Penang is Little Children on a Bicycle located at the shophouse on Armenian Street, George Town as part of the Penang Street Art Project. The little girl and her younger brother ride a bicycle with smiles on their faces which bring a happy aura to the Armenian Street.

Caning

Caning (鞭刑) is an official punishment in Malaysia, a court sentence only for men. Women, boys under 10, men older than 50 years old (except those convicted of rape) and people sentenced to death can not be caned. The maximum number of strokes that can be given is 24. Caning is also a common punishment in school for male students who have committed minor offenses.

Ban on Excessive Use of Lipstick

There is a ban on the excessive use of lipstick in Kuala Lumpur which was put into effect in 1996. The reasoning behind it was that the government thought it would lead to illicit sex problems within the city. Malaysia is an Islamic nation, so it's understandable when it comes to Islamic laws.

Task: Draw your mind-map on the "Malaysia in My Eyes" page based on the facts of Malaysia and then introduce Malaysia to your peers by using your mind-map.

★ 5C Reading on Malaysia

A. Read the following passage and underline the features of Baba-Nyonya culture.

In the early 15th century, Zheng He and his fleet traveled to the Indian Ocean. A part of them settled in today's Malaysia and intermarried with the local women. Their descendants are known as Peranakans (峇峇娘惹). The males are called Baba, and females Nyonya. Baba-Nyonya culture is a hybrid of the Chinese and local cultures, layered with Portuguese, Dutch and English influences due to colonization. These influences are reflected in their buildings, costume and cuisine.

Most of the buildings are two-story houses. Some are covered by Chinese style glazed tiles, decorated with Chinese style screens, lanterns, porcelain, and wooden furniture with marble and mother of pearl inlays. Baba-Nyonya also inlaid the wooden lattice windows with European style stained glass. Other European style elements, such as Dutch tiles, Victorian epergnes and lamps, Scottish cast iron handrails and Romanesque pillars can also be seen in the houses.

Kebaya is the costume of Nyonya. It is light and thin, fastened with 3 brooches, containing the Western style of low-cut and shoulder pad. Kebayas are colorful with Chinese traditional auspicious patterns, such as flowers, birds, fish, insects and phoenix. Combined with Chinese traditional hand embroidery and openwork embroidery, many styles were merged together.

Nyonya cuisine is a unique blend of Chinese cooking methods with Malaysian ingredients and recipes. It is tangy, aromatic and spicy. Typical Nyonya dishes are Nasi Lemak, Asam Laksa, Nyonya Kuih and Cendol. Nyonya cuisine emphasizes the matching between the tableware and the dishes. Baba-Nyonya peranakan porcelain is mainly pink and green, with typical Chinese traditional auspicious patterns of phoenix, lotus, peony, and so on.

你知道峇峇娘惹文化与中国文化的历史渊源吗?

B. Discuss the following questions based on the above reading material.

1. In which aspects has Chinese culture cast its influence on Baba-Nyonya culture?

2. How did Baba-Nyonya absorb and merge the essence of other cultures in terms of buildings?

3. How did Chinese Malaysians keep Chinese traditional culture and form the unique Baba-Nyonya culture?

PART III   Welcome Guests from the Land

★ *Project—Catering Services*

You are a waiter working at an influencer restaurant in Chongqing. A group of Malaysian tourists will have dinner here. Please discuss with your partners the do's and don'ts in Malaysia and decide what you should do to make them feel at home based on what you have known about Malaysian people, their cultures, customs and taboos.

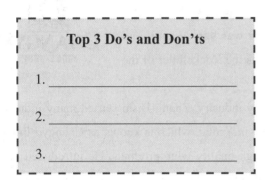

Top 3 Do's and Don'ts

1. _____

2. _____

3. _____

Your Goals

1. Respect the tourists' religious beliefs.

2. Offer high-quality catering services.

· *Tasks*

A. *Tell your partners the reasons why these do's and don'ts are listed top 3.*

B. *List as many do's and don'ts as you can and employ them into the services for Malaysian tourists. The following ones are for your reference.*

Reference for Do's and Don'ts in Malaysia

1. Dress appropriately at religious sites.

2. Remove your shoes before entering a Malaysian home.

3. Only wear a bikini on the beach.

4. Don't kiss or hug in public.

5. Never move objects using your feet.

6. Don't cross your legs.

7. Don't use the right forefinger to point at places, objects or people.

8. Don't put your hands inside your pockets.

9. Never hit your fist into a cupped hand.

10. Don't shake hands with Muslim women unless they stretch out their hands first. This is especially for men.

★ *The Land and the World*

Zhang Bishi—A Patriotic Chinese Malaysian

Born in a poor family in Dabu, Guangdong Province, Zhang Bishi was a patriotic overseas Chinese living in Malaysia. He went to Nanyang—today's Southeast Asia, to make a living when he was very young, and worked his way up as a water carrier to be known as the Rockefeller of the East.

With an ambition to vitalize his motherland by industry, Zhang Bishi started many industries in China. In 1892, he founded the Changyu Winery in Yantai, which is known as Changyu Pioneer Wine Company today, with the goal to produce high-quality wine products. He introduced grape vines and winemaking techniques from abroad, and employed lots of professional winemakers from countries with long histories of making wines, including Italy, Austria and France.

In 1915, Changyu wines won four gold medals and quality certificates at the Panama-Pacific International Exposition in San Francisco. This was the first time for a Chinese product to win an international exhibition award and made Changyu a globally known brand. Today Changyu Pioneer Wine Company is not only China's oldest and largest wine producer, but also among the top 10 worldwide.

Zhang Bishi is considered as the founding father of Chinese wines and the pioneer for China's industrial prosperity.

Guangludi, Former Residence of Zhang Bishi in Dapu County, Guangdong

Statue of Zhang Bishi

Cheong Fatt Tze—The Blue Mansion in Penang

Mind-map: Malaysia in My Eyes

Name: _____   Date: _____

KWL Chart

Topic: _____   Name: _____   Date: _____

Know	Wonder	Learned
What do you think you already know about Malaysia?	What do you wonder about Malaysia? Write your questions below.	Write what you've learned about Malaysia.

裁 切 线

Section 5　Vietnam

Learning Objectives

A flight to Hanoi is about 2 hours from Guangzhou, 3 hours from Singapore, roughly 12 hours from London and about 20 hours from New York with transfer.

After this section, you will be able to:

★ know the geographical features of Vietnam.

★ list the major cities and popular attractions in Vietnam.

★ apply Vietnamese social norms, taboos and unique features to serving inbound Vietnamese tourists, making them feel at home.

★ know the relationship of history, culture, festival and food between China and Vietnam.

"越"游越美之越南

越南位于中南半岛东侧、东南亚的中心地带，北靠中国，西接老挝和柬埔寨，东部和南部濒临中国南海，其国土呈现出狭长的S形状，有"太平洋阳台"的美誉，是丝绸之路的重要枢纽。河内是越南的首都，胡志明市是其最大城市；红河和湄公河为越南境内最大的两条河流，均发源于中国；肥沃的湄公河三角洲是其最为重要的水稻种植区；黄连山的主峰番西邦峰则为越南最高峰。

过去，越南以卫国战争的英雄精神而闻名世界，现在越南以一个和平、安全、有魅力的旅游目的地的形象而吸引国际游客。越南有着众多的物质和非物质文化遗产，比较著名的有下龙湾、美森谷地、会安古镇、顺化宫廷雅乐、雄王祭祀仪式等，旅游资源非常丰富。胡志明市中心保留了自西贡时代以来的风貌，为其赢得了"东方巴黎"的称号，而堤岸作为胡志明市最古老的地区，是越南华人的聚居地，唐人街亦位于此。旅游业已被确定为越南的支柱产业之一，越南在世界旅游大奖（World Travel Award）亚洲及大洋洲地区颁奖典礼上首次荣获"2018年亚太地区最佳旅游目的地"称号。

越南和中国山水相连，文化相通，风俗习惯相近，两国人民有着数千年交流接触的历史。近年来，中国对"一带一路"沿线国家的旅游投资已成为我国对外开放格局中的重要组成部分，随着相关政策的落地与配套设施的完善，"一带一路"沿线国家赴中国旅游热情不断高涨。2019年到中国旅游的外国游客人总人数3.0亿人次；按入境旅游人数排序，我国主要国际客源市场前20位的国家中越南位于第二，位于马来西亚、菲律宾、新加坡、印度、泰国等前列。两国间的旅游合作成为新亮点，促进了中越睦邻友好关系的发展。

Vietnam Facts

- **Name**: Socialist Republic of Viet Nam
- **Capital**: Ha Noi
- **Government**: Communist
- **Language**: Vietnamese
- **Population**: 96.2 Million (2019)
- **Currency**: VND 100 ≈ CNY 0.03 (2021)
- **National Symbols:** Five-Pointed Star on Red Field, Lotus Blossoms
- **National Day**: September 2 (Independence Day)

PART I   Let's Go

★ *First Glance*

Listen to a song, and then answer the following questions.

1. Do you want to go to Vietnam after hearing this song? Why?

2. Vietnam has undergone many changes over the years. Do you know any?

3. Which Vietnamese fact impresses you most in the song?

★ *Listening*

Listen to the song again and fill in the blanks with the lyrics you've heard.

Hello Vietnam

Tell me all about this _____ that is
difficult to say
It was given me the day I was born
Want to know about the _____ of
the empire of old
My eyes say more of me than what you dare
to say
All I know of you
Is all the _____ of war
A film by Coppola, the helicopter's roar
One day I'll touch your _____
One day I'll finally know your _____
One day I'll come to you

To say hello _____
Tell me all about my color
My hair and my little feet
That have carried me every mile of the way
Want to see your house, your _____
Show me all I do not know
Wooden sampans, floating _____, light
of gold…
And Buddha made of stone watch over me
My _____, they lead me through
the fields of rice
In prayer, in the light I see my _____
I touch my tree, my _____, my beginning

PART II   Explore the Land

• *Geography*

Vietnam is located in Southeast Asia. It is situated on the Indochinese peninsula and borders Cambodia (柬埔寨), China and Laos. The country is very narrow and long. It stretches over 1,650 kilometers from the north to the south. The capital city is Ha Noi.

Due to the shape, Vietnam has different climatic zones. The temperatures are generally higher in the southern parts than in the country's north.

Vietnam has many forested regions and rolling hills. High mountain peaks can be found in the northern parts of the country. The highest point of Vietnam is Fan Si Pan which is 3,143 meters high. The largest island is Pho Quoc (富国岛). The island is located in the Gulf of Thailand.

• *People*

Only 36% of the population lives in urban areas of the country. The majority of the people live in the Red River Delta in the north of the country and in the Mekong Delta and Ho Chi Minh City in the south.

The biggest city of the country is Ho Chi Minh City, formerly called Saigon, where more than eight million people live. Da Nang, Hai Phong, Can Tho and the capital city Ha Noi are big cities with more than one million inhabitants.

In Vietnam, the government recognizes 54 ethnic groups. The vast majority of people belong to the Viet people. The biggest ethnic minority groups are the Thai and Khmer people.

• *Language*

Languages spoken in Vietnam are diverse on par with its vast number of ethnicities. Almost each ethnic minority group has its own language such as Hmong, Muong, Khmer, and Tay. However, Vietnamese boasts the only official language which belongs to the Austro-Asiatic Languages and it is used in all primary schools in Vietnam. Despite that, words and accents can vary according to different regions from the north to the south. Vietnamese also inherits a strong influence from foreign languages like Chinese, French and English.

Some common expressions in Vietnam are:

Nyob zoo Xin chao (Hello).

Ua tsaug Cam on ban (Thank you).

Sibntsib dua Tam biet (Goodbye).

Kuv hlub koj Anh yeu em (I love you).

• *Attractions*

Ha Noi

Ha Noi is Vietnam's capital city. It is situated in the north of the country. The buzzing city is Vietnam's major trading center for centuries and it is fascinating to discover the historic past of the city. In the city's Old Quarter the streets are still named after the goods and wares that were once crafted and traded here, such as Hang Be Street—the street of the bamboo crafters, Hang Dao Street—the silk weaver street and Hang Tung Street, where barrels were once skillfully made.

Ho Chi Minh City

Ho Chi Minh City, or Saigon, is Vietnam's largest and most exciting city. It is a popular tourist destination due to its fascinating culture, classic French architecture, and sleek skyscrapers as well as ornate temples and pagodas. The city is also filled with rooftop bars that overlook and beyond, while fantastic restaurants offer a combination of French, Chinese, and local Vietnamese cuisine. Saigon had already been christened the "Paris of Asia".

Da Nang

Da Nang is the county's second biggest city. Due to its location at the Central Coast, the sandy beaches and nearby international airport, this is one of the most popular holiday destinations in Vietnam. It is easy to explore the nearby historic cities of Hue and Hoi An or the magnificent Marble Mountains from here. The Golden Bridge near the mountain resort of Ba Na Hill further inland from Da Nang is a wonderful new attraction to explore as well. The new sky bridge is 150 meters long and offers awesome views.

Hoi An

Hoi An (会安) is a UNESCO World Heritage Site. Hoi An Town is an exceptionally well-preserved example of a Southeast Asian trading port dating from the 15th to the 19th century. Its buildings and its street plan reflect the influences, both indigenous and foreign, that have combined to produce this unique heritage site.

Hue

The city in central Vietnam was once the national capital from 1802 until 1945. The Imperial

City of Hue (顺化) with its palaces and temples also houses the Forbidden City and the royal palace which was the emperor's home for many centuries.

PhuQuoc

PhuQuoc is Vietnam's largest island, which attracts visitors to its clear turquoise waters and stunning beaches. Here people can enjoy idyllic beaches, romantic sunsets, evergreen forests, and a serene atmosphere.

Ha Long Bay

Ha Long Bay (下龙湾) and its magical karst rock formations is among the most amazing wonders of the world. Nearby Van Don International Airport opened in December 2018 and now it is much easier to reach this popular tourist attraction. The bay is home to about 2,000 residents while already over 10 million tourists visit Ha Long Bay every year.

• *Vietnamese Food*

Many dishes in Vietnam consist of rice and vegetables as well as fish, seafood, chicken or beef. Soy sauce as well as fish sauce or shrimp sauce and rice products are the most common ingredients in Vietnamese dishes.

Typical Vietnamese dishes:

• **Nem** (越南春卷): Grilled pork meat skewers which have been marinated in fish sauce. They are often served with spicy chili sauce.

• **Canhchua** (酸菜汤): Sour soup with fish, tomatoes and vegetables as well as pineapple chunks.

• **Pho** (越南河粉): Traditional soup dish made with clear broth, spring onions and sprouts as well as sliced chicken or beef slices.

• **BanhBao** (越南包子): Vietnamese pastry dumpling with usually savory filling such as pork or chicken meat.

• **Xoi** (糯米饭): Sweet sticky rice cakes made with coconut milk and mung beans, often with added food coloring.

• *Unique Vietnam*

Non La

Non La (越南斗笠) is Vietnamese famous palm-leaf conical hat. It is a traditional symbol of Vietnamese people without age, sex or racial distinctions. Non La has its own origin, coming from a legend related to the history of rice growing in Vietnam. The story is about a giant woman from the sky who has protected humankind from a deluge of rain (倾盆大雨). She wore a hat made of four round shaped leaves to guard against all the rain.

Ao Dai

Ao Dai (奥黛) is Vietnamese traditional long gown. The modern Ao Dai we see today is tight-fitting, which accentuates and flatters the women's curves. Therefore, Ao Dai is interestingly considered to cover everything, but hide nothing, especially when it is made of thin or see-through fabric. Ao Dai, therefore, is an ideal souvenir for foreign tourists upon leaving Vietnam, to remind them of a beautiful country that they have been to.

Rice

For Vietnamese, rice can mean much more than a type of staple. It is not overstated to assert that rice is the most influential factor in Vietnamese traditional culture and a driving force for history. It is not just because rice is the most popular grain, which cannot be absent in any Vietnamese meal. It is also because rice feeds the population, and that it contains a hidden beauty that can adorn the already elegant Vietnamese culture. Rice is Vietnamese's unofficial symbol.

Bamboo Tree

Bamboo tree is a significant symbol in both Vietnamese culture and daily life. It exists almost everywhere in Vietnam, though mainly in rural areas. The solid, straight and high bamboo trees represent the resilience (不屈不挠) and bravery of the Vietnamese people. Also, as the bamboo trees often grow in clusters with a strong vitality, it represents the solidarity of Vietnamese people as well as their diligence and loyalty to their homeland.

Quan Họ Singing

Quan Họ (越南关荷调) has become a unique culture representing diverse culture of Kinh Bắc area. The images of young male and female in traditional dressing singing Quan Họ has been considered one of the most beautiful pictures of Vietnam. Although Quan Họ has been modified significantly, yet key elements, especially its music and rhythm are well preserved.

Royal Court Music

Imperial court music is an integral entertainment form in the Vietnamese court during feudal times. The most outstanding form of royal music is "refined music" or "nha nhac", which is recognized as a Masterpiece of Oral and Intangible Heritage by UNESCO. The refined music was first performed in the 13th century but until the Nguyen Dynasty could the royal music enjoy its golden age.

Vietnamese Noodles

When most foreigners think of Vietnamese cuisine, and Vietnamese noodle in particular, "Phở" instantly comes into their minds. In fact, "phở" is not the only one, though without doubt the most renowned, among many kinds of Vietnamese noodles including "phở", "bún", "miến", "hủ tiếu" and so on.

Task: Draw your mind-map on the "Vietnam in My Eyes" page based on the facts of Vietnam and then introduce Vietnam to your peers by using your mind-map.

★ *5C Reading on Vietnam*

A. Read the following passage about Tet Festival.

Vietnam inherited the lunar calendar from China, with its twelve-year cycle of years named after various animals, and continues to follow it. The lunar New Year and the season of spring start with the Tet Festival (越南春节), which usually falls in late January or early February. Typically public holidays will be granted for seven days. Tet is a time when  everyone wants to be at home with the family. The house will have been scrubbed clean and decorated; new clothing will be worn; presents will be exchanged.

 Before Tet there will be a rush to buy clothing, vast quantities of food, candles, and flowers. Practically every family forgets thrift and buys a large quantity of food for the Tet holidays, not only to eat but to place on the family altar for the ancestors. City streets are a riot of color with flowers and decorations on each shop and sidewalk stall. Among the items for sale are the traditional Tet trees—pink peach blossoms in the north, yellow apricot flowers in the south, and beautiful trimmed kumquat (金钱橘) trees everywhere.

Some things are considered to be very bad luck if done at Tet. One should never clean the house, insult others, misbehave, swear, or show any anger or grief. Breaking any dishes is also considered a bad omen.

你知道中国春节和越南春节的关系吗?

B. Discuss the following questions based on the above reading material.

1. Do you know any more similarities between Tet and Spring Festival?

2. How has Chinese Spring Festival influenced Vietnamese Tet?

3. Do you agree that the traditional festival is a bridge which makes people know each other better between China and Vietnam?

PART III   Welcome Guests from the Land

★ *Project—Tour Commentary*

You are a tour guide for a group of Vietnamese tourists. They are going to visit a traditional scenic spot—Tianfu Cheongsam Viewing Store. Please prepare a relevant tour commentary based on what you know about local Cheongsam. Also, you need to take Vietnamese culture and Ao Dai into consideration.

Some Must-Knows

1. _____

2. _____

3. _____

Your Goals

1. Make the tourists happy.

2. Give the tourists a deep impression of cheongsam to promote Chinese culture.

• *Tasks*

A. Tell your partner the reason why you choose these must-knows.

B. Prepare a 3-minute tour commentary based on your must-knows.

The Magic Words or Sentences You Might Need for the Presentation

Words:

cheongsam (旗袍)	female (女性)	garment (长袍)
mandarin collar (中式立领)	chinese knotted button (中国结扣)	slit (开口)
satin brocade (织锦缎)	embroidered (刺绣的)	style (款式)

Sentences:

1. The cheongsam, also known as Qipao or Chipao, is a traditional Chinese close-fitting dress…

2. Its main characteristics are…

3. It is usually made from… Some are even beautifully embroidered.

4. With time, the style of the cheongsam began to…

5. Ao Dai is thought to be influenced by…

★ *The Land and the World*

Vu Xuan Hong—Friendship Ambassador

Vu Xuan Hong, former President of the Vietnam Union of Friendship Organizations in Ha Noi, Vietnam. He was born on January 4, 1950, Ninh Binh. On behalf of Vietnam Union of Friendship Organizations, he made contributions to promoting China-Vietnam friendship. The development of China-Vietnam relations can't do without the support of the organizations.

On the afternoon of October 14, 2013, Premier Li Keqiang met with Vu Xuan Hong and spoke highly of the contributions made by the Vietnam Union of Friendship Organizations.

On June 30, 2016, Vu Xuan Hong was awarded the honorary title of Friendship Ambassador in Beijing.

Mind-map: Vietnam in My Eyes

Name: _____   Date: _____

KWL Chart

Topic: _____   Name: _____   Date: _____

Know What do you think you already know about Vietnam?	**Wonder** What do you wonder about Vietnam? Write your questions below.	**Learned** Write what you've learned about Vietnam.

裁 切 线

Chapter 3　East and South Asia

Section 1　South Korea

Learning Objectives

After this section, you will be able to:

★ know the geographical features of South Korea, especially the large number of successive mountain ranges.

★ learn the basic Korean language and list the special food culture.

★ apply South Korean social norms, taboos and unique features to serving inbound South Korean tourists, making them feel at home.

★ promote the image of Chinese tourism by relating China and South Korea from history, architecture, language and festivals.

茹古"韩"今之韩国

韩国位于东亚朝鲜半岛南部，总面积约10.329万平方千米，通用韩语，总人口约5200万（2021年），首都为首尔。韩国国名源于古时朝鲜半岛南部的部落联盟"三韩"（辰韩、马韩、弁韩），在中国东汉、三国时代，三韩的政权即被中原称为"韩国"，如《三国志》中记载："桓、灵之末，韩澨强盛，郡县不能制，民多流入韩国。"1919年大韩民国临时政府成立于中国上海，虽然改变政体，但仍沿用"韩国"的国名。1948年8月15日起朝鲜半岛南部的国名就被定为"大韩民国"，简称"韩国"。

韩国虽然境内无很多高山，但有许多风景美丽的丘陵和中低山。海拔400米以上的山峰有90余座，其中以雪岳山、智异山、汉山和五台山最为有名。美丽的溪谷遍布全国各地，瀑布众多，形成许多重要的旅游点。较大的温泉有14处，且附有设施完备的旅游和疗养机构。风光美丽的海滨浴场很多，其中条件较好的有55处。历史文化古迹也十分丰富。庆州、釜山和首尔都具有悠久的历史，城内有不少古代宫殿。全国有重要寺庙59座，以海印寺、松广寺和通度寺最为著名。

韩国是一个发达的资本主义国家，是APEC、世界贸易组织和东亚峰会的创始成员国，也是经合组织、二十国集团和联合国等重要国际组织成员。受新冠肺炎疫情影响，2020年2月韩国出入境人数为384.39万人次，环比减少50.9%，同比减少49.4%。数据显示，2月出境的韩国公民105.56万人次，环比减少58.1%，同比减少59.9%，入境的外籍人员71.94万人次，环比减少45.5%，同比减少42.2%。从2020前两个月入境的外国人国籍来看，中国最多，为62.62万人，其后是日本，为42.12万人次。出入境人员中有78.9%利用仁川国际机场，其次是金海机场（9.8%）、金浦机场（5.4%）等。

中韩两国近年来越来越感觉到维护地区和平与稳定的重要性，彼此为解决地区问题开展密切合作。因此，如何在接触中了解韩国基本国情，增进互信共识，拓展合作领域，深化合作层次是当代涉外旅游复合型人才思考的重要问题。

South Korea Facts

- **Name**: Republic of Korea
- **Capital**: Seoul
- **Government**: Presidential Republic
- **Language**: Korean
- **Population**: 52 Million (2021)
- **Life Expectancy**: 82.3 Years (2019)
- **Currency**: KRW 100 ≈ CNY 0.58 (2021)
- **National Symbols**: Siberian Tiger, Hibiscus Syracuse
- **National Day**: August 15

PART I　Let's Go

★ *First Glance*

Watch the video, and then answer the following questions.

1. Do you think tourism is developed in South Korea?

2. What else do you know about South Korea?

3. Do you know anything about South Korean food culture?

★ *Viewing and Listening*

Watch the video again and fill in the blanks with the attractions you've watched.

_____

_____

_____

_____

_____

_____

PART II Explore the Land

· *Geography*

South Korea is located in East Asia, on the southern half of the Korean Peninsula bounded by the Sea of Japan in the east, the Yellow Sea in the west and the Korea Strait in the south. In the north it shares its land boundary with the Democratic People's Republic of Korea. The other overseas neighbors of South Korea are Japan in the east and China in the west.

South Korea's terrain is mostly mountainous with only 30% lowland out of the total land area. The total area is 103,290 square kilometers. And it has 2,413 kilometers long coastline. The highest point in South Korea is Halla-san (汉拿山), an extinct volcano, which rises to 1,950 meters and is located on Jeju Island (济州岛)—the largest South Korean island. The climate in South Korea is temperate with more rainy summers than winters.

· *People*

South Korea is one of the most ethnically homogenous nations in the world. That means that almost everybody belongs to the same ethnic category. Over 99% of South Koreans identify as ethnically Korean. The largest group of ethnic minorities in South Korea, the Chinese, only number around 20,000 people. So South Korea is really home to the Koreans.

Most Koreans live in urban areas of the country. The lowlands around the capital city Seoul and Incheon are home to the majority the South Koreans. South Korea is one of the planet's most densely populated countries with a density of 503 people per square kilometer.

· *Language*

Korean is the national and official language in South Korea. In ancient times, Koreans started using Chinese characters to write. The Hangul alphabet was created in the 15th century, which made it easier for all Koreans to gain knowledge. And the Hangul alphabet became popular in the 19th century when Koreans started trying to shake off Chinese influences. There have been several attempts to abolish the use of Chinese characters in the past, but the solutions were always temporary. Today in South Korea, following government policy, students in secondary schools must learn 1,800 basic Chinese characters.

The most common ways to greet someone in Korean are:

Annyonghasyo! (Hi!)

Gomawoyo! (Thanks!)

Charchayo! (Good night!)

• *Attractions*

Seoul

Being the capital and largest city of South Korea, Seoul (首尔) is also its cultural and business center with stunning architecture, vibrant culture and a thriving economy. From modern skyscrapers and neon lights to Buddhist temples, palaces and pagodas, Seoul is a fascinating mix of old and new, which is the key to Seoul's allure and a central tenet of the city's identity. UNESCO World Heritage Site Changdeokgung Palace is a fine example of authentic ancient architecture, while Namsan Soul Tower is a much-loved landmark, which glances at the most beautiful images of Seoul.

Busan

Located in the southeast, Busan (釜山) is the second largest city and has become the largest industrial area of South Korea. Additionally, Busan boasts the fifth busiest sea port in the entire world. Known as the "Summer Capital of South Korea", the beaches, the restaurants, and cafes that dot the shoreline in Busan, are considered major tourist spots during summer months. Busan also has the world's largest department store, Shinsegae in Centum City. Busan is well known as a passionate baseball city as well as being well known for basketball, football, horse racing and cycling.

Incheon

Incheon (仁川) was inhabited since the New Stone Age. And today it's the third most populous city of South Korea. With a massive ice-free harbor and a world-renowned international airport, Incheon serves as a transportation hub by air and sea. Being South Korea's first free economic zone, it has gathered investment from large local companies and global enterprises. Incheon is not only a historically and economically significant place for Koreans, but also a cultural center with many attractions like Yeongjong Island and Ganghwa Island that offer visitors a unique blend of the modern and traditional, the past and future.

Gyeongbokgung Palace

Located in the heart of Seoul and built in 1395, Gyeongbokgung Palace (景福宫) is one of South Korea's most iconic buildings due to its long and storied history. Gyeongbokgung Palace, which means "palace greatly blessed by Heaven", was the first and largest of the five grand royal palaces built during the Joseon Dynasty.

The South Korean government has invested much time and effort into rebuilding, restoring, and maintaining the palace for future generations. These efforts include work to rebuild and restore the buildings that were destroyed during the Japanese occupation to restore this fabulous building back to the epitome of its former glory.

• **Jeju Island**

Jeju Island (济州岛) is a popular vacation spot for Koreans and foreigners. It remains the top honeymoon destination for Korean newlyweds. Despite attempts to market the island as "the Hawaii of Korea", climatologically and geographically it bears little in similarity to the Hawaiian Islands in the U.S. The island offers visitors a wide range of activities: hiking on Halla-san or Olle-Gil, catching sunrises and sunsets over the ocean, riding horses, touring all the locales from a favorite television K-drama, or just lying around on the sandy beaches.

• ***South Korean Food***

Food in South Korea is reflective of the many different cultural influences that have made their way into the lives of the Korean people like China, Japan, and other Asian mainland countries. It has become so popular that locals and tourists alike describe them as savory, spicy, hearty and nutritious delights.

Here are popular South Korean foods:

• **Kimchi** (泡菜): A popular Korean dish which is best described as a spicy, slightly sweet, pickled or fermented cabbage.

• **Haejangguk** (宿醉汤): Soup to chase a hangover which usually consists of dried napa cabbage, congealed ox blood and various vegetables in a hearty beef broth.

• **Bibimbap** (石锅拌饭): A Korean dish of rice with cooked vegetables, usually meat, and often a raw or fried egg.

• **Bulgogi** (韩国烤肉): Known as Korean BBQ beef, which is marinated thinly sliced beef, typically cooked over an open flame.

• **Soondubu Jjigae** (软豆腐炖): Known as soft tofu stew, a Korean stew made with silky soft, uncurdled tofu coated in a spicy and flavorful broth, to be served alongside a bowl of steamed rice.

• **Chimaek** (炸鸡与啤酒): A popular weekend or post-work delicacy. "Chi" is Korean for chicken and "Maek" is short for "maekju", which means beer.

• ***Unique South Korea***
Jikji

Written in Chinese characters by a Buddhist monk, Jikji is the abbreviated title of a Korean Buddhist document whose title can be translated into "Anthology of Great Buddhist Priests' Zen Teachings". Printed during the Goryeo Dynasty in 1377, Jikji is the world's oldest extant book printed with movable metal type.

UNESCO confirmed Jikji as the world's oldest metal-printed book in September 2001 and included it in the UNESCO Memory of the World Register. The ancient book is now kept at the National Library of France in Paris.

Hanbok

Hanbok (韩服) is the traditional attire of the Korean people. Its general design aims to create a delicate flow of lines and angles, which illustrates the softness and elegance of traditional Korean aesthetics. Traditional hanboks boasted vibrant hues that correspond with the five elements of the yin and yang theory. And its basic aesthetic framework is centered on the Korean fondness for naturalness, desire for supernatural protection and blessings, and the Confucian style dress code.

Cosmetic Surgery

South Korea has a big plastic surgery market, with one in three women aged between 19 and 29 reported to have gone under the knife. Plastic surgery is integrated into people's daily life. Parents often "gift" their children some form of surgery after they finish their national college entrance exams or when they become legal adults. Plastic surgery tourism is also a lucrative market. Revenue from plastic surgery tourists in 2014 was $107 million.

Korean Drama

Korean drama is television series in Korean language, made in South Korea. They are popular worldwide, partially due to the spread of Korean popular culture. Many Korean dramas have been adapted throughout the world, and some have had great impact on other countries.

Dongdaemun Market

Dongdaemun Market (东大门), a prominent landmark in South Korea, is a large commercial district comprised of traditional markets and shopping centers. It's South Korea's largest wholesale and retail shopping district, featuring 26 shopping malls, 30,000 specialty shops, and 50,000 manufacturers. All kinds of goods can be found here including clothes, electronics, office supplies and pet products, etc.

Chuseok

Celebrated on the 15th day of the 8th lunar month, Chuseok (秋夕节) is a three-day holiday and one of the most important ones in South Korea. Family members gather together, celebrate and show gratitude to their ancestors for the fruitful harvest. They hold memorial services on the morning of Chuseok, during which an offering is

prepared to their deceased ancestors, which consists of songpyeon, alcohol, and freshly harvested rice. They also visit their ancestors' graves and remove any weeds growing around them to show appreciation and respect to them, which is considered a familial duty and a sign of devotion.

Task: Draw your mind-map on the "South Korea in My Eyes" page based on the facts of South Korea and then introduce South Korea to your peers by using your mind-map.

★ 5C Reading on South Korea

A. Read the following passage and sum up the different activities between China and South Korea in traditional festivals.

The Dragon Boat Festival is a traditional Chinese festival that commemorates Qu Yuan, an ancient Chinese poet. In China, it takes place on the fifth day of the fifth month on the Chinese lunar calendar. However, China is not the only country where people can enjoy such a festival, many countries in Asia, also celebrate the Dragon Boat Festival annually in a different way.

In South Korea, the festival is known as "Gangneung Danoje Festival", which places sacrificial ceremony as its core, blending the concepts of Confucianism, Shamanism and Buddhism. It is celebrated in the town of Gangneung on the fifth day of the fifth lunar month and usually lasts for a month. Gangneung City has preserved traditional customs that South Koreans have practiced for more than a thousand years, and successfully bid for Gangneung Danoje Festival to be listed by UNESCO as an Intangible Cultural Heritage in 2005.

Today, Dano is one of the three major traditional holidays in South Korea. On that day, families in South Korea offer wormwood and muffins to their ancestors. People wear traditional costumes to attend ceremonies, watch swings and wrestling matches. Other traditional customs associated with the special day include eating rice cakes, making Dano fans, performing traditional mask dances, washing hair in water boiled with sweet flag, etc.

> 韩国江陵端午祭申遗成功对保护中国传统文化节日有何启示？

B. Discuss the following questions based on the above reading material.

1. Do you know why people in South Korea celebrate Dano Festival?

2. What are the differences and similarities between South Korea's Gangneung Danoje Festival and China's Dragon Boat Festival?

3. What should Chinese people do to protect the traditional culture and festivals, like the Dragon Boat Festival?

PART III   Welcome Guests from the Land

★ Project—Airport Drop Off

You are a tour guide for a group of South Korean tourists who are going back to South Korea. At the airport, you'd like to remind your guests about the rules for checked and carry-on luggage. Review the airport security policies and restricted items, and discuss with your partner wchich rules might be the most applicable to your South Korean guests.

Top 3 Security Reminders

1. _____

2. _____

3. _____

Your Goals

1. Make good impressions.
2. Make the tourists feel happy.
3. Improve professional skills and services.

· *Tasks*

   A. *Tell your partners the reasons why you want to remind the tourists of these top 3 securitiy reminders.*

   B. *Prepare a 3-minute presentation on your top 3 securitiy reminders.*

For Your Reference

- hand luggage restrictions/allowances 随身携带行李限制/限额
- take liquids through security 带着液体过安检
- the rules for electronic items and devices you're allowed to take on the flight 允许带上飞机的电子物品和设备的规则
- There are restrictions on what items can be taken in hand luggage and hold luggage when going through security and boarding a plane.
- Airport security staff will not let anything through that they consider dangerous.
- There are restrictions on the amount of liquids you can take in your hand luggage.
- If you do take liquids in your hand luggage, the containers must hold no more than 100 ml.

★ *The Land and the World*

Ban Ki-moon—The Bridge of China, South Korea and the World

Ban Ki-moon, born in June 13, 1944, South Korean diplomat and politician, who served as the eighth Secretary-General of the United Nations (UN).

Ban said that China has set a good example of how a committed and persistent government can transform economic development into increased quality of human life. The success of China, among other Asian countries, is not only proof of feasibility, but also a valuable lesson that will empower other developing countries on their way toward sustainable development.

Ban made the remarks in a pre-recorded speech delivered at a news conference in Beijing that released the Asia Poverty Reduction Report 2020, which said Asia has been leading the poverty reduction cause worldwide since 1990, to which China is a major contributor.

Ban has also repeatedly put forward the mechanism of common development, prosperity and stability for the sake of China and South Korea. He pointed out that the duty-free commodities in Seoul of South Korea are favored by Chinese tourists, which is beneficial to the development of South Korea's tourism market, the promotion of South Korea's economic development, and the stabilization of South Korean friendly relations.

Mind-map: South Korea in My Eyes

Name: _____ Date: _____

KWL Chart

Topic: _____   Name: _____   Date: _____

Know	Wonder	Learned
What do you think you already know about South Korea?	What do you wonder about South Korea? Write your questions below.	Write what you've learned about South Korea.

裁

切

线

Section 2   Japan

A flight to Tokyo is about 3 hours from Shanghai, 8 hours from Singapore, 13 hours from London, and 12.5 hours from New York.

Learning Objectives

After this section, you will be able to:

★ know the geographical features of Japan, especially the cause of frequent earthquakes.

★ list the typical landmarks and attractions in Japan.

★ apply Japanese social norms, taboos and unique features to serving inbound Japanese tourists, making them feel at home.

★ promote the image of Chinese tourism by relating China and Japan from history, architecture, language and food.

月异"日"新之日本

　　日本是一个位于东亚的岛国，有"日出之国""樱花之国""火山地震之邦"等称号。全国由北海道、四国、本州和九州四大岛及其他6800多个岛屿组成，面积37.8万平方千米，是亚洲面积最大的发达国家。人口约1.26亿（2021年），居世界各国第11位，在所有发达国家中排名第二，仅次于美国。居民多为大和族，通用日语，信奉神道教和佛教。首都东京是日本的政治、经济、文化中心，也是世界上最繁华和拥挤的城市之一。

　　日本被誉为极富自然美的地方，繁华的东京、古老的京都、圣洁的北海道，随处可见的有着浓郁东方特色的庭院和庙宇，都给旅游者留下了深刻印象。樱花、温泉和富士山几乎是日本的象征。日本旅游业非常发达，接待服务设施完善，国内旅游一直占据主导地位。近年来，政府致力于把日本建设成为一个旅游国家，积极促进国际旅游的发展。日本曾经使用"Yokoso Japan, Japan Endless Discovery"作为旅游宣传口号。

　　从1979年至2004年，日本一直是中国第一客源市场国家，2017年到中国旅游的日本游客为268万人次，2018年为269万人次，为中国第四客源国。日本来华旅游以观光休闲为主，商务旅行、经济考察与学术交流的人数增长较快，来华修学旅游的人数也有明显增加。随着日本游客对中国认识的逐渐加深，他们需要更多有文化内涵和个性化的旅游产品和服务。同时，随着中国政治、经济和文化的不断发展和进步，在接待日本入境游客时，也更应该思考如何讲好中国故事，让更多日本游客认识中国，乐游中国，爱上中国。

Japan Facts

- **Name**: Japan
- **Capital**: Tokyo
- **Government**: Constitutional Monarchy
- **Language**: Japanese
- **Population**: 126 Million (2021)

- **Life Expectancy**: 83.7 Years (2019)
- **Currency**: JPY 100 ≈ CNY 5.86 (2021)
- **National Symbols**: Crane, Cherry Blossom
- **National Day**: Feburary 11

PART I　Let's Go

★ *First Glance*

Watch the video, and then answer the following questions.

1. Do you want to go to Japan after watching the video?

2. Which Japan fact impresses you most in the video?

3. What do you know about Japan?

★ *Listening*

Listen to the audio and fill in the blanks with the words you have heard.

Japan is known as the "＿＿＿＿＿＿＿＿". Its flag is a red circle on a ＿＿＿＿＿＿＿＿. The red circle on the flag represents the belief that Japan was the first country to see the sun rising in the east each morning. Japan is an archipelago made of thousands of islands; however, 98% of the population lives on the ＿＿＿＿＿＿＿＿.

The four places mentioned are Hongshu, Shikoko, Kyushu, and Hokkaido. Hongshu is ＿＿＿＿＿＿＿＿＿＿ island. Hokkaido Island to the north is home to many ＿＿＿＿＿＿＿＿ and winter sports. ＿＿＿＿＿＿＿＿ like Fukouka are in Kyushu. Shikokou in the south is ＿＿＿＿＿＿＿＿ of the four major islands.

PART II   Explore the Land

• *Geography*

Located on the Asian continent, Japan is a chain of islands along the eastern coast of Asia, reaching from the northern coast of Russia to the South East China Sea.

The Japanese islands consist of 4 main islands and dozens of smaller isles. The largest of the four major islands is Honshu, which is also the seventh largest island in the world. The biggest cities are Tokyo (东京), Yokohama (横滨), Osaka (大阪) and Nagoya (名古屋).

The highest mountain in Japan is Mount Fuji, a dormant volcano, which last erupted in 1707.

Japan lies on the Pacific "Ring of Fire", a chain of volcanoes which are responsible for the most dramatic volcanic outbreaks and tsunamis in the recent years. In Japan, there are more than 108 active volcanoes.

• *People*

Japan is the oldest monarchy in the world and has an emperor. Naruhito, the reigning emperor is Japan's 126th emperor, in Japanese called "tenno". The emperor's wife is Empress Masako. The imperial palace is in Tokyo and this is the main residence of the imperial family.

The crown is usually handed down from father to his son or grandson. Naruhito was crowned in May 2019, after his father, Emperor Akihito, stepped down.

• *Language*

Japanese, or Nihongo, is spoken by about 128 million people worldwide. The Japanese language is complex because there are no singular and plural forms and there is no gender form and no articles are used.

There are only 48 sounds, so it is relatively easy to learn to speak, but learning how to write Japanese is quite a task.

There are three styles of writing the symbols. The biggest challenge is learning to write the characters.

The most common ways to greet someone in Japan are:

こんにちは Konnichiwa (Hi; Good afternoon).

お早うございます Ohayō gozaimasu/ Ohayō (Good morning).

こんばんは Konbanwa (Good evening).

· *Attractions*

Tokyo

Tokyo is Japan's capital and the world's most populous metropolis. It is also one of Japan's 47 prefectures, consisting of 23 central city districts and multiple cities, towns and villages west of the city center.

Prior to 1868, Tokyo was known as Edo. A small castle town in the 16th century, Edo became Japan's political center in 1603 when Tokugawa Ieyasu established his feudal government there. A few decades later, Edo had grown into one of the world's most populous cities. After the Meiji Restoration of 1868, the emperor and capital moved from Kyoto to Edo, which was renamed Tokyo ("Eastern Capital"). Large parts of Tokyo were destroyed in the Great Kanto Earthquake of 1923 and in the air raids of 1945.

Today, Tokyo offers a seemingly unlimited choice of shopping, entertainment, culture and dining to its visitors. The city's history can be appreciated in districts such as Asakusa and in many excellent museums, historic temples and gardens. Contrary to common perception, Tokyo also offers a number of attractive green spaces in the city center and within relatively short train rides at its outskirts.

Kyoto

Kyoto (京都) served as Japan's capital and the emperor's residence from 794 until 1868. It is one of the country's ten largest cities with a population of 1.5 million people and a modern face.

Over the centuries, Kyoto was destroyed by many wars and fires, but due to its exceptional historic value, the city was dropped from the list of target cities for the atomic bomb and escaped destruction during World War Ⅱ. Countless temples, shrines and other historically priceless structures survive in the city today.

Osaka

Osaka (大阪) is Japan's second largest metropolitan area after Tokyo. It has been the economic powerhouse of the Kansai Region for many centuries. Osaka was formerly known as

Naniwa. Before the Nara Period, when the capital used to be moved with the reign of each new emperor, Osaka was once Japan's capital city, the first one ever known.

In the 16th century, Toyotomi Hideyoshi chose Osaka as the location for his castle, and the city might have become Japan's political capital if Tokugawa Ieyasu had not terminated the Toyotomi lineage after Hideyoshi's death and moved his government to Tokyo.

Hakone

Hakone (箱根) is part of the Fuji-Hakone-Izu National Park, less than one hundred kilometers from Tokyo.

Famous for hot springs, natural beauty and the view of nearby Mount Fuji across Lake Ashinoko, Hakone is one of the most popular destinations among Japanese and international tourists looking for a break from Tokyo.

Mountain Fuji

Mount Fuji is the highest mountain in Japan, standing 3,776.24 meters. It is the second-highest island volcano in Asia, and the seventh-highest peak of an island on the earth. Mount Fuji is an active volcano that last erupted from 1707 to 1708.

Nara

Japan's first permanent capital was established in the year 710 at Heijo, the city now known as Nara (奈良). Nara is located less than one hour from Kyoto and Osaka. Due to its past as the first permanent capital, the city remains full of historic treasures, including some of Japan's oldest and largest temples.

· *Japanese Food*

The Japanese diet consists mainly of rice, fish, soy products and vegetables. Many dishes contain these ingredients and soups. Sushi, which contains raw fish such as salmon or tuna, is very popular.

Popular Japanese foods:

- **Sushi** (寿司): Raw fish and rice rolls.
- **Bento box** (便当盒): Lunch boxes often filled with sushi and other treats and snacks.
- **Ramen** (拉面): Egg noodles in a broth.
- **Soba** (荞麦面): Buckwheat noodles in a broth.
- **Tempura** (天妇罗): Light and crispy deep-fried food, such as vegetables, fish or meat.
- **Taiyaki** (鲷鱼烧): Sweet treats with various fillings in a fish shape.

· *Unique Japan*

Shinto

Shinto (神道教) is widely considered to be the native religion of Japan. While most locals would deny being religious at all, Shinto traditions and festivals play a huge role in everyday life. In Kyoto alone, there are over 400 Shinto shrines dedicated to various kami (deities).

Kimono

Traditional fashion such as the kimono (和服) is unique to Japan and that sets it apart from other cultures. Many locals still enjoy wearing traditional clothes for special occasions, including graduation, weddings, and festivals.

Anime and Manga

Astro Boy (《铁臂阿童木》), written in the 1950s, is one of the world's first manga cartoons (漫画). The comic was admired for its progressive style, and decades later, manga and anime would grow to become one of the country's most iconic exports. Japan's manga has a strong influence on the comic book artistry in both China and South Korea.

Bowing

The Japanese learn how and when to bow from a young age, and they use bows among themselves to mean anything from "thank you" to "I'm sorry".

Sumo Wrestling

Sumo wrestling (相扑) began in Japan hundreds of years ago, during the Edo Period, but its roots may go back even further to ancient Shinto rituals. Japan is the only country where sumo wrestling really caught on, and it is still the only place where you'll find the sport practiced on a professional level.

Tatami

Tatami (榻榻米) flooring originated as small, mobile seating for the nobility during the Heian Period. By the early Edo Period, even the lower classes started using tatami mats. They are not only comfortable but also high maintenance and must be replaced from time to time. They're now used primarily in Japanese-style rooms, such as those in tearooms, traditional restaurants, and inns.

Kawaii Culture

No place on earth appreciates cuteness as much as Japan does. From adorable mascots and warning signs to pop culture icons and advertisements, kawaiiness is one of the most prized attributes that a thing can have.

Task: Draw your mind-map on the "Japan in My Eyes" page based on the facts of Japan and then introduce Japan to your peers by using your mind-map.

★ 5C Reading on Japan

A. Read the following passage and underline the parts related with China.

Old Japanese is the oldest attested stage of the Japanese language. Through the spread of Buddhism, the Chinese writing system was imported to Japan. The earliest texts found in Japan are written in classical Chinese. Some of these Chinese texts show influences from Japanese grammar, such as the word order; for example, placing the verb after the object. In these hybrid texts, Chinese characters are also occasionally used phonetically to represent Japanese particles. The earliest text, the Kojiki, dates to the early 8th century, and was written entirely in Chinese characters.

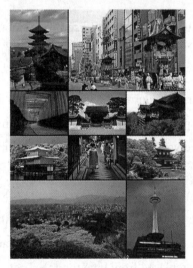

Kyoto (京都市) is the capital city of the Kyoto Prefecture in Japan. Located in the Kansai region on the island of Honshu, Kyoto forms part of the Keihanshin metropolitan area along with Osaka and Kobe. As of 2018, the city had a population of 1.47 million. The original city was arranged in accordance with traditional Chinese feng shui, following the model of the ancient Chinese capital of Chang'an. The Imperial Palace faced the south, resulting in Ukyō (右京区: the right sector of the capital) being on the west while Sakyō (左京区: the left sector) is on the east. The streets in the modern-day districts of Nakagyō (中京区), Shimogyō (下京区), and Kamigyō -ku still follow a grid pattern. Kyoto is considered the cultural capital of Japan and a major tourist destination. It is home to numerous Buddhist temples, Shinto shrines, palaces and gardens, some of which are listed collectively by UNESCO as a World Heritage Site.

你知道中国文字、语言及建筑对日本的影响吗?

B. Discuss the following questions based on the above reading material.

1. How has Chinese significantly influenced Japanese language?

2. Do you know any more similarities between Kyoto and Chang'an?

3. How do you understand that civilizations are colorful because of communication and rich because of mutual learning?

PART III Welcome Guests from the Land

★ *Project—Recommending Souvenirs*

You are a tour guide for a group of Japanese tourists. They want to buy souvenirs which will help them make the trip in China unforgettable and memorable experience. Please discuss with your peers and decide 3 things to recommend based on what you know about Japanese people and culture. Also, you need to take local Chinese culture into consideration.

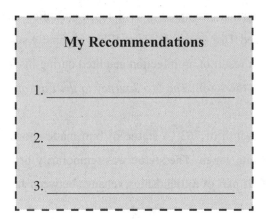

My Recommendations

1. _____

2. _____

3. _____

Your Goals

1. Make the tourists happy.
2. Make more international tourists know about China.

• *Tasks*

A. *Tell your partner the reason why you choose these three things.*

B. *Prepare a 3-minute presentation on your recommendation.*

The Magic Words or Sentences You Might Need for the Presentation

Words:

specialty (特产)	sichuan brocade (蜀锦)	tea set (茶具)
chopsticks (筷子)	jade bracelet (玉手镯)	cloisonné (景泰蓝)
silk scarf (丝巾)	chinese knot (中国结)	calligraphy and painting (书画)

Sentences:

1. The top 3 things / items that I want to recommend are…

2. The first one is… the second one is… and the last one is…

3. … is an art that is famous throughout the world.

4. Pieces of intricately made art can be bought to hang up on your wall, no matter what size.

5. It will remind you of the good trip in China and you'll never forget the joy, happiness and rich culture you have explored in China.

★ *The Land and the World*

Monk Jianzhen's Journey to Japan

Jianzhen or Ganjin in Japanese, was a Chinese monk who helped to propagate Buddhism in Japan. In the eleven years from 743 to 754, Jianzhen attempted to visit Japan six times. Jianzhen finally came to Japan in the year 754 and founded Tōshōdai-ji in Nara. When he finally succeeded on his sixth attempt, he had lost his eyesight as a result of an infection acquired during his journey. Jianzhen's life story and voyage are described in the scroll, *The Sea Journey to the East of a Great Bonze from the Tang Dynasty*.

Jianzhen died on the 6th day of the 5th month of 763. A statue of him made shortly after his death can still be seen at Tōshōdai-ji in Nara, Japan. The statue was temporarily brought to Jianzhen's original temple in Yangzhou in 1980 as part of a friendship exchange between Japan and China.

Jianzhen Monk Memorial Hall in Yangzhou

Jianzhen's Wooden Statue

Tōshōdai-ji Built by Jianzhen in Nara, Japan

Mind-map: Japan in My Eyes

Name: _____   Date: _____

KWL Chart

Topic: _____ Name: _____ Date: _____

Know	Wonder	Learned
What do you think you already know about Japan?	What do you wonder about Japan? Write your questions below.	Write what you've learned about Japan.

裁

切

线

Section 3   India

Learning Objectives

A flight to Delhi is 4.5 hours from Kunming, 14 hours from Tokyo, 8.5 hours from London and 13.5 hours from New York.

After this section, you will be able to:

★ know the geographical features of India.

★ list the typical landmarks and attractions in India.

★ better understand and communicate with Indian tourists by knowing geography, history, traditions and culture of India.

★ explore and discover more opportunities to promote China and India tourism industry.

菩提"印"记之印度

　　印度位于南亚次大陆，面积约298万平方千米，与北京时差两个半小时。印度是世界四大文明古国之一，公元前2500年至1500年之间创造了印度河文明。公元前1500年左右，原居住在中亚的雅利安人中的一支进入南亚次大陆，建立了一些奴隶制小国，确立了种姓制度，婆罗门教兴起。公元前4世纪崛起的孔雀王朝统一印度，中世纪小国林立，印度教兴起。公元8世纪阿拉伯人侵入，1206年建立德里苏丹王朝，引入伊斯兰文化。1600年英国侵入，建立东印度公司。1757年沦为英殖民地。1947年印巴分治，印度独立。1950年印度共和国成立，为英联邦成员国。印度的历史及地理环境决定了其在民族、语言、文化、宗教、饮食等各个方面呈现出多样性的特点。

　　印度是世界第二人口大国，也是金砖国家之一。印度三分之二的人口仍然直接或间接依靠农业维生，近年来服务业增长迅速，已成为全球软件、金融等服务业最重要出口国。全球最大的非专利药出口国，侨汇世界第一。印度1955年通过消除种姓歧视的宪法条款，各邦也制定了相应的法律。但在不少地方，尤其是广大乡村，种姓歧视还相当严重。

　　印度历史悠久、文化灿烂，生态多样，至今有29处世界自然与文化遗产，在世界旅坛中独具特色，堪称"神奇印度，梦幻之国"。旅游业是印度第三大创汇部门和重要就业创造部门。进入20世纪80年代以来，印度来华旅游人数逐步增长，来华旅游的主要目的是休闲、商务、购物。2015年，中印两国签署《关于旅游合作的协议》，建立联合工作机制，推进游客签证便利化。2015年在中国举办"印度旅游年"，2016年在印度举办"中国旅游年"。习近平主席在印度访问时宣布，为便利印度香客赴中国西藏神山、圣湖朝圣，中方同意增开乃堆拉山口的朝圣路线。印度也在大力开发佛教旅游线路，景点包括公元7世纪玄奘取经、在印度修行相关的景点。历史上东土大唐和西天佛国的美好回忆有望书写全球化旅游时代的新传奇。

India Facts

• **Name**: Republic of India

• **Capital**: New Delhi

• **Government**: Democracy

• **Languages**: Hindi, English

• **Population**: 1.32 Billion (2021)

• **Life Expectancy**: 68.3 Years (2019)

• **Currency**: INR 100 ≈ CNY 8.71 (2021)

• **National Symbols**: Lotus, Tiger, Peacock

• **Important Holidays**: Republic Day, Independence Day, Holi, Divali

PART I Let's Go

★ *First Glance*

Watch the video, and then answer the following questions.

1. How many Indian cultural symbols can you recognize in the video?

2. Which Indian fact impresses you most in the video?

3. Why are Indian cultures so diversified?

★ *Listening*

Listen to the passage and fill in the blanks with the words you have heard.

India—an influential nation in South Asia, also known as the _____, is home to the world's _____ population. It is a country of bulk variety, whether it concerns religious, cultural, or ethnic _____. It operates the world's most vigorous democratic republic, and has had a key voice in global affairs since its "creation" with the division of the Indian subcontinent shortly after the Second World War by the British Empire.

With a rapidly growing consumer base, and a swiftly rising overall _____ fueled by its young and increasingly educated population, India has begun its trip on the path to becoming a _____ world power within the next century.

PART II Explore the Land

• *Geography*

The Republic of India occupies most of the subcontinent of India in South Asia. It is the 7th largest country by geographical area. The country is surrounded by the Bay of Bengal in the east, the Arabian Sea in the west, and the Indian Ocean to the south. Currently India has 29 states and 7 union territories. New Delhi is the capital, and Mumbai is the largest city.

The country can be divided into three distinct geographic regions: the Himalayan (喜马拉雅山脉的) region in the north, which contains some of the highest mountains in the world, the Gangetic Plain (恒河平原), and the plateau region in the south and central part. Its three great river systems—the Ganges, the Indus, and the Brahmaputra—have extensive deltas and all rise in the Himalayas.

The climate of India varies significantly across the country. Some areas are tropical, warm and humid while other areas have desert conditions and the northern locations experience temperate weather patterns.

• *People*

India is the second-most populous country with over 1.32 billion people. Indian society is structured around the families people are born into and where they are born. Individuals inherit their social position and stay within it throughout life.

A caste, or jati (meaning "birth"), is the level within the social system that determines who people will marry and often even what line of work they can pursue, where they can live and what they can eat. There are more than 2,000 jati and they fall within four recognized caste groups, or varnas:

• Brahmans (婆罗门)—priests and the most educated.

• Kshatriyas (刹帝利)—warriors and landowners.

• Vaishyas (吠舍)—merchants.

• Sudras (首陀罗)—craftsmen and workers.

A fifth, unofficial group, the Panchama (潘查摩) were historically called the "Untouchables" and in more recent years the Dalit or "Oppressed".

Caste has been the predominant feature of Indian social system. The Constitution, has taken a great step towards the dilution of caste and casteism. Caste and casteism have been playing important factor in social, economic, cultural and political life in India. As caste system has deep historical roots, it cannot be abolished.

• *Language*

Do you know that India has 22 official languages? If two unknown Indians meet randomly on the street, there would only be a 36% chance that they would understand each other. And that 36% depends a lot on their ethnicity and place of origin. Hindi is the most widely spoken language and primary tongue of 41% of the people. English enjoys the status of subsidiary official language but is the most important language for national, political, and commercial communication. For many people in India, English is no longer a foreign language because, after almost 100 years of colonization, Indians made it their own. For cultural and linguistic reasons, Indian English is very different from Standard English, and is best known as "Hinglish".

Here are some simple expressions in Hindi:

Namaste. (Hello.)

Dhanyawad. (Thank you.)

Bahut achchha. (Very Good.)

• *Attractions*

Delhi

The city of Delhi (德里) actually consists of two components: Old Delhi, in the north, is the historic city. New Delhi, in the south, is the capital of India since 1947 which was built in the first part of the 20th century as the capital of British India. Old Delhi and New Delhi are just two faces of the same coin. They perfectly showcase the incredible blend of tradition and modernity of the city. Delhi is home to some of the most stunning temples, mosques and forts. These include the Red Fort, Jama Masjid and the Baha'i Lotus Temple.

Mumbai

Located along the sea, Mumbai (孟买) was once known as Bombay. It is the biggest city in India, and the country's financial center. With endless opportunities for exploration, the city's most notable attraction is the Gateway of India, built in 1911 to commemorate a royal visit.

Jaipur

Jaipur (斋普尔) is commonly known as the "Pink City" due to its stunning buildings which were painted pink in 1876 to welcome the Prince of Wales and Queen Victoria. Jaipur is also the biggest city in the state of Rajasthan, and its capital. Together with Agra and Delhi, it is part of the famous Golden "Triangle" which attracts thousands of Indian and international tourists every year.

Jim Corbett National Park

Jim Corbett National Park is a world-famous tiger reserve and home to a wide variety of majestic animals such as leopards, elephants, boars, jackals, mongooses and so on. The park encompasses a total area of approximately 520 square kilometers. There is a mixed variety of flora and fauna in its breathtaking landscapes. Named after the legendary tiger hunter turned naturalist Jim Corbett (1875-1955), the proud destination Jim Corbett National Park was the first national park of India.

Taj Mahal

The Taj Mahal (泰姬陵) is an enormous mausoleum complex commissioned in 1632 by the Mughal (莫卧儿) emperor Shah Jahan to house the remains of his beloved wife. It is an outstanding example of Mughal architecture, which combined Indian, Persian and Islamic influences. At its center is the Taj Mahal itself, built of shimmering white marble that seems to change color depending on the daylight. This stunning marble mausoleum is part of the Seven Wonders of the World.

• *Indian Food*

Food in India has been influenced by various civilizations. The food and cooking styles are different from region to region. Cows are considered holy by the Hindu, and thus many Indians will not eat beef. Muslims do not eat pork, so in the northern regions where most Indian Muslims live, pork will not be served. Food is eaten by Indians traditionally with the right hand; the left hand is only used for serving oneself. However, many Indians today also use cutlery such as forks and spoons.

Here are some popular Indian dishes:

• **Curry** (咖喱饭): Come in all guises and are made with lots of spices. The ingredients of the curries are chosen according to season and regional availability of products, so there will be fish curry in the southern state of Kerala, while the lamb curry is popular in the northern Kashmir region.

• **Roti** (烤饼): The simplest of many kinds of flatbread eaten as a staple food in India. It's made using fine whole-wheat flour and water and cooked on a griddle. Indian people tear off pieces of roti and use them to scoop up mouthfuls of other foods.

• **Biryani** (印度炒饭): A northern Indian dish influenced by Persian cuisine. It is a rice dish with chicken and vegetables, herbs and spices. The whole dish is often sealed under a pastry crust before baking.

• *Unique India*

Colorful Clothes

Indian clothing is renowned throughout the world, for its hand-woven textiles, ethnic wears, richly embroidered fabrics, authentic drapes in exclusive designs. Traditional Indian clothing for women are the saris (纱丽) or the salwar kameez and also Ghaghra Cholis. For men, traditional clothes are the Dhoti, Lungi or Kurta.

Holi

Holi is a famous Hindu festival that is celebrated in every part of India with utmost joy and enthusiasm. The festival is typically celebrated in March, on the full-moon day of Phalgun, marking the onset of spring and the end of winter. On the day of Holi people play with colors. One of the most popular lines used during Holi is "Bura na mano, Holi hai!" (Don't be sad / angry, it is Holi.)

Yoga

Yoga is associated with the rich heritage and the great ancient culture of India. Yoga means "to unite" in Sanskrit and describes a way to live healthily. Yoga teaches discipline through meditation and helps to stay focused and calm our bodies.

The Holy Cow

In Hinduism, a cow is considered a sacred animal, given the status of a goddess or a mother. Many religious people feed a cow on a daily basis or even make generous donations for the cow shelters. In many states of India, cow meat is banned and consuming it is equal to sin.

Mehendi / Henna

Mehendi (印度手绘) is a Hindi and Arabic word derived from a Sanskrit "mendhika", which referred to the henna (散沫花) plant. The use of henna is considered auspicious in many cultures, especially by the Hindus. A special Mehendi ceremony is conducted where the bride applies Mehendi on her hands as customary pre-wedding rituals.

Indian Classical Dance

India has a very rich culture of dance and music including traditional, classical, folk and tribal dance styles. In Indian culture, classical dance has a lot of significance, because it serves as a fabulous way to express the innate feelings of the heart.

Bollywood

Bollywood is the nickname for the Indian film industry located in Mumbai. Movies are three to four hours long, including dozens of songs and dances, top stars, the story of boy meets girl, lots of action, and always a happy ending. Films like *Dangal*, 3 *Idiots*, and *Hindi Medium* are very popular in China.

Task: Draw your mind-map on "India In My Eyes" page based on the facts of India and then introduce India to your peers by using your mind-map.

★ *5C Reading on India*

A. Read the following passage and get to know the importance of chai.

THE INDIAN "MASALA TEA"

Chai is the national drink of India. It is a way of life in India. A day for most Indians is incomplete without a cup of this warm and aromatic drink. India is the second largest producer of tea in the world as well as the second largest exporter of tea after China. When the British came to India, they established tea plantations as an alternative to the expensive Chinese tea they were habituated to consuming.

No matter where in India, people are not very far from a chai stall, little roadside shacks that go by different names in different parts of the country. Tea sold at these humble outlets is often the cheapest and most delicious. This sweet, spicy, milky beverage is ideal refreshment in every kind of weather.

Chai is a staple in every household in India and every household has its own recipe for chai. So there's no one right way to make chai. But a typical masala chai has black tea, ginger, cardamom, cinnamon, black pepper, cloves, and sugar mixed with water and whole milk. Each ingredient, when used correctly, plays a vital role in crafting the perfect cup of chai.

你对印度茶的历史有没有更多的了解? 如何做到鉴往知来?

B. Discuss the following questions based on the above reading material.

1. How popular is chai in India?

2. Do you know the major flavor of Indian chai?

3. How was chai introduced to India, and what can we learn from it?

PART III *Welcome Guests from the Land*

★ *Project—Meeting Guests at the Airport*

You are a local tour guide from CITS at Shuangliu International Airport to pick up an inbound travel group of 20 guests from India. They set off from Delhi and the trip is 5 hours long. Mr. Ravi is the tour leader. Please discuss with your peers the procedure you should follow to receive the group. Then, role-play the situation with your partner.

Procedure You Should Follow

1. _____

2. _____

3. _____

Your Goals

1. Offer a friendly greeting.
2. Check the luggage.
3. Board the bus.

· *Tasks*

    A. *Tell your partner the procedure you should follow to receive the group.*

    B. *Role-play the situation.*

The Magic Words or Sentences You Might Need for the Role-play

Words:

landed (已降落)	international passenger (国际航班旅客)	arrivals (进港、到达)
delayed (延误)	luggage claim (行李领取处)	airlines (航空公司)
passport (护照)	airport terminal (机场候机楼)	flight number (航班号)

Sentences:

1. Hi, everybody. My name is... On behalf of CITS, I'd like to welcome you all to Chengdu.

2. Did you have a pleasant trip? / You must be very exhausted after a long journey.

3. Do we need to wait for any of your baggage?

4. Have you all got your baggage? Good, now let's go to the motor coach. Please follow me and my flag.

5. Our motor coach is waiting outside. Shall we go now?

6. Well, is everybody here now? Come this way, please. The coach is waiting outside the airport.

★ *The Land and the World*

Xuan Zhang—The Chinese Buddhist Traveler to India

Xuan Zhang (Hsuan-Tsang), the Chinese pilgrim visited India during the reign of Harsha. He made an extensive tour of different parts of North and South India, recording minute details of the standard of living of the people, their social, economic life, religion and culture, etc. He spent about 14 years, from 630-644 A.D., in Harsha's capital. Harsha came to admire him for his deep devotion to Buddha and his profound knowledge of Buddhism.

Xuan Zhang took with him from India 657 volumes of valuable manuscripts, carried by twenty horses of his escort party. Back in Chang'an, he set himself to translate some of those manuscripts into Chinese, assisted by several scholars. About 74 Buddhist works were translated during his life time which proved of immense value to Chinese people.

Xuan Zhang compiled all his experiences in a book titled *Si-Yu-Ki* or *Great Tang Records on the Western Regions* (《大唐西域记》). The descriptions he has left of the places he saw and their inhabitants give us a valuable insight into the India of those days. Xuan Zhang was indeed an ancient ambassador of peace between China and India.

Mind-map: India in My Eyes

Name: _____ Date: _____

KWL Chart

Topic: _____ Name: _____ Date: _____

Know	Wonder	Learned
What do you think you already know about India?	What do you wonder about India? Write your questions below.	Write what you've learned about India.

Chapter 4   The Pacific

Section 1   New Zealand

A flight to Auckland, the largest city in New Zealand, is 13 hours from Chengdu. A flight to Wellington, the capital, is 19 hours from Guangzhou, 12 hours from Beijing and 3 hours from Sydney.

Learning Objectives

After this section, you will be able to:

★ know the geographical features of New Zealand, especially its location in southern hemisphere.

★ understand the Maori culture in New Zealand.

★ apply New Zealand social norms and unique features to serving inbound New Zealand tourists, making them feel at home.

★ analyze the traits of tourism industry in New Zealand through the film-induced tourism.

★ promote the image of Chinese tourism by relating China and New Zealand from movies, television works or live webcasts as the integration between culture and tourism.

怦然"新"动之新西兰

"神话般的中土世界"新西兰，位于大洋洲，与澳大利亚为邻，海岸线长6900千米。除了南岛和北岛，还有七百多座小岛。新西兰地广人稀，自然风光秀丽，阳光和雨水充沛，全国气候温和，四季差别不太明显，是北半球人躲避严寒和酷暑的理想去处。新西兰是多民族、多文化、多语言国家，约3/4的人口来自欧洲，约17%为毛利人，其余人口来自太平洋岛国和亚洲。

新西兰是农业国家，以羊和奶制品著称。酿酒业和电影业是新西兰重要的新兴工业，《指环王》一夜之间让新西兰成为人们趋之若鹜的"魔戒"之国。旅游业是新西兰的支柱产业，2019年旅游业对新西兰GDP贡献率为15%，就业贡献为19.8%，创汇20.6%，为新西兰第一大创汇产业。

中国与新西兰于1972年12月22日建立外交关系后，双边关系发展顺利。2009年4月，两国签署《旅游事务对话与合作安排》，新西兰来华旅游人数不断增长，到2018年达14.6万人次，来华游客中观光度假比例约占1/4。中国已成为新西兰第五大出国旅游目的地。目前，中国是新西兰第二大客源国和成长最快的海外旅游市场。2019年中新旅游年则更进一步加强中国和新西兰两国旅游业关系，并为双方创造更多商业机会带来绝佳机遇。

随着中新两国在政治、经济和文化各领域的深入交往，在接待新西兰入境游客时，更应该思考如何持续维护双边友好关系，吸取新西兰影视文化促进旅游业发展的经验，树立文旅融合新观念，讲好中国故事，让更多新西兰游客感悟中国文化，爱上魅力中国。

New Zealand Facts

- **Name**: New Zealand
- **Capital**: Wellington
- **Government**: Constitutional Monarchy
- **Languages**: English, Maori
- **Population**: 5.11 Million (2021)

- **Life Expectancy**: 81.6 Years (2019)
- **Currency**: NZD 100 ≈ CNY 483.59 (2021)
- **National Symbols**: Silver Fern, Kiwi
- **National Day**: February 6 (Waitangi Day)

PART I　Let's Go

★ *First Glance*

Watch the video, and then answer the following questions.

1. What is the unique aspect of New Zealand that impresses you most? And why?

2. Can you write down the titles of some movies that were shot in New Zealand?

★ *Viewing and Listening*

Watch the video and write down the corresponding hot activities of each picture.

_____

_____

_____

_____

_____

_____

PART II Explore the Land

· *Geography*

New Zealand is a country in the southern hemisphere and belongs to Oceania. It consists of two main islands: North Island and South Island. The islands are separated by the waters of the Cook Strait. There are also about 700 smaller islands.

Surrounded by the South Pacific Ocean and lies to the southeast of Australia, New Zealand lies on the Ring of Fire and there are numerous volcanos on North Island. The main cities in New Zealand are: Auckland, Christchurch, Wellington, Hamilton and Tauranga. More than half of the population of New Zealand lives in these five cities.

· *People*

New Zealand is one of the least densely populated countries in the world. The majority of New Zealanders are of European descent and about 15% are of Asian origin and about 8% are from the Pacific islands.

New Zealand's first or indigenous people are the Maori people. They make up about 17% of New Zealand's population today. Most of the Maori people live in the region of Rotorua.

· *Language*

English is the dominant language in New Zealand. Only about 4% of the population speaks the Maori language. Small groups of New Zealanders also speak Samoan, Hindi, Chinese or other languages as home language.

Maori is the language of the indigenous Maori people of New Zealand; it's also one of New Zealand's offcial languages.

The most common phrases in Maori are:

"Nau mai" means "Welcome".

"Kia ora" means "Hello".

"Kei te pēhea koe?" means "How are you"?

"Ko wai tōu ingoa?" means "What's your name"?

"He roa te wā kua kitea" means "Long time no see".

• *Attractions*
Auckland

Auckland is New Zealand's most populous city and is a multi-cultural hub of food, music, arts and culture. Known as Tāmaki Makaurau, Auckland sprawls over volcanic hills and around twin harbors, offering a stimulating mix of natural wonders and urban adventures.

Auckland offers an urban environment where most people live within half an hour of beautiful beaches, hiking trails and a dozen enchanting holiday islands. More than just a city, Auckland is a whole region full of things to see and do.

Rotorua

Rotorua is a geothermal wonderland (地热奇境) with bubbling mud pools, clouds of steam, and natural hot springs perfect for bathing and relaxing in. The city offers a raft of attractions and experiences for everyone from adventure-seekers to those just looking to unwind.

Waitomo Caves

Waitomo Caves is one of the must-see natural attractions. The area's name comes from the Maori words wai (water) and tomo (hole).

Waitomo Caves have been drawing tourists since the late 1800s after the subterranean (地下的) network was discovered by a local Maori chief. Today, thousands of visitors each year come to Waitomo to marvel at the incredible limestone (石灰岩) formations and glowworms (萤火虫) hidden in its depths.

Christchurch

Christchurch is the largest city in the South Island. The urban area is home to 377,200 residents, and the territorial authority has 385,500 people, which makes it the second-most populous city in New Zealand after Auckland and before Wellington. Christchurch is the city of exploration, where urban regeneration and heritage thrive. The city is constantly evolving, always giving locals and visitors something new to explore.

Hobbiton Movie Set

Hobbiton Movie Set was a significant location used for *The Lord of the Rings* film trilogy and *The Hobbit* film trilogy. It is situated on a family run farm about 8 kilometres west of Hinuera and 10 kilometres southwest of Matamata, in Waikato, and is now a Tolkien tourism destination, offering a guided tour of the set.

Queenstown

Queenstown is a resort town in the southwest of New Zealand's South Island. It has an urban population of 16,000. The town is built around an inlet called Queenstown Bay on Lake Wakatipu, a long, thin, Z-shaped lake formed by glacial processes. Queenstown is a hub of adventure, thrumming with adrenaline (肾上腺素) and an unique sense of fun.

· *New Zealand Food*

New Zealanders' main diet is Western food. They have a large demand for meat and dariy products, loving to eat meat and drink thick soup. New Zealand cuisine uses the abundant fresh meats, fish, vegetables and fruit in a creative manner.

New Zealand cuisine draws inspiration from Europe, Asia and Polynesia.

Here are popular New Zealand foods:

• **Mutton**: New Zealanders love eating mutton, and the flavor of mutton is various. One-year-old lambs taste tender, which are very popular with the local people.

• **Seafood**: New Zealand's unique geographical environment brings it tasty seafood, such as black-edged abalone (黑边鲍鱼), salmon, green mussel, crayfish (lobster), oysters and tutatua and pipi (New Zealand shellfish).

• **Pavlova** (帕洛娃): It's the most representative New Zealand dessert. It is made from white cream and fresh fruit or berries spread on meringue (蛋白霜).

• **Haangi** (杭伊): A Haangi is a traditional Maori meal that is cooked by steaming food which is usually placed underground. Cooking a haangi is a long process that sometimes takes many hours.

· *Unique New Zealand*

Maori Culture

Maori culture is an integral part of life in New Zealand, influencing everything from cuisine to customs, and language. The first group of Maori people came to New Zealand more than 1,000 years ago from their mythical Polynesian homeland of Hawaiki. Today, one in seven New Zealanders identify as Maori. Their history, language and traditions are central to New Zealand's identity.

Many Maori cultural practices are kept alive in contemporary New Zealand. All formal Maori gatherings include a formal reception of visitors, speeches and songs, and food cooked in earth ovens on preheated stones. Carved houses, which serve as centers of meeting and ceremony in Maori villages, are still being built.

Extreme Activities

It's no secret that New Zealand is the country pumped with adrenaline. New Zealand extreme activities range from jumping off a bridge with a rubber band, to zigzagging your way through braided rivers.

Bungy Jumping

New Zealand is proud to be the home of modern bungy jumping. It is one of the most popular tourist attractions. Everyone from schoolboys to grandmothers can strap "rubber bands" to ankles and take a daredevil (惊险的) leap from platforms and bridges around New Zealand.

Skydiving

Skydiving is the sport of jumping from an airplane and typically executing a prolonged free fall before deploying a parachute. A consistent favorite skydiving place is Fox Glacier, an 8-mile-long glacier located in the remote Westland Tai Poutini National Park on the West Coast of New Zealand's South Island. As people free fall, knees in the breeze, they can marvel at the view of the wild coastline along the Tasman Sea and the snowy rugged peaks of the Southern Alps.

Luge Ride

Rotorua offers the biggest luge ride in the country, while Queenstown offers the steepest one. This half go-cart half slide is a lot of fun when done with 2-3 competitive mates.

Kiwi

The kiwi is a unique and flightless bird in New Zealand. It has loose hair-like feathers, strong legs and no tail. It is the national symbol of the country and the word "Kiwi" has become synonymous with "New Zealander".

Home of Middle-earth

When the first *Lord of the Rings* movie was released in 2001, New Zealand became known as the home of Middle-earth. Tourists may explore many film locations and join tours and activities for the chance to see the film locations and step inside the imaginative mind of Tolkien. The landscapes of Middle earth™ came alive after they were featured in *The Lord of the Rings* film trilogy from 2001-2003.

Task: Draw your mind-map on the "New Zealand in My Eyes" page based on the facts of New Zealand and then introduce it to your peers by using your mind-map.

★ 5C Reading on New Zealand

A. Read the following passage and think about the new way to develop our current tourism industry.

About New Zealand

When the first *Lord of the Rings* movie was released in 2001, New Zealand became known as the Home of Middle-earth. The dramatic scenery, consisting of golden plains, towering mountains and enchanting valleys, plays a part in creating the mythical world of Middle-earth as seen in *The Lord of the Rings* and *The Hobbit* film trilogy. *The Lord of the Rings* and *the Hobbit* films have boosted tourism and economic growth in New Zealand. In the year after the release of the first Hobbit film in 2012, the number of visitors in New Zealand added to 13%. It has been estimated that the economic benefits of Hobbit films to New Zealand's tourism industry are between $50 million and $500 million annually.

About China

With 58 million fans worldwide, the Chinese Internet celebrity, Li Ziqi is using the technology to preserve the old way of living, and with it, her videos have gone viral both at home and abroad.

Li's YouTube videos center on her life with her grandmother in the rural parts of Sichuan Province. In the videos, Li, often dressed in graceful traditional garments, rises at sunrise, rests at sunset, plants seeds and harvests flowers, cooks Chinese dishes and crafts bamboo furniture. Much of the popularity of her videos can be attributed to the attraction of Chinese culture. Li's overseas followers have praised her videos for showing the amazingly picturesque, simple and elegant side of China's rural life.

"She told the stories of China's culture and that of China," the official Sina Weibo account of China Central Television noted. In this technology-dominated era, changes can happen in the blink of an eye. Possibly it will be a new idea of developing the tourism of Sichuan, even China.

> 请思考如何打造文化旅游的本土品牌？

B. Discuss the following questions based on the above reading material.

1. How do you connect movies with tourism in China? Can you list something and discuss the details with your peers?

2. What is the most important factor for making a local tourism brand?

PART III   Welcome Guests from the Land

★ Project—Check-in at the Hotel

You are a receptionist at a five-star hotel. A New Zealander guest arrives, and you're supposed to help him check in. Make sure you behave professionally, gracefully and impressively. Discuss with your partners how you would structure the dialogue.

Top 3 Questions I Need to Ask
1. _____
2. _____
3. _____

Receptionist Job Description

A hotel receptionist, sometimes called a hotel desk clerk, is a person who works at the front desk of a hotel, greeting and assisting guests. Receptionists are typically responsible for everything from helping people make reservations to managing available rooms, issuing room keys, and solving any problems that may arise during the course of a stay. In most cases, he or she is the first person that guests will interact with at the hotel, which makes the role one of some importance.

· Tasks

A. Tell your partner the reason why you ask these three questions.

B. Make a dialogue to greet the guests and help them check in. You can use the useful sentences as reference.

The Sentences You Might Need for the Dialogue

1. Good afternoon. Welcome to ×× (hotel). May I help you?
2. Do you have a reservation with us, Mr. ×× ?
3. Just a moment please. I'll check our reservation record.
4. Thank you for waiting, Mr. ×× . Your reservation is for a twin from March 5th to 7th for three nights. Is that right?
5. Could you fill out the registration form, please?
6. How would you like to make payment?
7. You can just skip that, and I'll fill it in for you later on.
8. May I see some identification?
9. Please sign at the Cashier's counter when you check out.
10. Have an enjoyable stay./Please enjoy your stay here.
11. If I can be of any help, please just let me know.
12. Here are your room keys and meal coupons.

★ *The Land and the World*

Rewi Alley—Our Old Friend Forever

Rewi Alley, Lùyì Àilí, born in New Zealand on December 2, 1897, is a writer, educator, social reformer, potter, and member of the Communist Party of China. He came to China on April 21, 1927 and has lived in China for a long time since then. He stood together with the Chinese people sharing happiness and woe and worked hard for the liberation and construction of the Chinese people for 60 years.

In the 1930s, Rewi Alley organized the production of self-help products in Shanghai, supplied military and civilian supplies during wartime, and supported the people's guerrilla warfare under the leadership of the Communist Party of China. In 1942, he and the British George Hogg founded the Baili Technology School in Shuangshepu, Shan'xi Province. In 1944, the school was moved to Shandan County, Gansu Province. The teaching policy of part-work and part-study, combining theory with practice, was deeply welcomed by the local people. In 1953, the school moved to Lanzhou. Over the years, the school has trained a large number of technical workers for China's petroleum industry and made great contributions to the cause of China's revolution and construction.

After the founding of People's Republic of China, Rewi Alley devoted himself to maintain world peace and friendship among the people of all countries. He has made important contributions to developing the friendship between the Chinese people and the people of New Zealand and other countries, and enhancing the understanding of the achievements of China's socialist construction. He has won the respect and affection of the Chinese, New Zealanders and the international friends.

Mind-map: New Zealand in My Eyes

Name: _____   Date: _____

KWL Chart

Topic: _____   Name: _____   Date: _____

Know	**Wonder**	**Learned**
What do you think you already know about New Zealand?	What do you wonder about New Zealand? Write your questions below.	Write what you've learned about New Zealand.

栽

切

线

Section 2   Australia

Learning Objectives

A flight to Sydney is about 10 hours from Chongqing, 7.5 hours from Jakarta, 20 hours from London and 20 hours from New York.

After this section, you will be able to:

★ know the geographical features of Australia, especially its location and ecotourism.

★ list the typical landmarks and attractions in Australia.

★ apply Australian unique features to serving inbound Australian tourists, making them feel at home.

★ promote the image of Chinese tourism by relating China and Australia from environment, business, trade and education.

"澳"妙无穷之澳大利亚

澳大利亚全称为澳大利亚联邦（The Commonwealth of Australia），位于南半球的南太平洋上，是世界上唯一国土覆盖整个大陆，与世界其他国家隔离的大陆岛国。季节的更替同北半球地区完全相反，一月是炎热的夏天，七月则是飘雪的冬日。大陆东侧是太平洋，西侧是印度洋，与西北方的印尼和东南方的新西兰隔海相望。领土面积769.2万平方千米，是世界第六大国。全国划分为6个州和2个领地，三个时区。澳大利亚物产丰富，被称为"骑在羊背上的国家""坐在矿车上的国家"和"手持麦穗的国家"，总人口有约2569万（2020年），人口密度仅约为每平方千米2人，英国及爱尔兰后裔占74%，亚裔占5%，土著人占2.7%，其他民族占18.3%。作为典型的移民国家，被社会学家喻为"民族的拼盘"。

澳大利亚旅游资源丰富，著名的旅游城市和景点有悉尼、墨尔本、布里斯班、阿德莱德、珀斯、大堡礁、黄金海岸和达尔文等。尽管国内游客仍是主导，海外游客人数总体呈上升趋势，新西兰、英国、美国是澳大利亚传统客源国，近年来中国游客增长迅猛。2010年8月，澳大利亚旅游局在中国推出最新旅游宣传语——"澳大利亚，尽是不同（There is nothing like Australia.）"并一直沿用至今；2017年是"中澳旅游年"，中、澳两国积极开展了一系列双边旅游交流活动。2018年，澳大利亚共接待130万中国游客，中国游客数升至国际游客榜首。

澳大利亚是中国传统的旅游客源市场，一直稳居我国主要客源市场第11位左右。2018年旅华游客达75万，其中川渝接待澳大利亚游客量约占三分之一。中国政治稳定、经济发展，为世人瞩目；随着两国政府和人民之间友好往来的增加，宣传力度加大，使澳大利亚人对中国的认知程度有所更新和提高，中国的历史、文化和古迹，还有现代文明的魅力吸引着不同年龄段澳大利亚人，是旅华人数增长的坚实基础。

Australia Facts

- **Official Name**: The Commonwealth of Australia
- **Capital**: Canberra
- **Government**: Democracy
- **Language**: English
- **Population**: 25.69 Million (2020)
- **Currency**: AUD 100 ≈ CNY 475.76 (2021)
- **National Symbols**: Golden Wattle, Opal, The Commonwealth Star
- **National Animals**: Kangaroo, Emu
- **National Anthem**: Advance Australia Fair
- **National Day**: January 26 (Australia Day)

PART I Let's Go

★ *First Glance*
Watch the video, and then answer the following questions.

1. Is it different from what you've known about Australia? In which ways?

2. What impresses you most after watching the video?

3. What is the title of the video and what does 8D mean here?

★ *Listening*
Listen to the audio and fill in the blanks with the words you have heard.

International travelers will be digitally immersed in Australia's iconic _____.

A series of new immersive videos will transport viewers from around the world into the heart of some of Australia's most breathtaking _____ and keep them dreaming of all of the experiences awaiting them when they are able to travel to Australia again.

Harnessing innovative 8D audio technology, the six videos take viewers on a sensory journey, immersing them in the unique sights, _____ and textures of iconic destinations such as Uluru, Sydney Opera House, Fraser Island and the Daintree.

The videos have each been themed by color—blue, red, and magenta, green, black and white—to evoke a range of feelings and emotions, and showcase the _____ and vibrancy found in Australia, and provide inspiration for future holiday plans.

Tourism Australia Managing Director Phillipa Harrison said the videos would give travelers around the world a taste of what it's like to experience _____ firsthand, but from the comfort of their homes.

PART II Explore the Land

· *Geography*

Australia is the smallest continent lying between the Pacific and Indian Oceans in the southern hemisphere. The mainland of Australia is not only the largest island in the world but also the flattest continent.

Australia is separated from Indonesia to the northwest by the Timor and Arafura Seas, from Papua New Guinea to the northeast by the Coral Sea and the Torres Strait, from the Coral Sea Islands Territory by the Great Barrier Reef, from New Zealand to the southeast by the Tasman Sea, and from Antarctica in the far south by the Indian Ocean. The country's interior consists of arid and semi-arid areas which are referred to as "outback (澳大利亚内陆荒原地带)". About 70% of Australia is outback, while the coastal plains are more fertile and house the majority of Australia's population. About 35% of Australia's land area is covered by deserts.

· *People*

The population of Australia consists of more than 270 ethnic groups. Until the mid-20th century, however, Australian society was regarded as essentially British—or at any rate Anglo-Celtic. The ties to Britain and Ireland were scarcely affected by immigration from other sources until then. Although some nine-tenths of Australia's population is of European ancestry, more than one-fifth is foreign-born, and there is a small but important (and growing) aboriginal population.

Of those born overseas, about half were born in Europe. Among the larger non-European groups are New Zealanders and Chinese. The growth in immigration, particularly Asian immigration beginning in the last decades of the 20th century, combined with a subsequent flow of refugees from the Balkans, altered the cultural landscape, imbuing Australia with a cosmopolitanism that it lacked in the mid-20th century. Despite the country's long-standing Anglo-Celtic heritage, the Chinese and the Italians, have had an important presence in Australia since the 19th century.

· *Language*

Though Australia has no official language, English is regarded as the national language. Even so, Australia is a linguistically and culturally diverse country with influences from more than 160 spoken languages. Australian English has a unique accent and vocabulary. In the 2011 census, 76.8% Australian spoke English at home. Mandarin is the biggest non-English dialect spoken in Australia. Early European settlement in Australia almost eradicated the indigenous languages, and few of these aboriginal languages have survived today.

Several common ways to greet in Australia are:

G'day, mate!

Hey mate!

G'day, how's it going?

· *Attractions*

Sydney

Sydney is the capital city of the state of New South Wales, and the most populous city in Australia and Oceania. As of June 2019, Sydney's estimated metropolitan population was more than 5 million, meaning the city is home to approximately 20% of the country's population. The iconic Opera House is one of the world's most famous landmarks. Then there is the Harbor Bridge, the magical setting of the Sydney Botanical Garden, Darling Harbor, the Rocks and much more to explore.

Melbourne

Melbourne, with a population of more than 4 million, is the second largest city of Australia. It is famous for being capable of showing "four seasons in one day" and has a temperate climate with distinct seasons and usually mild weather, lots of trendy restaurants, shops and art galleries along the Murray River, good to visit year-round.

Adelaide

Adelaide, capital of South Australia, referred to as "the city of churches", is a gateway to some of Australia's best wine country and is believed to be the home to Australia's best restaurant, hotel, wine, gin and beach. Once considered a sleepy city, Adelaide has undergone a rapid transformation with a booming small-bar scene, world-class art and music, and a festival calendar to rival that of any other Australian city.

• Great Barrier Reef

Off the east coast of Queensland, the Great Barrier Reef, the greatest mass of coral, is one of the seven wonders of the natural world and one of world's foremost tourist attractions. Pulling away from it, and viewing it from a greater distance, people can understand why. It is larger than the Great Wall of China and the only living thing on earth visible from space. It is great for snorkelling and diving.

• Uluru-Kata Tjuta National Park

Uluru-Kata Tjuta National Park (乌鲁鲁-卡塔丘塔国家公园) is located toward central

Australia in the southwestern corner of the northern territory. The national park boundary encompasses an area of 1,333.7 square kilometers. It is home to Australia's renowned Uluru, and Kata Tjuta, both sandstone monoliths with Uluru being the more popular and most renowned natural feature.

Uluru, giant monolith, also known as Ayers Rock, rising from seemingly nowhere in the deep center of Australia, is one of the world's great natural wonders. It lies 335 kilometers southwest of the nearest large town, Alice Springs. It stands at a massive 348 meters tall and measures a lengthy 9.4 kilometers in width. The sandstone that makes up Uluru is estimated to be around 600 million years old. Uluru is a sacred site to the Anangu tribes of Central Australia, the indigenous peoples of the Western Desert.

• *Australian Food and Drink*

As a modern nation of large-scale immigration, Australia has absorbed culinary contributions and adaptations from various cultures around the world, including British, European, Asian and Middle Eastern.

Aboriginal Food

The Aborigines have been living off the land here in Australia for literally thousands of years. It is quite astounding how many native plants, berries and creatures can be eaten. There are still traditional tribes throughout Australia living off the land. But the majority of Aboriginals now live a more Western lifestyle and a more Western diet.

Seafood

When it comes to seafood, Australians like to keep it simple. It's not uncommon to find a silver bucket of cold cooked shrimp offered on menus as a "bucket of prawns". Served with a glass of chilled white wine or a beer, this is a popular snack at pubs across Australia. Local, fresh oysters also feature on most menus within sight of the ocean.

Barramundi (澳大利亚肺鱼), white, firm-fleshed fish, similar in taste to snapper, is hugely popular in Australia. Locally farmed Atlantic salmon and ocean trout (鲑鳟鱼), Tasmania specialties are highlights of any gourmet trip.

Salt and pepper squid, traditional Vietnamese spiced, fried seafood, is found throughout Australia in beer gardens, regional pubs, beach side takeaways and refined city eateries. This delicious dish is served in multitude of ways—for example, with salad and deep-fried sweet potato wedges, or with a touch of chili, lemon dipping sauce and a side of steamed rice.

Meat Pie

A pastry case full of mince or diced mean and rich gravy (肉汁), the once humble meat pie has been a part of Australian working-class history for decades. Traditionally made of beer and topped with tomato sauce, this quick takeaway snack can be found in many service stations and convenience stores across the country. Local bakeries can be found in almost every neighborhood in Australia, usually several varieties of meat pie, from classic beef and gravy to creamy scallop pie, lamb shank pie or vegetable pie.

• *Unique Australia*

Singularity

The most striking characteristics of the vast country are its global isolation and the aridity of much of its surface. Visitors from the northern hemisphere are at first overwhelmed by the vast, uninhabited land and by the grey charred bush, and tall, pale trees. It still retains some of the mystical quality it had for the first explorers searching for inland seas and great rivers, and it remains a symbol of Australia's strength and independence.

Australia's isolation from other continents explains much of the singularity of its plant and animal life. Its unique flora and fauna include hundreds of kinds of eucalyptus trees (桉树) and the only egg-laying mammals on the earth, the platypus and echidna. Other plants and animals associated with Australia are various acacias and dingoes, kangaroos, koalas, and kookaburras.

Aboriginal People

Australia's first or indigenous people are usually referred to as the aboriginal people of Australia. They make up about 2.8% of Australia's population today. The indigenous Australians are said to be direct descendants of migrants from Africa who left the African continent about 75,000 years ago. They have migrated over the Australasian continent until they settled in Australia around 60,000 years ago.

Today aboriginal people live in all main cities in Australia but most of them still live in the desert areas of the Australian outback. The aboriginal people are highly skilled in arts and crafts. Aboriginal Australians struggle to retain their ancient culture and fight for recognition. The state of Victoria is currently working toward a first-of-its-kind treaty with its aboriginal population that would recognize aboriginal Australians' sovereignty and include compensation.

TAFE

TAFE (Technical and Further Education) is a government-run system that provides education after high school in vocational areas, like beauty, design, childcare, accounting, business, recruitment, IT, and many more. While university teaches a broad range of theories, TAFE focuses on specific skills for a particular workplace. For example, a Certificate IV in aged care teaches all the skills

needed to work in aged care—either at a client's home or an aged care facility.

Task: Draw your mind-map on the "Australia in My Eyes" page based on the facts of Australia and then introduce Australia to your peers by using your mind-map.

★ *5C Reading on Australia*

A. Read the following piece of news.

TSYDNEY, Jan. 23, 2020 (Xinhua)—The world-famous sails of the iconic Sydney Opera House turned red on Thursday, to celebrate the Lunar New Year and welcome the Year of Rat.

Now the largest Spring Festival anywhere outside Asia, Aussies have fallen in love with the traditions of the Lunar New Year and it's expected that over 1.5 million people will attend more than 100 events over the 16-day period.

"Lunar New Year has become an integral part of our calendar in New South Wales (NSW) State and is widely celebrated by East Asian and Southeast Asian communities," NSW Premier Gladys Berejiklian said.

Originally beginning 24 years ago, Sydney's first Lunar New Year festival was a rather modest affair. With a lot of help and hard work from community organizers, the yearly event has now become a showpiece for Australia's rich multicultural success.

Another highlight of the 2020 Sydney Lunar Festival will be the returning Lunar Lanterns exhibition, with 12 larger-than-life illuminated artworks representing all the animal signs of the zodiac.

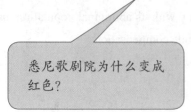

悉尼歌剧院为什么变成红色？

Seeing the event as a way to further build ties with Australia's Asian neighbors, Berejiklian said, "Festivals such as Lunar New Year bring us all together and enable us to learn more about each other's rich traditions and cultures."

B. Discuss the following questions based on the above news.

1. How much do you know about Sydney Opera House?

2. Why was it turned completely red?

3. In which way can we see the influence of Chinese culture on Australia?

PART III   Welcome Guests from the Land

★ *Project—Designing Welcome Cards*

You are a Front Office Manager of a hotel. A group of Australian tourists will come and stay in your hotel next month. You hope to design welcome cards to make their stay unforgettable and memorable. Please discuss with your peers and finish the card based on what you know about Australian people and culture. Also, you need to take local Chinese culture into consideration.

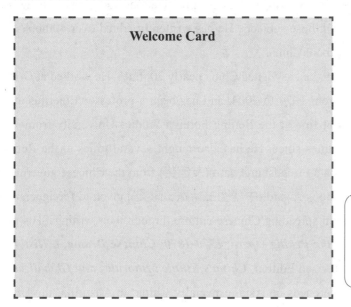

Welcome Card

Your Goals

Make the tourists feel at home and know about China.

· *Tasks*

    A. *Find 3 welcome cards from different hotels and compare with yours. Tell your peers why you design yours in this way.*

    B. *Prepare a brief presentation about your card.*

Case Study

★ *The Land and the World*

Professor Colin Mackerras—Friendship Award Winner

Professor Colin Mackerras (Chinese name "马克林"), is a specialist on Chinese history, musical theater and ethnic minorities, as well as Australia-China relations and Western images of China, and has published widely on all those subjects. He has written or edited over 40 books and authored nearly 200 scholarly papers about China.

Born in Sydney, Australia, in 1939, he has visited China nearly 70 times. He worked at Griffith University in Queensland Australia from 1974 to 2004, and has been a professor Emeritus at the University since retirement. He taught first at the Beijing Foreign Studies University from 1964 to 1966 and has taught there many times since. He has also taught several times at the Renmin University of China in Beijing. He won a Friendship Award (友谊奖) from the Chinese government in 2014 and in 2016 a Special China Book Award (中华图书特殊贡献奖), given to foreigners who have made outstanding contributions in spreading Chinese culture through their writings. His most important books include *The Rise of the Peking Opera, 1770-1870*; *Chinese Drama, a Historical Survey; Western Images of China*, Revised Edition; *China's Ethnic Minorities and Globalization*. He has also attended numerous conferences on Asia, especially China, in Australia, the United States, the Netherlands, Canada, Switerland and the United Kingdom.

Professor Colin Mackerras and His Books

Mind-map: Australia in My Eyes

Name: _____   Date: _____

KWL Chart

Topic: _____   Name: _____   Date: _____

Know	Wonder	Learned
What do you think you already know about Australia?	What do you wonder about Australia? Write your questions below.	Write what you've learned about Australia.

裁 切 线

Chapter 5   The Americas

Section 1   The United States of America

Learning Objectives

A flight to New York is 10 hours from Beijing, 13 hours from Tokyo, 7 hours from London and 12 hours from Seoul.

After this section, you will be able to:

★ know the geographical features of the US especially the locations of major cities like Washington DC, New York and Los Angeles.

★ list the typical landmarks and attractions in the US.

★ apply the US social norms, taboos and unique features to serving the inbound US tourists, making them feel at home.

★ analyze the reasons for the measures adopted during COVID-19 epidemic and BLM protests in the US.

"美"不胜收之美国

美国全称美利坚合众国，位于北美大陆，面积937万平方千米，是世界第四领土大国，美洲第二领土国家。领土包括美国本土、北美洲西北部的阿拉斯加和太平洋中部的夏威夷群岛。落基山脉纵贯南北，中西部以山地高原为主，东部以平原低地为主。中部的密西西比河是境内最长、流域面积最广、水量最大、利用价值最高的大河。美国本土的气候大部分地区属大陆性气候，南部属亚热带气候，阿拉斯加属极圈内寒冷气候区，夏威夷属热带气候区。

美国幅员辽阔，地貌多姿，气象万千，集森林、湿地、湖泊、河流、草原、沙漠、高山、火山、峡谷、冰雪、海洋于一体，风光旖旎，美不胜收，旅游资源丰富，同时还有现代化的大都会，现代化的科学和文化以及让人流连忘返的各类主题公园，加上便捷的海、陆、空交通服务，使得美国的旅游收入多年稳居世界第一。

美国是稳居世界前列的入境旅游市场，2014年7476.7万人次，1772.4亿美元；2017年7590万人次，居世界第三位，外汇收入达2107.49亿美元，居世界第一位，接待入境游客人数与全国人口之比为23:100。主要国际客源国为加拿大和墨西哥，接待国际游客最多的城市前三分别是纽约、洛杉矶和迈阿密。美国也是世界上最大的客源产出国，2015年7300万人次，支出1200亿美元；2017年7976.7万人次，支出1530亿美元。主要出境旅游目的地为墨西哥、加拿大、英国、法国、意大利、德国、中国和日本，出行以观光旅游和探亲访友为主要目的，占70%，其次为商务出行。

中国作为东方文明古国，历史文化悠久、自然和人文旅游资源丰富，对美国游客有着独特的吸引力，因此如何在接待美国游客的过程中，展现泱泱大国的气度是值得每个旅游从业人员思考的问题。

America Facts

- **Name**: The United States of America
- **Capital**: Washington D.C.
- **Government**: Constitution-based Federal Republic
- **Language**: English
- **Population**: 333 Million (2021)
- **Life Expectancy**: 79.3 Years (2019)
- **Currency**: USD 100 ≈ CNY 648.17 (2021)
- **National Symbols**: American Bison, Bald Eagle, Oak Tree, Rose
- **National Day**: July 4

PART I Let's Go

★ First Glance

Watch the video, and then answer the following question.

1. Why do you think Troy University has Terracotta Warriors on campus?

2. What are the Sichuan cultural symbols?

3. How would you do to let more American visitors know more Sichuan culture?

★ Viewing and Speaking

Watch the video again and fill in the blanks, and then discuss with your peers your thought on the symbolic importance of Terracotta Warriors at Troy University.

Over the past _____ I've had the pleasure to visit China more than 25 times. Today _____ Terracotta Warriors stand proudly on our campus. We believe that collection of warriors represents the _____ display of warriors outside of Xi'an. I think it's particularly important to help our students to understand the world around them. Our Terracotta Warrior plays an important role in the _____ of our students.

The _____ between China and the United States is extremely important, not only to the people of both countries but to people of the world. We believe the _____ built upon trust and mutual understandings are _____. We also believe that Troy University is _____.

PART II   Explore the Land

· *Geography*

The United States of America (USA), also known as the United States (US) or America, is situated mostly in central North America. It is the world's fourth largest country in size and nearly the third largest in terms of population after China and India. Located in North America, the country is bordered on the west by the Pacific Ocean and to the east by the Atlantic Ocean. Along the northern border is Canada and the southern border is Mexico. It is a union of states. Of the 50 states of the USA, 49 are located on the American mainland and one state, Hawaii, is located in the Pacific Ocean.

More than twice the size of the European Union, the United States has high mountains in the west and a vast central plain. The lowest point in the country is in Death Valley which is at –86 meters and the highest peak is Denali (Mt. McKinley) at 6,198 meters.

· *People*

The USA is a multi-racial and multi-ethnic country. It is home to people of all different ethnic groups, different religions and different mother tongues. Christianity is the largest religion, and about 67% of all Americans are its followers. Judaism is the 2nd largest. The state officially categorizes its population into six groups: white (76.4%), black / African American (13.4%), Native American / Alaskan Native (1.3%), Asian (5.8%), Native Hawaiian and Pacific Islander (0.3%), and two or more races (2.8%).

· *Language*

English is the most commonly used language in the USA. However, more than 300 languages are spoken in the country. 78% of all American say that they speak only English. About 13% speak mainly Spanish.

The three major differences between British and American English are in pronunciation, vocabulary and spelling.

The most common ways of greeting in the United States are:

Good morning: Slightly on the formal side.

Mornin' / Morning: A more casual version of "good morning".

Hey: One of the most common greetings in the US that can also be used in the plural, as in: "Hey guys" and "Hey ya'll" (ya'll is used in many of the southern US states as a plural "you all" form).

Hi/Hi there: Very common phrases used in all situations.

How's it goin' / going?: A question inquiring about how the other person is doing. Listen for a positive or negative response indicating how their day has been.

How are you? / How are you doing? / How are ya?: These phrases show that people are interested in the person. Most Americans generally always respond positively with "good".

Yo / What's up?: Usually used by younger people.

· *Attractions*

New York City

New York City has been described as the cultural, financial, and media capital of the world, significantly influencing commerce, entertainment, research, technology, education, politics, tourism, art, fashion, and sports. Home to the headquarters of the United Nations, it is an important center for international diplomacy. New York is also home to the highest number of billionaires of any city in the world. Many districts and landmarks in New York City are well known, including Time Square, Statue of Liberty and Broadway Theater. "I Love New York" is both a logo and a song that have been used since 1977 to promote tourism in New York City.

New York City is home to the headquarters of the National Football League, Major League Baseball, the National Basketball Association, the National Hockey League, and Major League Soccer. New York has been described as the "Capital of Baseball". Also, the famous new Yankee Stadium is here.

Washington D.C.

Washington, D.C., known as D.C. or just Washington, is the capital city of the US. It is one of the most visited cities in the US, with over 20 million visitors in 2016. The often-visited landmarks are the National Mall, Lincoln Memorial and the United States Capitol. The Smithsonian Institution is an educational foundation chartered by Congress in 1846 that maintains most of the nation's official museums and galleries in Washington. Its collections are open to the public free of charge. The most visited museum in Smithsonian Institution is the National Museum of Natural History on the National Mall.

Golden Gate Bridge

Golden Gate Bridge (金门大桥), a suspension bridge spanning the Golden Gate in

California, links San Francisco with Marin county to the north. The bridge is one of the most internationally recognized symbols of San Francisco and California. The Frommer's travel guide describes the Golden Gate Bridge as "possibly the most beautiful, certainly the most photographed bridge in the world". At the time of its opening in 1937, it was both the longest and the tallest suspension bridge in the world, with a main span of 1,280 meters and a total height of 227 meters.

Yellowstone National Park

Yellowstone National Park is an American national park located in the western US. It was the first national park in the US and is also widely held to be the first national park in the world. The park is known for its wildlife and its many geothermal features, especially Old Faithful geyser (老忠实间歇泉), one of its most popular. Hundreds of species of mammals, birds, fish, reptiles, and amphibians have been documented, including several that are either endangered or threatened. In 1978, Yellowstone was named a UNESCO World Heritage Site.

Grand Canyon National Park

Grand Canyon National Park (大峡谷国家公园), located in the northwestern Arizona, is the 15th site in the United States to have been named as a national park. The park's central feature is the Grand Canyon, a gorge of the Colorado River, which is often considered one of the Wonders of the World. The park, which covers 4,926.08 square kilometers, received more than six million visitors in 2017, which is the second highest count of all American national parks after Great Smoky Mountains National Park. The Grand Canyon was designated a World Heritage Site by UNESCO in 1979. The park celebrated its 100th anniversary on February 26, 2019.

Theme Parks

Some describe the US as the land of theme parks. People from different places and of different ages can always have fun in these diverse theme parks. There are plenty of places to enjoy a calming Ferris wheel, ride a classic wooden rollercoaster, or scream your head off on a rollercoaster.

Famous and most visited top 3 theme parks in the US are:

Universal Studios: Los Angeles, California and Orlando, Florida.

Walt Disney World Resort: Orlando, Florida.

Busch Gardens: Tampa Bay, Florida and Williamsburg, Virginia.

• *American Food*

American food is primarily Western in origin, but has been significantly influenced by indigenous American Indians, African Americans, Asians, Europeans, Pacific Islanders, and Hispanic Americans, reflecting its history as a melting pot of different cultures. Some popular American foods are hot dog, apple pie, Thanksgiving dinner, cheeseburger, Reuben sandwich, Philly cheese steak, nachos, Chicago-style pizza, Delmonico's steak, etc.

• *Unique USA*

Checks and Balances

Checks and balances, principle of government under which separate branches are empowered to prevent actions by other branches and are induced to share power. Checks and balances are applied primarily in constitutional governments. For example, Checks and Balances in the Constitution. The House of Representatives has sole power of impeachment, but the Senate has all power to try any impeachment. Any bills that intend to raise revenue must originate in the House of Representatives, but the Senate also has to approve the bill. Congress has the power to set and collect any taxes or duties.

Broadway Theater

Broadway theater, also simply known as Broadway, refers to the theatrical performances, located in the Theater District and the Lincoln Center along Broadway, in Midtown Manhattan, New York City. Broadway and London's West End together represent the highest commercial level of live theater in the English-speaking world. Most Broadway shows are musicals. The top 3 Broadway musicals are the Phantom of the Opera, Hamilton and Chicago.

American Sports

Sports are an important part of culture in the US. American football is the most popular sport to watch, followed by baseball, basketball, ice hockey and soccer, which make up the 5 major sports.

Sports are particularly associated with education in the US, with most high schools and universities having organized sports, and this is a unique sporting footprint for the US college sports competitions play an important role in the American sporting culture, and college basketball and college football are as popular as professional sports in some parts of the country.

The Super Bowl is the annual championship game of the National Football League (NFL). It is among the world's most-watched sporting events and frequently the most-watched American television broadcast of the year.

Hollywood

Hollywood (好莱坞) is home to many famous television and movie studios and record companies. It is a popular destination for nightlife, tourism, and is home to the Hollywood Walk of Fame. Many historic Hollywood theaters are used as venues and concert stages to premiere major theatrical releases and host the Academy Awards. Hollywood still attracts millions of visitors each year who travel there to pay homage to their favorite stars.

Task: Draw your mind-map on the "The United States in My Eyes" page based on the facts of the US and then introduce the US to your peers by using your mind-map.

★ *5C Reading on the United States*

A. Read the following information on Coronavirus in the US.

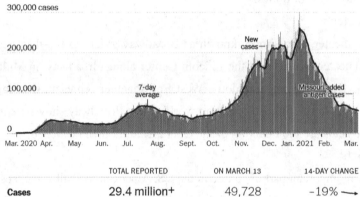

Coronavirus in the US:

Latest Map and Case Count

Updated March 14, 2021, 8:09 P.M. E.T.

	TOTAL REPORTED	ON MARCH 13	14-DAY CHANGE
Cases	29.4 million+	49,728	−19% →
Deaths	534,460	1,846	−31% →
Hospitalized		43,254	−25% →

Day with reporting anomaly. Hospitalization data from the US Department of Health and Human Services, 14-day change trends use 7-day averages.

At least 1,846 new coronavirus deaths and 49,728 new cases were reported in the United States on March 13. Over the past week, there has been an average of 55,215 cases per day, a decrease of 19 percent from the average two weeks earlier. As of Sunday evening, more than 29,460,900 people in the United States have been infected with the coronavirus according to a New York Times database.

和同学讨论并分享感受。

B. Discuss the following questions based on the above reading material.

1. How do you feel when you see the numbers listed above?

2. How will COVID-19 impact tourism industry?

PART III   Welcome Guests from the Land

★ *Project—Recommending Local Food*

You are a waiter working at Chengdu Kempinski Hotel. You meet a group of American tourists who are interested in Sichuan food. They want to have a try but don't know what is good for them. Recommend food which they might like. Discuss with your peers the reason for your recommendation.

My Recommendation

_____

_____

_____

_____

_____

Your Goals

1. Recommend the right famous Sichuan dishes.
2. Respect different food cultures.

· *Tasks*

A. *Discuss with your partner the reasons for choosing your dishes.*

B. *Write down the English name for these dishes and then discuss with your partner whether American guests would like them and why.*

火锅 _____

红烧肥肠 _____

糖醋里脊 _____

回锅肉 _____

水煮鱼 _____

麻婆豆腐 _____

★ *The Land and the World*

Ieoh Ming Pei—
A Master in Blending Cultures Who Never Forgot His Chinese

Ieoh Ming Pei, born on April 26, 1917 in Guangzhou, was a Chinese American architect. He came to the United States in 1935 with plans to study architecture. Pei was known for his strikingly contemporary, elegant, and functional buildings. They can be found throughout the United States and in other countries, including Canada, France, and Japan.

Pei, who died at the age of 102, was an important name in his field, with his buildings built all over the world. When he was a child, he learned basic knowledge about architecture from his father. Pei made innovations in architecture, and won the Thomas Jefferson Memorial Medal for Architecture. He built the Allied Bank Tower in Dallas, Texas, as well as the Louvre Pyramid, which is the main entrance to the Louvre Museum in Paris.

Pei, a master in blending different cultures, never forgot his Chinese roots. He was highly influential in helping Chinese architects and landscapers imagine how Chinese architecture could be modernized while retaining its traditional elements.

Pei has made important contributions to the mutual understanding between the Chinese and American people and the exchange of Eastern and Western cultures for a long time.

Mind-map: The United States in My Eyes

Name: _____   Date: _____

KWL Chart

Topic: _____   Name: _____   Date: _____

Know	Wonder	Learned
What do you think you already know about the United States?	What do you wonder about the United States? Write your questions below.	Write what you've learned about the United States.

裁 切 线

Section 2　Canada

Learning Objectives

A flight to Ottawa is around 13 hours from Shanghai, 1 hour from New York, 8 hours from London and 21 hours from Singapore.

After this section, you will be able to:

★ know the geographical features of Canada, especially the Great Lakes.

★ have a better understanding of the uniqueness of Canada.

★ know more typical landmarks and attractions in Canada.

★ apply Canadian social norms, taboos and unique features to serving inbound Canadian tourists, making them feel at home.

★ know the importance of enhancing Sino-Canadian tourism cooperation and attracting more Canadian tourists to China.

惊喜交"加"之加拿大

加拿大位于北美洲最北部，西抵太平洋，东迄大西洋，北至北冰洋，海岸线长24万多千米，是世界上海岸线最长的国家。加拿大与美国南部和西部边界长达8891千米，是世界上最长的两国陆地边界。面积998万平方千米，位居世界第二。人口3800万（2020年），主要为英、法等欧洲后裔，土著居民约占3%，其余为亚非拉裔等，信奉天主教和基督教，官方语言为英语和法语。加拿大有"枫叶之国""移民之国"的称号，首都渥太华。

加拿大森林广袤，雪山、湖泊、岛屿和苔原众多，民族多样、文化多元，自然和人文旅游资源极其丰富，是全球最受欢迎的旅游目的地之一。加拿大旅游业年均产值超过900亿加元，约占国内生产总值的2%，2019年创下接待2210万国际游客的新纪录。以"Canada for Glowing Hearts"作为旅游宣传口号，加拿大计划在2025年打造成世界旅游大国。

旅游合作是近年中加两国关系发展的新亮点。中加两国自然风光迥异、文化传统有别，旅游资源互补性强，市场潜力巨大。2016年9月中加两国宣布2018年为中加旅游年。2017年中国赴加游客69.45万人次，增长率为11.9%，中国成为加拿大增速最快的客源国市场。2018年，加拿大位列中国游客最满意目的地榜单第七，游客最满意购物目的地榜单第二。加拿大游客来华人数也逐年增加，2017年加拿大赴华游客80.5万人次，2018年84.9万人次，加拿大是中国第十二大客源国。中国内地是加拿大来亚太地区仅次中国香港的第二大旅游目的地。加拿大是我国拟开拓的重点客源国市场之一。接待加拿大游客时，应思考如何宣传我国自然、人文景观，吸引更多加拿大游客来华，让加拿大游客了解古老和现代中国，促进两国相互理解，增进友谊，互利互惠。

Canada Facts

- **Name**: Canada
- **Capital**: Ottawa
- **Government**: Constitutional Monarchy
- **Languages**: English, French
- **Population**: 38 Million (2020)

- **Life Expectancy**: 82.2 Years (2019)
- **Currency**: CAD100 ≈ CNY 517.50 (2021)
- **National Symbols**: Beaver, Maple Leaf
- **National Day**: July 1

PART I Let's Go

★ *First Glance*

Watch the video, and then answer the following questions.

1. What can visitors experience in the north of Canada?

2. Can you list any of the most popular destinations in central Canada? What are they?

3. Why do a large number of people immigrate to Canada each year?

★ *Viewing and Listening*

Watch the video again and fill in the blanks with the words you have heard.

As one of the commonwealth countries, Canada, known as "the country of maple _____", is a federal Constitutional Monarchy with _____ as its capital city and Toronto being the _____ city. Currently Queen Elizabeth Ⅱ is the head of state while the prime minister is the _____ of government. Due to the settlements of both France and Britain, the official languages are English and _____. Geographically, located in the most northernmost part of North _____, its 10 provinces and 3 territories extend from the Atlantic to the _____ and northward into the Arctic Ocean, bordering the _____ to the south and northwest which is the world's longest _____ between 2 nations. At 9.98 million square kilometers, Canada is the _____ largest country in the world.

PART II *Explore the Land*

· *Geography*

Located in the North American continent, Canada borders the Atlantic Ocean in the east, the Pacific Ocean in the west and the Arctic Ocean in the north. It shares a land border of 8,891 kilometers long with the USA in the south and in the northwest.

Canada houses about three million lakes, which are more than all the other countries in the world combined. The largest lake that is entirely in Canada is Great Bear Lake. Lake Superior, the largest lake in North America, is shared with the USA. Canada shares the largest waterfalls of the world by water volume. The McKenzie River (麦肯齐河) is Canada's longest river. The highest mountain is Mount Logan with 5,959 meters, which is also the second highest peak of the North American continent.

Canada is the second largest country in the world. It is also among the ten most sparsely populated countries. Canada is home to 17 UNESCO World Heritage Sites.

· *People*

Almost 90% of all Canadians live within 160 kilometers of the Canada-USA border. Most of the Canadian families have roots in England and France, as during the French and British colonized the country and thus many families immigrated into Canada. Almost 40% of the Canadians refer to belonging to the English, Scottish or Irish ethnic groups and about 13% are refer to belonging to the French ethnic group. Among the aboriginal people in Canada are the Métis, the Indians (the First Nations People) and the Inuit. Together they comprise less than 5% of Canada's total population.

· *Language*

English and French are both official languages of Canada. Almost half of the people can speak both of them. The majority of Canadians speak English as first language, but in Quebec City, French is the dominant language. The largest immigrant group speaks Chinese because of the growth in Chinese immigration since the 1980s. Cree is the most common of the native languages.

Several most commonly used little words in Canada are:

Eh?—The word is the classic term used in everyday Canadian dialect to indicate that people don't understand something, can't believe something is true or if they want the person to respond. For example, "It is a very nice day out today eh?" "Yes, it is."

Sorry—A handy little word used to express pardon, excuse, apology, or shock and horror, etc. For example, "Sorry, I didn't hear what you said."

Loonie—A loonie, the Canadian $1 coin, gets its name from the picture of the Canadian bird, the loon, which appears on one side of the coin. For example, "I'm short a loonie for the TTC (Toronto Transit Commission)."

• *Attractions*

Ottawa

Standing on the south bank of the Ottawa River, Ottawa is the capital and the fourth largest city in Canada. It was originally a trading and lumbering community that grew into a town of regional significance. Today, Ottawa is home to the federal government. People can tour iconic Parliament Hill, visit national museums, and take a paddle, cruise or skate on the Rideau Canal (里多运河)—a UNESCO World Heritage Site, or participate activities including cycling, rafting, hiking and skiing. And no matter the season, events like Winterlude, the Canadian Tulip Festival and Bluesfest fill the city with excitement and beauty.

Quebec City

Quebec City is known for its classical architecture and a distinctive European feel. It is one of the oldest cities in Canada with a history of over 400 years. The Historic District of Old Quebec's fortified city walls were designated a UNESCO World Heritage Site in 1985.

Tourism has been a mainstay of the economy for over 150 years. In winter, skiing is especially popular on the slopes of the Laurentian Mountains only a few miles from the city. The Mont Sainte-Anne center has been the scene of World Cup skiing tournaments as well as mountain bike world championships.

Toronto

Toronto is the largest and most populous city in Canada, the financial and commercial center of the country, and an important international trading center. Prior to the arrival of Europeans, a number of First Nations peoples had already inhabited here. In 1793 British colonial officials founded the Town of York on what was then the Upper Canadian frontier. That village grew to become the city of Toronto in 1834, and through its subsequent evolution and expansion, Toronto has emerged as one of the most liveable and multicultural urban places in the world.

Canadian National Tower

Canadian National Tower (CN Tower) is the broadcast and telecommunications tower in

Toronto. Standing at a height of 553 meters, it was the world's tallest freestanding structure until 2007. CN Tower is Toronto's most distinctive landmark and a major tourist attraction including observation decks, a revolving restaurant at 351 meters and an entertainment complex.

Horseshoe Falls

Horseshoe Falls is the largest of Niagara Falls' three waterfalls and a highlight of this internationally famed tourist attraction. Horseshoe Falls, also known as the Canadian Falls, is around 57 meters tall, approximately 790 meters wide and one of the world's highest-volume waterfalls.

Yellowknife Northern Lights

Known as "the world capital of northern lights", Yellowknife is one of the best places in the world to see northern lights. It lies just 512 kilometers from the Arctic Circle and enjoys clear weather during most of the winter. Its dark, long and crisp winter nights are perfect for viewing beautiful northern lights. The city of Yellowknife is equipped with special northern lighthouses which scatter throughout the city, alerting people to go out and marvel at the skies colored with dancing lights.

• *Canadian Food*

Canadian diet is similar to that of Americans and Europeans, with a heavy focus on processed grain and dairy products, farm-grown beef and chicken, certain cooked or fresh fruits and vegetables.

Popular Canadian foods are:

• **Tourtiere** (肉饼): Savoury pie made with ground beef and spices.

• **Nanaimo Bars**: Tremendously sweet, no-bake layered bar cookie.

• **Poutine** (肉汁奶酪薯条): French fries topped with fresh cheese curds and brown gravy.

• **Butter Tart**: Tart with a filling of butter, eggs, brown sugar, and, typically, raisins.

• **Montreal Smoked Meat**: Deli meat made by salting and curing beef brisket with spices.

• **BeaverTails**: Thick piece of deep-fried dough covered with cinnamon and sugar or chocolate spread and banana slices.

• *Unique Canada*

Most Educated Countries

According to the OECD (经济合作与发展组织), Canada is the most educated country in the world (2020), with 56.71% of adults have earned some kind of degree after high school.

Medicare

Medicare is Canada's publicly funded health care system. It offers free essential medical services for all Canadian citizens and permanent residents. Under this system, all Canadian residents have reasonable access to medically necessary hospital and physical services without paying out-of-pocket. It is one of the best systems in the world. There are multiple models of primary care delivery available.

Polar Bear Jail

Canada has the only polar bear jail in the world, which is located in Churchill, the world's polar bear capital. In fact, it is a secure facility serving as holding center for problem polar bears that repeatedly turn up in Churchill and pose a danger to the residents. The bears are held here for at least 30 days and fed only snow and water to stop them from returning to town in search of food.

UFO Landing Pad

Built as part of the Canadian centennial celebration in 1967, the UFO landing pad is designed to gather information about UFOs. St. Paul, Alberta has an official UFO landing welcome site. Weighing just over 130 tons, the large flat concrete structure contains a time capsule to be opened on the 100-year anniversary of the pad's opening in 2067.

In the 1990's, a rounded, saucer-shaped tourist information center was opened on the site containing a museum of UFO memorabilia including photographs of alleged landing sites, mysterious cattle mutilations, and crop circles.

Maple Syrup

Maple syrup is a popular natural sweetener that is claimed to be healthier and more nutritious than sugar. It is made by tapping sugar maple trees, then boiling the sap to produce a thick syrup.

Canada produces 71% of the world's maple syrup, 91% of which is produced in Quebec. Maple syrup is synonymous with Canadian culture ever since the country's indigenous people taught early settlers how to harvest sap and boil it to make syrup.

Ice Wine

Ice wine is a dessert wine made from frozen grapes. A wine can only be labeled as "ice wine" if it is made from naturally frozen grapes that were harvested from the vine. Canada is the largest producer of ice wine. It produces more ice wine than all the other countries combined.

Apology Act

Canadians are so polite that they had to introduce an Apology Act. In 2009, an act was passed which made apologies inadmissible in court. So, saying "sorry" meant "an expression of sympathy or regret" not "an admission of fault or liability in connection with the matter to which the words or actions relate".

Task: Draw your mind-map on the "Canada in My Eyes" page based on the facts of Canada and then introduce Canada to your peers by using your mind-map.

★ 5C Reading on Canada

A. Read the following passage and underline the significance of the garden.

Modeled after the garden home of a Ming Dynasty (1368-1644) scholar, hand-made with no power-tools, glues or screws, the Dr. Sun Yat-sen Classical Chinese Garden has been dubbed "the best urban garden in the world" by National Geographic. It is undoubtedly Chinatown's main attraction of Vancouver. As a place to experience Chinese heritage and history, the garden is the first of its kind outside China, and the biggest outside of Asia.

Rooted in ancient Chinese Taoist philosophy of pursuing peace and harmony between man and nature, the garden was fashioned to employ the four essential elements—flowers, water, rocks and architecture. Each aims to install tranquility and harmony through their creation of balance amongst contrary forces, or yin and yang as it is known in Chinese philosophy. This balance first manifests itself in the contrast between the garden's tranquility, peace and quietness, and its surrounding urban hustle-bustle environment. It can also be found in the harmony between the water and the rocks, and the different colors of the carefully selected plants.

The Dr. Sun Yat-sen Classical Chinese Garden was constructed as a joint venture between the Canadian and Chinese governments in 1986 for the Expo' 86 World's Fair to promote Chinese culture, maintain and enhance the understanding between China and the West. It is named after Dr. Sun Yat-sen, the founding father of the Republic of China, who overthrew the Qing Dynasty in the Xinhai Revolution. He spent a considerable amount of time in Vancouver's Chinatown, raising money to fund the revolution.

你知道中加两国在温哥华修建中山公园的意义吗？

B. Discuss the following questions based on the above reading material.

1. How has Chinese Taoist philosophy of pursuing peace and harmony between man and nature manifests itself in the Dr. Sun Yat-sen Classical Chinese Garden in Vancouver?

2. What's the significance of building the Dr. Sun Yat-sen Classical Chinese Garden in Vancouver?

3. How does the beauty of Chinese classical designs cast its influence on Vancouver?

PART III   Welcome Guests from the Land

★ *Project—Tour Commentary*

You are a tour guide for a group of Canadian tourists. They want to visit Jiuzhai Valley. Please discuss with your partners the 3 must-knows you'd like to introduce about Jiuzhai Valley based on the local scenery, culture and customs, and then write a tour commentary. Also, you need to take Canadian people and culture into consideration.

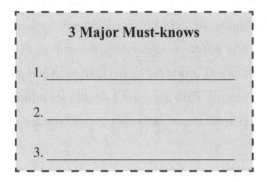

3 Major Must-knows

1. _____

2. _____

3. _____

Your Goals
1. Make the tourists enjoy their trip.
2. Promote the local attractions and specialties.

• *Tasks*

A. Tell your partners the reasons why you choose these three must-knows.

B. Prepare a short tour commentary based on your three must-knows.

The Magic Words or Sentences You Might Need for the Presentation

Words:

yak meat (牦牛肉)   rhododendron (杜鹃花)   Tibetan Buddhism (藏传佛教)

chang (青稞酒)   the Pearl Shoal (珍珠滩)   cordyceps sinensis (冬虫夏草)

yak butter tea (酥油茶)   altitude sickness (高原反应)

travertine topped waterfall (钙化瀑布)

Sentences:

1. The top 3 must-knows that I want to introduce are…

2. … has been likened to a land from a fairy tale.

3. The local food and drink traditionally include barley, yak meat and mutton.

4. The Nuo Ri Lang Waterfall is the widest travertine topped waterfall in the world.

5. The water, the soul of Jiuzhai Valley, is so crystal, clear and rich in colors that it has earned the reputation, so well expressed in the saying "Those who have visited Jiuzhai Valley will no longer appreciate the water landscape again".

★ *The Land and the World*

Isabel Crook—A Lifelong Friend of China

Isabel Crook was born in 1915 to a Canadian missionary family in Chengdu, Southwest China's Sichuan Province. Spending most of her childhood there, Crook was deeply interested in tremendous changes in China. Later, Crook returned to Canada for higher education and graduated from the University of Toronto with a master's degree in anthropology. When returned to China, Crook began carrying out field research in rural parts of Sichuan Province.

Crook became a member of the Communist Party of Great Britain after meeting her husband David Crook in China in the early 1940s. In 1947, Crook and her husband observed and studied the revolutionary land reform taking place in China. In 1948, the couple was invited to work as teachers in a newly established foreign affairs school in Hebei Province. They were the first foreign teachers at the school and brought Western teaching methods and ideologies to the classroom. The school was the forerunner of today's Beijing Foreign Studies University, which has seen more than 400 ambassadors and 1,000 counselors walk through its doors.

Crook has witnessed a large portion of the changes China has experienced since the founding of the People's Republic of China in 1949. In 2019, Crook was awarded the Medal of Friendship for her contribution to supporting China's socialist modernization, promoting exchanges and cooperation between China and foreign countries, and safeguarding world peace.

Mind-map: Canada in My Eyes

Name: _____   Date: _____

KWL Chart

Topic: _____   Name: _____   Date: _____

Know	Wonder	Learned
What do you think you already know about Canada?	What do you wonder about Canada? Write your questions below.	Write what you've learned about Canada.

裁 切 线

Section 3   Brazil

Learning Objectives

A flight with transfer to Brasilia is about 30 hours from Hong Kong, 44 hours from Chongqing, 30 hours from Tokyo, 19 hours from London and 21 hours from New York.

After this section, you will be able to:

★ know the geographical features and uniqueness of Brazil.

★ understand the China-Brazil ties in various ways.

★ list the major attractions and landmarks in Brazil.

★ apply Brazilian social norms, taboos and unique features to serving inbound Brazilian tourists, making them feel at home.

★ know the influence of Chinese craftsmanship, culture and spirit of sustainable development in Brazil.

桑"巴"国度之巴西

巴西全称巴西联邦共和国，位于南美洲东部，东濒大西洋；领土面积约851.49万平方千米，居世界第5位。首都巴西利亚有最年轻的"人类文化遗产"之美誉。官方语言为葡萄牙语。人口约2.1亿（2020年），有大量混血种人。大多数巴西人信奉天主教，文化具有多元融合的特点。巴西地处热带和亚热带气候带，享有得天独厚的自然条件。它是全球淡水资源最丰富的国家；"地球之肺"亚马孙雨林覆盖了其近一半的国土。巴西经济实力居南美洲首位、世界第12位；与俄罗斯、印度、中国、南非并称为金砖国家（BRICS）。

巴西旅游业久负盛名，旅游总收入位列全球第12位。多姿多彩的桑巴狂欢，星光熠熠的足球冠军，脍炙人口的烤肉盛宴，美不胜收的天使之城都是其旅游名片。然而巴西的魅力远不止于此，它还拥有鬼斧神工的山川地貌、独具魅力的热带风光。境内有世界上最长的河流——亚马孙河，世界规模最大、最壮观的瀑布群——伊瓜苏瀑布，世界最大的沼泽湿地——潘塔纳尔湿地。海岸线上有众多美丽的小岛，合称为"巴西大西洋岛屿"，它们被联合国列入世界自然遗产，是南大西洋热带海岛的活标本。知名旅游城市包括：里约热内卢、圣保罗、萨尔瓦多、巴西利亚、马瑙斯、黑金城等。

随着金砖国家合作机制的影响力不断释放，旅游交流成为金砖国家经贸合作的新增长点。金砖国家旅游市场成为世界旅游格局中的重要力量，中国和巴西也相互成为重要客源国和目的地。

Brazil Facts

- **Name**: Federative Republic of Brazil
- **Capital**: Brasilia
- **Government**: Multiparty Federal Republic
- **Language**: Portuguese
- **Population**: 210 Million (2020)
- **Currency**: BRL 100 ≈ CNY 124.92 (2021)
- **National Symbols**: Jaguar, Macaw, Cattleya Orchid
- **National Day**: September 7

PART I Let's Go

★ *First Glance*

Watch the video about the Lencois Maranhenses National Park, and then answer the following questions.

1. What's your opinion of the scenery shown in the video?

2. What do you want to know about the sustainable development of tourism in Atins (阿廷斯)? Write your thoughts in the KWL chart.

★ *Listening*

Listening to the audio and fill in the blanks with the words you have heard.

Rio de Janeiro has become a popular tourist destination because of its beaches, climate, and _____ events. Located along Brazil's east coast, Rio is recognized as one of the world's most beautiful cities. The waters of the _____ and Guanabara Bay provide a sparkling backdrop for the city, while coastal mountains and hills _____ its landscape. The Sugar Loaf landmass and the soaring statue of Christ the Redeemer atop Mount Corcovado provide iconic _____ for the city. Rio de Janeiro's roots and traditions perhaps are shown best through the world-renowned Carnival, held _____ before Lent. Rio's celebration is recognized as the world's largest Carnival festival. The festivities include music, pageants, parties, and street parades filled with vibrantly costumed dancers _____ to samba rhythms. Samba schools perform a vital role in the celebration of Carnival, providing dancers, costumes, and floats.

PART II Explore the Land

· *Geography*

Brazil locates in the central eastern part of South America and occupies half the continent's landmass. It is South America's biggest and the fifth largest country in the world, exceeded in size only by Russia, Canada, China, and the United States.

Brazil covers a wide range of tropical and subtropical landscapes, including wetlands, savannas, plateaus, and low mountains. Brazil contains most of the Amazon Basin, which has the world's largest river system and the world's most-extensive rainforest. The Amazon, the Parana River (巴拉那河), the San Francisco River (圣弗朗西斯科河) are among the biggest rivers in Brazil. The country borders the Atlantic Ocean and has an almost 7,500 kilometers long coastline. It is known for its powdery white-sand beaches as well as plentiful coral-fringed tropical islands.

· *People*

Brazil is the country with the fifth largest population in the world, after China, India, the USA and Indonesia. Most Brazilians live in urban centers, mainly along the Atlantic coast and in the major cities.

Brazil has one of the most diverse populations in the world. People of Portuguese or other European descent account for nearly half of the population, although people of mixed ethnic backgrounds form an increasingly larger segment. Major ethnic groups include people of African descent, Native Americans, people of mixed ancestry and people of Asian descent. Brazil also has the largest Japanese community outside Japan.

· *Language*

Brazil is the only Portuguese-speaking country in South America. The Brazilian Portuguese is slightly different to the Portuguese spoken in Portugal. The pronunciation sounds different and some of the words are used only in Brazil. Many Brazilians can speak English or Spanish, and in some states, the local also speak indigenous languages (土著族群语言) and other languages.

Here are some basic words and useful expressions for tourists:

Olá or oi (Hello.)

Por favor (Please.)

Obrigado (Thank you by male speakers.)

Obrigada (Thank you by female speakers.)

Beleza (OK. / Good.)

• *Attractions*

Historic Town of Ouro Preto

Founded at the end of the 17th century, the Historic Town of Ouro Preto (欧鲁普雷图古镇) was the center of the gold rush and Brazil's golden age in the 18th century. On September 5,1980, the town became Brazil's first cultural property entered on the World Heritage List. The town covers the steep slopes of the Rich Valley. Along the original winding road and within the irregular layout following the outline of the valley lie squares, public buildings, houses, fountains, bridges and churches which together form an outstanding evidence to its past prosperity.

Brasilia

The capital of Brazil, created out of nothing in the central western part of the country from 1956 to 1960, was a landmark of 20th century urbanism because of its unique city plan and architecture, as well as its vital role in the development of the Brazilian national modernization. The city made its inclusion on UNESCO's World Heritage Sites in 1987.

Iguacu National Park

Iguacu National Park (伊瓜苏国家公园) is created to preserve one of the world's largest and most impressive waterfalls, extending over some 2,700 meters. It is home to many rare and endangered species of flora and fauna (动植物群), among them the giant otter and the giant anteater. The clouds of spray produced by the waterfall are beneficial to the survival of vegetation and wildlife. It is a World Heritage property of outstanding universal value.

Atlantic Forest South-East Reserves

The Atlantic Forest South-East Reserves (大西洋东南热带雨林保护区) are located in the Brazilian states of Paraná and São Paulo, representing one of the largest and best-preserved areas of the Brazilian Atlantic forests, and one of the most threatened biomes (生物群落) of the world. The 25 protected areas that make up the site display great biological wealth. From mountains covered by dense forests, down to wetlands, coastal islands with isolated mountains and dunes, the region comprises a rich natural environment of great scenic beauty. It was entitled the Natural World Heritage in 1999.

Recife

Recife is Brazil's fourth largest city. It stands out as a major tourist attraction of the northeast states, both for its beaches and for its historic sites, dating back to both the Portuguese and the Dutch colonization (殖民) of the region. The city is located at the confluence (交汇处) of the Beberibe and Capibaribe rivers before they flow into the South Atlantic Ocean. It is a major port on the Atlantic. Its name is a reference to the stone reefs that are present by the city's shores, and it is also nicknamed "Venice of Brazil" because of its over 50 bridges and many waterways.

· *Sports*

The people in Brazil love being outdoors, the main sports are football, volleyball and water sports.

Football is the nation's most popular sport, and Brazilians are highly excited fans. Brazil has hosted the FIFA World Cup 2 times, in 1950 and 2014. Brazil has won the world cup 5 times, in 1958, 1962, 1970, 1994 and 2002. Brazil has produced some of the best players throughout the history of the game, such as Pelé, Ronaldo, Rivaldo, Ronaldinho and Neymar.

Volleyball is the second most popular sport in Brazil, because of the country's great successes in Volleyball World Championship (世界排球锦标赛) since the mid-20th century. And Brazilian championships of beach volleyball draw thousands of spectators and television coverage on a world scale.

With roughly 7,500 kilometers of coastline, surfing is part of the daily life and embedded in the culture, especially in coastal cities. The good climate in Brazil means that surfing conditions remain favorable almost all year round, and there are good spots for both beginners and advanced surfers.

· *Unique Brazil*

Carnival

Brazil is known for its cheerful and vibrant atmosphere during Carnival time starting on the Friday before Ash Wednesday. Carnival is celebrated with the parades of the various samba schools. The communities are usually widely involved as drumming, dancing and marching are practiced all year round for this special annual event. Carnival is celebrated in many cities such as in Sao Paolo, Salvador or Rio de Janeiro. The Samba School Parade (桑巴舞学校游行) is the centerpiece of Rio de Janeiro's Carnival. The four-day celebration is the most famous and energetic Brazilian holiday.

Christ the Redeemer

Christ the Redeemer Statue is one of the new Seven Wonders of the World. Located in Rio de Janeiro, the statue was created in 1931 to pay a tribute to Jesus Christ. It stands at the summit of Mount Corcovado which makes it one of the largest Art Deco (装饰派艺术) statues in the world.

Sugarloaf Mountain

Sugarloaf Mountain is located in the heart of Carrabassett Valley and is surrounded by Maine's Western Mountains. As a natural landmark, it reminds people of the sailors who come to Guanabara Bay. As a geological landmark, it reminds people of the geological site precisely dating the history of our planet. And, as a touristic landmark, the cable cars opened on Sugarloaf have projected Brazil's name worldwide.

Brazilian Coffee

Brazil has been the largest producer of coffee in the world since 1840. Brazilian coffee comes from a wide variety of regions and climates within Brazil. A great high-quality Brazilian coffee is often soft, nutty, low acid and chocolatey. There is a very special type of Brazilian coffee called Jacu Bird Coffee (肉垂凤冠雉咖啡), or known as Bird Poop Coffee worldwide. The Jacu bird is a native bird to Brazil, and it feeds on ripe coffee cherries. Workers collect the bird's droppings before processing. In terms of coffee tasting, drinkers of this coffee comment that Jacu Bird Coffe is a full-bodied, sweet coffee that has a hint of cinnamon and a smooth, clean aftertaste.

Teatro Amazonas

A Brazilian national treasure, the historic Teatro Amazonas (亚马孙歌剧院) in Manaus was built in the late 19th century. In order to achieve the desired luxury and refinement, most of the materials used in the construction were brought from Europe. This magnificent theater, crowned with a tiled mosaic (马赛克) dome in the colors of the Brazilian flag, features operas and other artistic performances. The theater has become urban landmarks representative of a time of flourishing commerce and culture, which lasted to the present day in the urban center of Manaus.

The 2016 Olympic Games

The 2016 Summer Olympics was a major international sport and cultural event from August 5, 2016, to August 21. The host city was Rio de Janeiro, Brazil. The 2016 Summer Paralympic Games was also held in the same city and organized by the same organizing committee. The Rio Games were the 28th occurrence of the Modern Olympic Games. The event marked the first time that either the Summer or the Winter Olympics was held in South America.

Zerão

Zerão stadium, known in English as "the Big Zero", is a famous football field. Opened in 1990, the stadium was so delicately designed that the midfield line fell exactly on the equator (赤道), meaning each half lies on a different hemisphere (半球).

Task: Draw your mind-map on the "Brazil in My Eyes" page based on the facts of Brazil and then introduce Brazil to your peers by using your mind-map.

★ *5C Reading on Brazil*

A. Read the following passage and be aware of Chinese companies' contributions to Brazil's infrastructure.

Brazil's railway system spreads across 30,000 kilometers, but the system is underused and almost entirely focused on cargo shipments. Suffering from years of under-investment and lack of maintenance, passenger transport, outside of urban metro areas, is near non-existent.

As Brazil turns its attention to trains, many rail companies in China have made great contribution to Brazilian railway development. CRRC Corp Ltd (中国中车股份有限公司) supplied rail cars for the 2014 FIFA World Cup in Brazil. During the 2016 Rio Summer Olympics, the key Olympic transport line featured China-made trains. More than half the subway trains running in Rio de Janeiro's metro system were Chinese products which helped to link the city's many tourism districts. China has increasingly gotten involved in Brazilian rail projects and plans: the upgrade for the Western Railway Line; the Twin Ocean Railway Cooperation connecting Peru's Pacific coast to the Brazilian Atlantic; the Chinese-funded Amazonian railway; the TAV Project linking tourist cities like Rio de Janeiro, Sao Paulo and Campinas.

After the 11th BRICS summit in Brasilia, China has moved actively toward including Brazil in its global Belt and Road Initiative, meanwhile Brazil considers China its largest trading partner and greatest partner for investments. The two countries have developed mutual interests in many sectors such as energy, transportation, agriculture, electricity generation and transmission, as well as tourism.

> 中国高铁走进巴西，通过"中国制造"加深两国友谊。你知道中国企业落户巴西，为促进当地就业、改善民生所做的贡献吗？

B. Read the above passage and do the follow-up research.

1. Search with keywords "The Belo Monte Cooperation" via Xuexi.cn and study the report. And then find out China's contribution to Brazil's sustainable development.

2. Read the Keynote Speech of the Second Belt and Road Forum for International Cooperation, and find relevant information about tourism.

3. Search for tourist attractions along the train route from Rio de Janeiro to Sao Paulo.

PART III Welcome Guests from the Land

★ Project—Enjoying Sichuan Opera

You are a tour guide for a group of Brazilian tourists. The guests are looking forward to enjoying Sichuan Opera. Aiming to make this cultural activity unforgettable, you are supposed to give a brief introduction to Sichuan Opera. Please take Brazilian art forms into consideration, such as Baila Brazil, Samba and Capoeira, which can make them relate Sichuan Opera with their arts.

Baila Brazil　　　　　**Samba**　　　　　**Capoeira**

• Tasks

A. *Discuss how to attend Sichuan Opera for the first time with a partner, and then conclude at least 3 tips to make sure the guests can enjoy themselves as possible as they can.*

B. *Prepare a brief presentation on Sichuan Opera.*

The Magic Words or Sentences You Might Need for the Presentation

Words:

fire-blowing (喷火)　　　　　　　　face-changing (变脸)

elaborate makeup (精致的装扮)　　　high-speed acrobatics (迅捷的杂技)

high-pitched singing (高昂的唱腔)　　Plum Performance Award (梅花表演奖)

handcrafted costumes and props (手工制作的服装和道具)

Sentences:

1. Sichuan Opera is a traditional folk drama art.

2. Sichuan Opera combines singing, poetry and performing…

3. Sichuan Opera features different singing styles from… and folk song melodies…

4. The singing is performed in the Sichuan dialect.

5. The artistic skills include…

6. Emerging as an urban dance movement from Uberlândia in Brazil, Baila Brazil is a fusion of percussion, rhythmic drumming, and classical dance.

7. Samba is characterized by simple forward and backward steps and tilting, rocking body movements.

8. Capoeira is a Brazilian martial art disguised as a dance of African origin and performed to musical instruments and traditional Brazilian music.

★ *The Land and the World*

> **Famous Footballer Reborn in China—Ai Kesen**

Born Elkeson de Oliveira Cardoso in Maranhão in Brazil, but reborn in China as Ai Kesen (艾克森), the striker made history September 2019 when he became the first person without any known Chinese ancestry to play for China's national football team. The unlikely journey began on Christmas Eve 2012, when Guangzhou Evergrande announced they had signed Ai Kesen. Fast forward to 2019, with 5 Chinese Super League wins, 2 AFC Champions League wins and well over 100 goals later, and it was safe to say Ai Kesen had achieved legend status in China.

China was not an immigrant country, and its naturalization management is extremely strict. However, Ai Kesen was eligible for naturalization having lived in China for 5 years consecutively, and he was granted citizenship in 2019. "I want a new challenge", he said on social media, "I want to see where my limits are. I am very happy in China; it is my home. I want to say to the world: I have officially started a new journey—I'm Chinese! I want to return the love of the Chinese people over these seven years. I hope to get your support, as always. I accepted this challenge without hesitation."

With China's push toward hosting and winning a World Cup by 2050, and with China National Football Team struggling in qualification for the 2022 World Cup in Qatar, Ai Kesen determined to devote his talent to pursue national glory in the World Cup for China.

Mind-map: Brazil in My Eyes

Name: _____   Date: _____

KWL Chart

Topic: _____   Name: _____   Date: _____

Know	Wonder	Learned
What do you think you already know about Brazil?	What do you wonder about Brazil? Write your questions below.	Write what you've learned about Brazil.

裁

切

线

Chapter 6   Europe

Section 1   Britain

A flight to London, Britain is 11 hours from Chengdu, 13 hours from Singapore, 11 hours from Thailand and 8 hours from New York.

Learning Objectives

After this section, you will be able to:

★ know the geographical features of Britain, especially the four constituent parts.

★ list the typical landmarks and attractions in Britain.

★ apply British social norms, taboos and unique features to serving inbound British tourists, making them feel at home.

★ promote the image of Chinese tourism by relating China and Britain from tea culture, diplomatic relations and social attitudes.

含"英"咀华之英国

英国，曾盛极一时的"日不落帝国"，是由大不列颠岛上的英格兰、威尔士和苏格兰以及爱尔兰岛东北部的北爱尔兰以及一系列附属岛屿共同组成的联邦制西欧岛国，全称为"大不列颠及北爱尔兰联合王国"。本土位于欧洲大陆西北面的不列颠群岛，被北海、英吉利海峡、凯尔特海、爱尔兰海和大西洋包围。除本土之外，其还拥有十四个海外领地，总人口超过6680万（2019年）。通用英语，居民多信奉基督教新教。首都伦敦是英国的政治、经济、文化中心，是世界第一大金融中心，与纽约和中国香港并称为"纽伦港"，它也是全世界博物馆、图书馆和体育馆数量最多的城市。

英国是个有着深厚文化底蕴的国家，文物古迹众多，人文资源丰富。"万城之花"伦敦、"北方雅典"爱丁堡、大学城牛津、剑桥、古色古香的约克城、莎翁故乡斯特拉特福都是享有世界声誉的旅游名城。华兹华斯笔下静谧梦幻的湖区，拥有天空岛和尼斯湖的纯净高地，悠闲舒适的沿海度假小城，每一处都值得探寻游览。

英国是世界近代旅游业的发源地。1840年，托马斯·库克首次组织的火车专列旅游活动，标志着旅游业首先在英国诞生。英国是当今世界上旅游业最发达的国家之一，740多亿英镑的旅游业年产值，占世界旅游收入的5%左右。中英两国密切的贸易往来带动了两国商贸旅游和娱乐旅游的合作，双边游客互相往来频繁。

近年来，英国来华旅游人次不断增长，2009年达52.88万人次，居中国主要客源市场第12位，是欧洲来华旅游人数最多的国家，2018年来华旅游人次增至60.8万。因此，英国这个客源市场潜力非常大，但不会自然增长。对此，我们应该根据英国人的特点，分析来华旅游障碍，加强对外宣传，树立中国最安全、最有魅力的国家形象，让那些有支付能力的英国人对中国产生兴趣，来中国旅游。同时，我们要不断优化旅游大环境，不断创新完善旅游产品，加强国际旅游人才的培养，创造一个更加成熟的旅游市场。

Britain Facts

- **Name**: The United Kingdom of Great Britain and Northern Ireland
- **Capital**: London
- **Government**: Constitutional Monarchy
- **Population**: 66.8 Million (2019)
- **Language**: English
- **Currency**: GBP 100 ≈ CNY 898.04 (2021)
- **National Symbol**: Lion

PART I Let's Go

★ *First Glance*

Watch the video, and then answer the following questions.

1. Do you want to go to Britain after watching the video?

2. Which British fact impresses you most in the video?

3. What do you gain from this video about Britain?

★ *Viewing and Listening*

Watch a video about London and fill in the blanks with the words you have heard.

London is situated in the _____ of England in the _____. Home to over 8 million people, the capital of the UK has been an important financial, _____ and cultural center for hundreds of years. Of many _____ England has given to the world, none has been greater than her language and _____. And if ever there's a city that read like an epic saga, it's London.

The story of London began in Bronze Age, but it didn't really get going until the _____ withdrew in the 5th century.

London is very easy to navigate _____, and is compact enough to _____ on foot.

This world city is filled with iconic symbols, and one of the most easily recognizable is _____, an impressive reminder of London's rapid expansion in the _____.

PART II Explore the Land

· *Geography*

The United Kingdom of Great Britain and Northern Ireland, commonly known as Britain or the United Kingdom, is located off the northwestern coast of mainland Europe. It has coastlines along the Atlantic Ocean, the North Sea, and the English Channel. The United Kingdom consists of England, Scotland, Wales and Northern Ireland, and it also has 13 British overseas territories throughout the world.

The landscape becomes increasingly mountainous towards the north, rising to the Grampian Mountains (格兰扁山脉) in Scotland, the Pennines (奔宁山脉) in northern England, and the Cambrian Mountains (寒武纪山) in Wales.

With a total area of 243,610 square kilometers, the United Kingdom is about half the size of Spain, or slightly larger than half the size of California. It was part of the European Union from 1973 and left the EU on January 31, 2020.

· *People*

The United Kingdom is a country with a diverse and multiethnic (多种民族的) population. People from all over the world have made this country their home.

The United Kingdom has population of over 66.8 million which ranks 22rd most populous country in the world. The population makeup of UK is: England (84.25%), Scotland (8.2%), Wales (4.7%), and Northern Ireland (2.8%). White British is the predominant (主要的) race in the UK. The United Kingdom is also the 7th most densely populated country in the Europe.

In terms of population distribution, almost one-third of the population lives in England's southeast, which is predominantly urban and suburban. London is the capital city of UK, with population over 8 million, the population density of which is just over 5,200 per square kilometer.

• *Language*

The main language spoken in the UK is British English. Scots, Welsh and Irish are also spoken. There are also four Celtic languages spoken: Scottish Gaelic, Irish Gaelic, Welch and Cornish. The ancient languages are still spoken in England but only by small groups of people.

English is widely used in the UK in different dialects (方言) in addition to several regional languages. The English language emerged from the Anglo-Saxon kingdoms of medieval England. The language's development has been ongoing for over 1,400 years. Today, 98% of the inhabitants of the UK are English speakers. English ranks as the third most widespread languages in the world. Different organizations recognize it as either an official or co-official language including the EU and the UN.

"Please", "sorry" and "thank you" are the common words basically dominated all of social interaction in Britain. It's so rooted into their blood that often bum into things in the daily life.

• *Attractions*

London

London, the capital of the United Kingdom, is one of the four world-class cities, alongside New York, Paris, and Tokyo. By far Britain's largest metropolis, London is also the country's economic, transportation, and cultural center. Since the establishment of the city by the Romans more than 2,000 years ago, London has had great influence in the world.

From 1801 to the beginning of the 20th century, as the world's empire, London became the largest city in the world for its outstanding achievements in the field of technological inventions. In March 2016, Wealth Report was released and London ranked third among the most expensive cities in the world. In September 2018, the 2018 World Tourism City Development Rankings were published in a comprehensive ranking, and London ranked first. London offers excellence in its facilities and attractions, such as British Museum, Buckingham Palace, London Eye and Tower Bridge.

Buckingham Palace

Buckingham Palace was acquired by King George Ⅲ in 1761, as a private residence for Queen Charlotte and became known as the Queen's House.

During the 19th century it was enlarged, principally by architects John Nash and Edward Blore, who constructed three wings around a central courtyard. Buckingham Palace became the London residence of the British monarch on the accession of Queen Victoria in 1837.

Located in the city of Westminster, the palace is often at the center of state occasions and royal hospitality. It has been a focal point for the British people at times of national rejoicing (欢喜) and mourning.

The British Museum

The British Museum, in the Bloomsbury area of London, is a public institution dedicated to human history, art and culture. Its permanent collection of some eight million works is among the largest and most comprehensive in existence, having been widely collected during the era of the British Empire. It documents the story of human culture from its beginnings to the present. It was the first public national museum in the world.

Tower Bridge

Tower Bridge is a combined bascule and suspension bridge in London, built between 1886 and 1894. The bridge crosses the River Thames and has become a world-famous symbol of London. As a result, it is sometimes confused with London Bridge, about 0.5 miles upstream. Tower Bridge is one of five London bridges owned and maintained by the Bridge House Estates, a charitable trust overseen by the City of London Corporation.

The Palace of Westminster

The Palace of Westminster, also known as the Houses of Parliament or Westminster Palace is where the two Houses of the Parliament of the United Kingdom meet. The palace lies on the north bank of the River Thames in the London borough of the City of Westminster, close to other government buildings in Whitehall.

Big Ben is the nickname for the Great Bell of the striking clock at the north end of the Palace of Westminster; the name is frequently extended to refer to both the clock and the clock tower. The official name of the tower in which Big Ben is located was originally the Clock Tower; it was renamed Elizabeth Tower in 2012 to mark the Diamond Jubilee of Elizabeth Ⅱ, Queen of the United Kingdom.

Stonehenge

Stonehenge is one of the wonders of the world, which is believed to have been built from 4000 BC to 2000 BC. The whole monument is oriented towards the sunrise on the summer solstice (夏至). It's the most prehistoric monument on earth. It consists of an outer ring of vertical Sarsen (砂岩) standing stones, each around 13 feet high, seven feet wide, and weighing around 25 tons, topped by connecting horizontal lintel (过梁) stones. Now as a World Heritage Site, Stonehenge and all its surroundings remain powerful witnesses to the once great civilizations of the Stone and Bronze Ages.

Hadrian's Wall

Stretching 73 miles from coast to coast, Hadrian's Wall, a UNESCO World Heritage Site, was built to guard the wild northwest frontier of the Roman Empire. Today people can explore the Wall's rich history and its dramatic landscape at over twenty English heritage sites.

• *Britain Food*

Food and soft drinks are among the main manufactured goods in the Britain. The British love diversity in food, many foreign restaurants like Indian, Chinese, Thai and Italian are so popular in London. Typical English breakfast is with fried egg, sausages, bacon, black pudding, baked beans, tomatoes and toast. Eating out is now much more common in Britain.

Popular Britain foods:

• **Fish and Chips** (炸鱼和薯条): Deep fried fish or fish fingers with French fries that have been soaked with vinegar, raw fish and rice rolls.

• **Bangers and Mash** (香肠土豆泥): Sausages and mashed potatoes.

• **Black Pudding** (血肠): Sausage or sliced meatloaf of pigs blood and fat that has been mixed with pepper or spices and cooked or fried.

• **Yorkshire Pudding** (约克郡布丁): Similar to a flat round roll, eaten usually with the main meal and vegetables, not a dessert.

• **Haggis** (苏格兰羊杂碎肚): Traditional Scottish dish made with lamb's offal (liver, lungs, heart) minced with onions and spices. This dish is often served with mashed potatoes and mashed turnips.

• *Unique Britain*

Constitutional Monarchy

Monarchy is the oldest form of government in the United Kingdom. In a monarchy, a king or queen is Head of State. The British Monarchy is known as a constitutional monarchy. This means that, while the Sovereign is Head of State, the ability to make and pass legislation resides with an elected Parliament.

British Royal Family

In legal terms of the UK, the Queen is head of the executive and the Head of State; she is an integral part of the government's legislature (立法机关); she is also "supreme governor" of the established church.

Queen Elizabeth Ⅱ became Queen of the United Kingdom and Head of the Commonwealth on February 6, 1952. She is head of the British Royal Family, has 4 children, 8 grandchildren and 8 great-grandchildren.

The British Royal Family is the group of close relatives of the Monarch of the United Kingdom. Despite a lot of the British royal dynasty after dynasty, but in fact, they are near or far between the blood relationship, royal blood has never stopped.

Industrial Revolution

The Industrial Revolution was a period of major industrialization and innovation that took place during the late 1700s and early 1800s. The Industrial Revolution began in Great Britain and quickly spread throughout the world. The main features involved in the Industrial Revolution were technological, socioeconomic, and cultural. Although the Industrial Revolution occurred approximately 200 years ago, it is a period that left a profound impact on how people lived and the way businesses operated.

The Red Double Decker Bus

The red double decker buses, considered as an iconic symbol of England and Great Britain, had dominated English transport for over a century.

Traditionally red in color, these buses have two decks, and the earliest models did not have a roof on the second level. They were, therefore, used by travel agencies to allow tourists to view the many attractions of the country, through time-saving city tours.

Double-deckers are no longer used in general transportation and have now converted to camping homes and mobile holiday homes and some even as mobile cafes. One Route master, in particular, has been transformed into a mobile theater.

British Sunday Roast

The Sunday roast is a British tradition. Many British restaurants and pubs serve this delicious meal on Sundays. They can usually choose from beef, pork, lamb or chicken. It's served with roast potatoes and a variety of vegetables to compliment the roast meat.

Cultural Taboos

Although the United Kingdom has a generally open culture, there are some behaviors that are best avoided, particularly at the beginning of a relationship.

Behaviors to avoid:

• Greeting strangers with a kiss: British people only kiss their close friends or relatives.

• Gestures such as backslapping and hugging strangers.

• Spiting in public.

• Asking personal or intimate questions such as "How much money do you earn?" or "Why did you divorce?"

• Talking loudly in public.

• Picking nose in public.

• Eating off a knife when having a meal.

Task: Draw your mind-map on the "Britain in My Eyes" page based on the facts of Britain and then introduce Britain to your peers by using your mind-map.

★ 5C Reading on Britain

A. Read the following passage about the afternoon tea in Britain.

One thing that British and Chinese cultures share is a love for fine tea. Today, when we think of Western tea culture, we often think of the English and china tea cups.

The earliest record of tea in England is The Travels of Lin Xiaodeng, published in 1598. At that time, the British called tea Chaa. Tea originated in China, and the British East India Company initially traded tea with China through Dutch ports. In 1637, the English arrived in the East, and then they began to trade directly with Chinese merchants.

Afternoon Tea

People believe that an English duchess, Anna, the 7th Duchess of Bedford (1788-1861) first introduced the idea of afternoon tea. In the 18th and 19th centuries, the English ate only two main meals each day—breakfast and a heavy supper that would last for several hours in the evening. As a result, people often got very hungry during the long wait between these two meals. To solve this problem, the Duchess came up with the clever idea of inviting some friends to join her for an afternoon meal between four and five o'clock. This meal included cakes and sandwiches, and tea was served to wash down the food.

In order to make this afternoon meal important, fine china cups and plates, silver teapots, knives, forks and spoons were used. Soon, afternoon tea parties became popular social occasions.

Today, afternoon tea parties continue to play an important part in the social life of wealthy people in modern Britain.

> 你知道中英两国茶文化的异同吗？试举例说明。

B. Discuss the following questions based on the above reading material.

1. How has Chinese tea significantly influenced Britain's social life?

2. Do you know any more differences of tea culture between Britain and China?

3. Do you know the history of Chinese tea? And how do you understand that "the moon is bright in at home"?

PART III   Welcome Guests from the Land

★ *Project—Seeing Off at the Airport*

You are a tour guide for a British tourist. You want to send him a gift at the airport to make his trip in China unforgettable and memorable. Please pick up 1 item from the following based on what you know about British people and culture. Also, you need to take local Chinese culture into consideration.

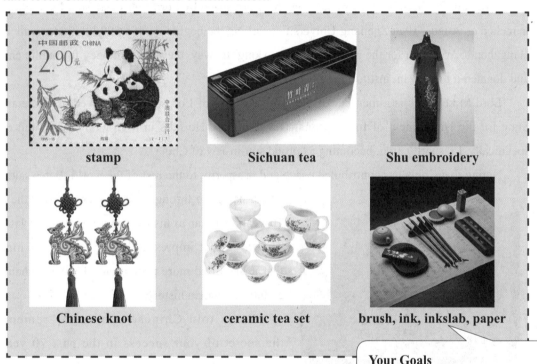

stamp   Sichuan tea   Shu embroidery

Chinese knot   ceramic tea set   brush, ink, inkslab, paper

Your Goals

Make the tourist feel at home and know more about China.

• *Tasks*

A. *Tell your partner the reason why you choose the item as the gift.*

B. *Write down at least 3 rules of giving gifts in Britain you have known.*

For Example:

Don't send the lilies to the British, because it means death.

Your Suggestions:

1. _____

2. _____

3. _____

★ *The Land and the World*

Lord Bates Walks for Peace and Prosperity

"Walking for Friendship", a month-long hike organized by Lord Bates and Mrs. Li Xuelin, was launched on August 19 at Zhejiang University, marking the beginning of a 500-kilometer walk from Hangzhou to Wenzhou for the married couple. Along the way, they raised money for public charity and donated it to relevant institutions.

Lord Mike Bates is a member of the British House of Lords and has served as Secretary of State for the Department of International Development. He falls in love with China, and more specifically, Li, shortly after, becoming a "proud son-in-law of China".

Noting that China has contributed peace and prosperity to the rest of the world, Bates said that

China has gone through a long journey over the past 70 years, similar to his own journey over the last 10. The thing that impresses him most about China is that it has lifted more people out of poverty than any country in human history.

Bates told Chinese people to "remember the secret of your success in the past 70 years", emphasizing that this extraordinary success was built on three things. "Firstly, on economic prosperity; Secondly, on engaging through economic trade and friendship with other countries around the world; Third and finally, through peace. We wish you more of the same over the next thirty and seventy years."

That's for the best wishes for the People's Republic of China.

Mind-map: Britain in My Eyes

Name: _____   Date: _____

KWL Chart

Topic: _____   Name: _____   Date: _____

Know	Wonder	Learned
What do you think you already know about Britain?	What do you wonder about Britain? Write your questions below.	Write what you've learned about Britain.

裁 切 线

Section 2   France

A flight to Paris is 10 hours from Beijing, 14 hours from Singapore, 1.5 hours from London and 8 hours from New York.

Learning Objectives

After this section, you will be able to:

★ know the geographical features of France.

★ list the typical landmarks and attractions in France.

★ apply French social norms, taboos and unique features to serving inbound French tourists, making them feel at home.

★ build up cultural confidence by understanding the common cultural characteristics of China and France.

文雅之"法"之法国

　　法兰西共和国，简称"法国"，古称"高卢"，位于欧洲西部，西濒大西洋，南濒地中海，西北隔英吉利海峡与英国相望。面积55万平方千米，是欧盟面积最大的国家。人口约6706万（2020年1月，不含海外领地），通用法语，大部分居民信奉天主教。法国是发达的工业国家，是欧盟最大的农业生产国，也是世界主要农产品和农业食品出口国，葡萄酒享誉全球。服务业和旅游业高度发达。首都巴黎，素有"艺术之都""时尚之都""花之都""浪漫之都"和"花都"之称，不仅是法国政治、经济、商业和文化中心，也是著名的旅游胜地。

　　法国是世界主要发达国家之一，是世界第一大旅游接待国。在法国，香水、时装、葡萄酒被誉为三大精品，是法国人的骄傲。法国旅游局官方宣传标语是"Rendez-vous en France（Meet You in France）"。法国目前拥有世界遗产45项，位列全球第五，仅次于德国。卢浮宫、埃菲尔铁塔、凯旋门和巴黎圣母院等标志性旅游景点享誉世界，地中海和大西洋沿岸风景区及阿尔卑斯山区都是举世闻名的旅游胜地，此外还有一些历史名城、卢瓦尔河畔的古堡群、布列塔尼和诺曼底的渔村、科西嘉岛等。秀丽迷人的自然风光、底蕴深厚的人文景观、完备有效的政府政策使得法国旅游业位居世界前列。

　　1981年法国来华游客2.14万人次，到2017年增至49.37万人次，在欧洲客源国中一直位列前三，是中国重要的客源市场之一。法国来华旅游以观光休闲和会议商务为主。目前，国内旅游项目、产品及度假型旅游地的开发不能满足游客需求，因此应该加强对法国游客需求和偏好的了解，开发适合法国游客的旅游项目和产品。

France Facts

- **Name**: The French Republic; La République Française
- **Capital**: Paris
- **Government**: Unitary Semi-Presidential Republic
- **Language**: French
- **Population**: 67.06 Million (2020)
- **Life Expectancy**: 82.4 Years (2019)
- **Currency**: EUR 100 ≈ CNY 776.16 (2021)
- **National Symbols**: Rooster, Iris
- **National Day**: July 14
- **Motto**: Liberty, Equality, Fraternity

PART I Let's Go

★ *First Glance*

Watch the video, and then answer the following questions.

1. What's your impression of France?

2. Which part impresses you most in the video?

3. Which city in France attracts you most? Why?

★ *Viewing and Listening*

Watch the video again and fill in the blanks with the words you have heard.

France seduces travelers with its _____ culture, classic French cafes, quirky markets and bistros with their *plat du jour* chalked on the board. France is also about world-class architecture and art. Its _____ landmarks are known the world over. Yet there are still _____ stars to be discovered and rediscovered. The country's cultural repertoire is staggering in volume and diversity with the likes of the Eiffel Tower and the French Riviera to enjoy.

High season runs July and August. Visit in spring for warm weather or autumn for grape _____. Travel costs in France can range from less than 120 Euro a day if you enjoy a dorm bed and lunch menus, more than 200 a day for a double room in a top-end hotel with dinner. France rail _____ is first-class, but a car is great for _____ villages and rural landscapes impossible to visit with public transport. Weekends of endless possibilities punctuate the gentle rhythm of _____life, sipping coffee on cafe terraces, road trips to Beaujolais and Burgundy. And other regions are so different that they could be another country. France's sheer _____ never ceases to amaze.

PART II Explore the Land

• *Geography*

France is the third largest country in Europe, with territory in Western Europe and several overseas regions and territories. The European part of France is called Metropolitan France and it is located at the western end of Europe. It is bordered by the North Sea in the north, the English Channel in the northwest, the Atlantic Ocean in the west and the Mediterranean Sea in the southeast.

The main mountain ranges are the Alps, the Pyrenees and the Jura. Located in the Alps, Mont Blanc lies along the French-Italian border, and it is the highest mountain in Europe at 4,810 meters above the sea level. The main rivers are the Loire (卢瓦尔河), the Rhone (罗纳河) and the Seine (塞纳河). Corsica (科西嘉岛) in the Mediterranean Sea is the largest island in France.

Paris is the largest city and main cultural and commercial center. Other major urban centers include Marseille, Lyon, Lille, Nice, Toulouse and Bordeaux.

• *People*

France has a population of about 67.06 million according to UN data. It ranks number 22 on the list of countries by population and ranks number 4 in Europe. French people are mainly Latin today identified by their use of Romance Language.

French celebrities:

• Napoleon Bonaparte, emperor of the French.

• Joan of Arc, the heroine of France.

• Marie Curie, physicist and chemist, the first woman to win a Nobel Prize.

• René Déscartes, mathematician, philosopher and writer.

• Voltaire, one of history's greatest writers and philosophers.

• Claude Monet, painter, whose painting style was later termed Impressionism.

• Victor Hugo, one of the greatest and best-known French authors of all times.

• *Language*

The official language is French. It is spoken by about 87 million people worldwide as their mother tongue. About 285 million other people use it. It is the second most widely learned foreign language in the world, with almost 120 million students, according to the French Ministry of Foreign Affairs and International Development.

The most common ways to greet someone in French are:

Bonjour. (Good morning. / Hello.)

Ça va? (How are you?)

Enchante. (Nice to meet you.)

• *Attractions*

Paris

Known as the "Flower Capital" of the world, with a history of more than 1,400 years, Paris is not only the political, economic and cultural center of France, but also of Western Europe. The city possesses an indefinable unity of atmosphere that has writers, poets, and painters for centuries, so it sometimes called the "City of Art" and the "City of Light" in tribute to its intellectual excellence as well as to its beautiful appearance.

In Paris, visitors can visit more than 60 museums or attractions. Here are some landmarks in Paris:

• The Eiffel Tower is one of the most famous landmarks in the world, which symbolizes Paris. The tower consists of 18,000 sturdy iron sections (weighing over 10,000 tons) held together by 2.5 million rivets. Reaching 324 meters in height, the tower was the world's tallest building until the Empire State Building was built.

• The Louvre Museum is the world's largest art museum and a historic monument in Paris. As a central landmark of the city, it is located on the right bank of the Seine. Approximately 38,000 objects from prehistory to the 21st century are exhibited here, including the Mona Lisa and the Venus de Milo statue.

• The Arc de Triomphe is one of the most famous monuments in Paris, standing at the western end of the Champs-Élysées at the center of Place Charles de Gaulle. It honors those who fought and died for France in the French Revolutionary and Napoleonic Wars, with the names of all French victories and generals carved on its inner and outer surfaces.

Notre Dame de Paris (巴黎圣母院), meaning "Our Lady of Paris", referred to simply as Notre-Dame, is a Catholic cathedral in the Middle Ages, which began to construct in 1163. The cathedral was considered to be one of the finest examples of French Gothic architecture and one of the most widely recognized symbols of the city of Paris and the French nation. Approximately 12 million people visit Notre-Dame annually, making it the most visited monument in Paris.

Provence

Provence is a large region in southeastern France, bordering the Mediterranean Sea and Italy. It has Marseille, Nice, Arles, Avignon and other famous cities. Provence is famous for the lavender. Large purple flower fields are the best representative. It is also the home of Van Gogh's famous painting Sunflower.

Nice, the cultural capital set on the south east coast of Mediterranean Sea, is the second most popular French city after Paris. It is easily accessible; being less than 6 hours from Paris by train, and the airport is located just minutes away from the city.

Marseille, the oldest and the second largest city in France, is the capital of Provence and the largest seaport in France. For thousands of years, goods from the East have been imported to the Western world from here. Different faiths and cultures such as Islam and Catholicism exchange and merge here, which is exactly the charm of Marseille. Marseille is one of the most visited cities in France.

Cannes

Cannes, a charming town, is famous for the Cannes Film Festival. It is also the host city of the annual Midem (国际音乐博览会), and Cannes Lions International Festival of Creativity (戛纳国际创意狮节).

Chamonix-Mont-Blanc

Mont Blanc in the French Alps is an unforgettable sight. As the highest mountain peak in Europe, Mont Blanc soars to 4,810 meters. Thanks to its elevation, Mont Blanc (White Mountain) is always blanketed in snow. Chamonix is a great base for skiing, hiking, rock climbing, and outdoor adventures or just relaxing.

• *French Food*

French cuisine is renowned for being one of the finest in the world. Ingredients which often include bread, eggs, and cheese are mixed a way so unique that each ingredient tastes like never before. In November 2010, French cuisine was added by the UNESCO to its lists of the world's "Intangible Cultural Heritage".

A meal often consists of three courses: starter, sometimes soup, main course, cheese course and dessert, sometimes with a salad offered before the cheese or dessert. Wine and spices are two important features of French cuisine.

Famous French foods:

• **Pâté de foie gras** (鹅肝酱): Foie gras is French for "fat liver" and this pâté is made from the livers of specially fattened geese or duck.

• **Escargot** (蜗牛): A dish of cooked land snails, usually served as an appetizer in Spain and France.

• **Beef bourguignon** (勃艮第牛肉): This hearty stew is rich with beef and vegetables cooked in good red wine and finished with baby onions or shallots, button mushrooms and smoked lardons.

• **French onion soup**: A type of soup usually based on meat stock and onions, and often served with croutons and cheese on top.

- **Baguette** (法棍): It is a long thin loaf of French bread commonly made from basic lean dough.

• *Unique France*

Perfume and Fashion

France is famous for perfume and fashion. In terms of international perfume sales, France takes the lead, garnering about 30% of the world market. Fashion has been an important industry and cultural export of France since the 17th century. Today, Paris, along with London, Milan, and New York City, is considered one of the world's fashion capitals. Haute couture (高级时装) is the most refined fashion, and it is a symbol of French luxury. There are only 14 designers who bear the label of Haute couture. Christian Dior, Chanel, Ellie Saab and Versace are some of the big names who produce Haute couture.

Vintage Wines

France has a rich tradition of grape growing, or wine-making. Grape and wine varieties from this country are often named after the region where they are grown or produced. Four of the most prominent wines produced are Champagne, Bordeaux, Burgundy and Condrieu.

Art and Literature

The word "culture" actually comes from France. People will see beautiful French art everywhere in France. There are many of history's most influential artist, including Claude Monet, Camille Pissarro, and even Vincent Van Gough, who was born in the Netherlands, but died in France. Voltaire, Flaubert and Victor Hugo are regarded as some of the world's most significant thinkers of all times. France won many Noble Prizes.

Tour de France

It is an annual multiple stage bicycle race primarily held in France, also occasionally making passes through nearby countries. The race is 21-days long and covers approximately 3,500 kilometers of routes.

Films

France has the second-largest film exports in the world, only surpassed by the United States. The country also features prominently in global film markets, and with over 0.212 billion tickets being sold nationwide in 2016, France is the world's third largest film market, only exceeded in ticket sales by the United States and India.

Task: Draw your mind-map on the "France in My Eyes" page based on the facts of France and then introduce France to your peers by using your mind-map.

★ *5C Reading on France*

A. Read the following passage and underline the parts related with China.

"Special" is the word used to describe China-France ties. What are the specialties in China-France ties?

The "firsts" France made with China. ***The first*** major country in the West that established the diplomatic relationship with the People's Republic of China. ***The first*** major Western country to have established the comprehensive strategic partnership and institutionalized the strategic dialogue to sign an inter-governmental science and technology cooperation agreement with China. ***The first*** Western country to open direct flights with China. ***The first*** country to exchange with China in hosting the cultural year and setting up cultural centers.

BRI infuses new vigor into bilateral cooperation. In March 2014, Xi paid his first visit to France as president and the first city he chose to visit was Lyon, one of the final stops of the ancient Silk Road trade routes. In January 2018, Macron paid his first visit to China and his first stop was Xi'an city, the beginning of the ancient Silk Road. During Macron's China visit, he said France values bilateral cooperation under the framework of the Belt and Road Initiative (BRI), and called on Europe to participate in the project.

Work-study program in France. 2019 also marks the 100th anniversary of work-study program, a documentary co-produced by China and France has premiered in Paris on the occasion of the 100th anniversary of China's work-study program in France.

Nearly 100 years ago, groups of Chinese young people harboring the dream of saving the nation, traveled far away abroad to learn new ideas. Many of them chose France as their destination, among whom were Zhou Enlai, Deng Xiaoping and Chen Yi, the founders of the People's Republic of China, as well as scientists like Qian Sanqiang and Yan Jici, artists like Xu Beihong and Xian Xinghai, litterateurs like Ba Jin and Qian Zhongshu.

你能说说"一带一路"倡议对中法关系的发展有什么意义吗？

B. Discuss the following questions based on the above reading material.

1. Why are China-France ties special?

2. Do you know what BRI means to the relationship between China and France?

3. Discuss the significance of friendly exchanges and mutual cultural communication between China and France.

PART III   Welcome Guests from the Land

★ *Project—Introducing Itinerary on the Tour Bus*

You are a tour guide for French tourists. They are taking the airport bus to the hotel. You need to introduce the itinerary in Chengdu to them. Work with your peers to design the one-day tour itinerary in Chengdu and then make a brief introduction. When you discuss the activities to do, you need to take French culture and characteristics into consideration.

<table>
<tr><th colspan="2">Schedule for One-day Tour in Chengdu</th></tr>
<tr><th>Time</th><th>Attractions and Activities</th></tr>
<tr><td></td><td></td></tr>
<tr><td></td><td></td></tr>
<tr><td></td><td></td></tr>
<tr><td></td><td></td></tr>
<tr><td></td><td></td></tr>
</table>

· *Tasks*

A. Tell your partner the reason why you choose the specific attraction or activity.

B. Make a presentation to introduce the itinerary briefly.

The Magic Words or Sentences You Might Need for the Presentation

Words:

Jinli Pedestrian Street	Wuhou Temple (武侯祠)
Du Fu Thatched Cottage (杜甫草堂)	Kuanzhai Alley (宽窄巷子)
Wenshu Temple (文殊院)	Chunxi Road
People's Park	Sichuan Cuisine Museum
Jinsha Site Museum	Chengdu Research Base of Giant Panda Breeding

Sentences:

1. We are now on our way to... I'll tell you about the schedule after you check into the hotel.

2. Tomorrow's itinerary will include the following attractions: ...

3. The first attraction we are going to visit is... the second one is… and the last one is…

4. ... is famous for it's..., and... will be a great experience.

5. You will have the opportunity to taste authentic Sichuan cuisine and snacks in... at lunchtime, and dinner will be a feast of hot pot.

★ *The Land and the World*

Sinologist Joël Bellassen—Chinese Language Communicator

Joël Bellassen (白乐桑), French Sinologist, is a professor of Chinese at National Institute for Oriental Languages and Civilizations and the first Inspector-General in the field of Chinese Language Teaching at the Ministry of Education (France). He was among the first batch of students sent to China after the establishment of diplomatic relations. On graduation, he became France's first Chinese-language teacher at the kindergarten and

Host the Belt and Road Language and Culture Forum

primary school level. He was appointed as the very first Inspector-General of Chinese language teaching in 2006. Joël has since devoted himself to promoting Chinese language learning in France.

Joël in the Chinese Countryside in the 1970s

Joël says, "China, like France, is a very ancient country with a long history. Both value their historical records and cultural heritage. French people pay great respect to countries with history. It was in this frame of mind that I started to learn this remote language".

Today, 600 middle schools are offering Chinese courses, making Chinese the first language ever to enjoy such rapidly increasing attention in foreign-language education in France. Surpassing Portuguese, Hebrew and Arabic, Chinese has risen to fifth place as the foreign language most used in France. His efforts are one of the reasons France is able to keep its lead in Europe in Chinese teaching.

Joël believes Chinese language learning has a bright future in France, and he often says, "You will definitely come into contact with China in the future." In France, Chinese language and culture transmission is like a satellite moving fast on the right track and constantly speeding up.

Mind-map: France in My Eyes

Name: _____   Date: _____

KWL Chart

Topic: _____ Name: _____ Date: _____

Know	Wonder	Learned
What do you think you already know about France?	What do you wonder about France? Write your questions below.	Write what you've learned about France.

裁

切

线

Section 3   Germany

A flight to Frankfurt is 10 hours from Beijing, 12 hours from Singapore, roughly 1.4 hours from London and about 7.3 hours from New York.

Learning Objectives

After this section, you will be able to:

★ locate the geographical situation of Germany and its bordering countries.
★ list major cities and attractions in Germany.
★ apply German unique features to serving inbound German tourists, making them feel at home.
★ know the long-term cooperation in different fields between China and Germany.

"德"才兼备之德国

德国位于斯堪的纳维亚半岛，坐落于欧洲中部，东邻波兰、捷克，南接奥地利、瑞士，西接荷兰、比利时、卢森堡、法国，北接丹麦，濒临北海和波罗的海，是欧洲邻国最多的国家。德国国土面积357582平方千米，如果按地理面积计算，是继法国、西班牙和瑞典之后的欧盟第四大国。地势北低南高，可分为四个地形区：北德平原，中德山地，西南部莱茵断裂谷地区，南部的巴伐利亚高原和阿尔卑斯山区。主要河流有莱茵河、易北河、威悉河、奥德河、多瑙河。居民中30%信奉新教，31%信奉罗马天主教。德语为通用语言。

德国是一个诞生了贝多芬、歌德等众多杰出伟人的国度，是一个以强大的汽车制造业闻名世界的经济体，也是一个以啤酒和香肠为饮食代表的国家。德国以其悠久浓厚的文化历史和如画般的自然风光，吸引着来自世界各地的游客。德国旅游资源丰富，境内有40余处世界文化和自然遗产，既有历史古迹、城市地标，也有重要的工业设施和非同寻常的自然景观。如此魅力之国让德国成为世界上境外游目的地人数第七多的国家。

中德两国于1972年建立外交关系以来，在政治、经贸、教育、旅游等领域开展了广泛的合作与交流。在国家主席习近平提出"一带一路"倡议后，德国政府在欧洲国家中率先予以积极回应。2013年以来，依托"一带一路"倡议蓝图，中德两国的合作与交流迎来了新的发展契机。2019年到中国旅游的外国游客总人数3.0亿人次；按入境旅游人数排序，我国主要国际客源市场前20位的国家中德国位于第十六，位于英国、朝鲜、法国和意大利前列。2020年8月，作为"云游中国"主题系列活动的一部分，德国柏林中国文化中心在其官网、微信公众号及社交媒体账号上，推出熊猫主题视频短片、图片展以及熊猫主题旅游线路等内容，让疫情防控期间居家的德国民众，有机会"走进"中国四川的自然山水，感受大熊猫故乡的独特魅力。

Germany Facts

- **Name**: The Federal Republic of Germany
- **Capital**: Berlin
- **Government**: Democracy, Republic
- **Language**: German
- **Population**: 83.12 Million (2020)
- **Currency**: EUR 100 ≈ CNY 77.78 (2021)
- **Flag Colors**: Black, Red, Gold
- **Major Cities**: Munich, Cologne, Frankfurt, Hamburg, Leipzig, Bremen
- **National Symbol**: Eagle

PART I   Let's Go

★ *First Glance*

Watch the video, and then answer the following questions.

1. Do you want to go to Germany after watching the video?

2. Which German fact impresses you most in the video?

3. Do you agree that Germany is a dream destination as mentioned in the video? Why?

★ *Viewing and Listening*

Watch the video again and write down the corresponding aspect of each picture.

_____

_____

_____

_____

_____

_____

PART II Explore the Land

• *Geography*

Germany is located in the center of Europe and shares borders with 9 countries: Denmark, Poland, Czech Republic, Austria, Switzerland, France, Luxemburg, Belgium and the Netherlands. It is the second most populous country in Central Europe after Russia and many immigrants live and study in Germany.

The Baltic Sea, the North Sea and the lowlands form the natural borders in the north of Germany and the southern Germany borders are formed by the Alps Mountains and Lake Constance.

The highest mountain in Germany is the Zugspitze (which means windy peak) with 2,963 metres. Germany's highest mountain is one of Germany's top attractions and many tourists visit the mountain top every year.

• *People*

Germany is a remarkably cohesive (团结的) ethnic community in which 91.5 percent of the population are native German. Today almost one in every ten Germans comes from a foreign country—more than at any time in Germany's history. The largest ethnic minority are Turkish, who started to come to Germany in the 1950s to work. About two-thirds of Germans are Christians.

• *Language*

The official language is German. The schools teach a form called standard German, and most Germans use it at least for writing and reading. Some people, especially older Germans and people who live in rural areas, speak local dialects in everyday life. Germans from Munich and from Berlin have considerable difficulty in understanding one another if they speak their local dialects. In the northern Germany in particular, a form of German known as Low German is very different from standard German, and it has been used by some writers and poets. The influence of television, radio, and other mass media, however, has helped to spread the use of standard German.

Some common expressions in Germany are:

Guten tag. (Hello.)

Danke. (Thank you.)

Auf wiedersehen. (Goodbye.)

Ich liebe dich. (I love you.)

• *Attractions*

Berlin

Berlin is the capital city and cultural center. When people think of, the first thing that probably comes to mind is its most famous landmark—the Brandenburg Gate. A symbol of division for decades, the monument has always been at the heart of a major city bursting with ideas, inspiration, art, culture and creativity. In Berlin, visitors can enjoy all the classic hotspots, or take a break from the hustle and bustle, and head towards the wide-open city lakes and green spaces for some action-packed outdoor activities.

Munich

Lifestyle is a priority in Munich (慕尼黑). It might be down to the clear blue skies or simply the city's beauty, but one thing's for certain: The people of Munich always like to show their best side, whether they're in a beer garden, on one of the exclusive shopping streets, or in Bayern Munich's stadium.

Neuschwanstein Castle

The Neuschwanstein Castle (新天鹅城堡) is one of the most visited castles in Germany and one of the most popular tourist destinations in Europe. Every year over 1,300,000 people cross its gate. The castle is located in Bavaria, near the town of Fussen. The Neuschwanstein Castle looks like a fairytale castle. This fairytale look of the Neuschwanstein Castle inspired Walt Disney to create the Magic Kingdom.

Cologne Cathedral

Cologne Cathedral is a Catholic cathedral in Cologne, North Rhine-Westphalia, Germany. It is Germany's most visited landmark, attracting an average of 20,000 people a day. At 157 meters, the cathedral is currently the tallest twin-spired church in the world, the second tallest church in Europe after Ulm Minster, and the third tallest church in the world. It is the largest Gothic church in Northern Europe and has the second-tallest spires. The towers for its two huge spires give the cathedral the largest facade of any church in the world.

Schwarzwald (Black Forest)

The Black Forest is a large forested mountain range in the state of Baden-Württemberg in Southwest Germany. It is bounded by the Rhine Valley to the west and south. Its highest peak is the Feldberg with an elevation of 1,493 meters above sea level. The region is roughly oblong in shape, with a length of 160 kilometers and breadth of up to 50 kilometers. Black Forest is a tourist attraction in Germany. It is famous for cuckoo clock, black forest cake, and black forest ham, honey and pig elbow.

Heidelberg Castle

Heidelberg Castle (海德堡城堡) is a ruin in Germany and landmark of Heidelberg. The castle ruins are among the most important Renaissance structures north of the Alps. The castle has only been partially rebuilt since its demolition in the 17th and 18th centuries. It is located 80 meters up the northern part of the Königstuhl hillside; and thereby dominates the view of the old downtown.

Rügen

Rügen (吕根岛), Germany's largest island, is located in the northeast of the country off the Baltic Sea. Rügen has been one of Germany's most popular travel destinations for centuries; Bismarck, Sigmund Freud, Thomas Mann, and even Albert Einstein all vacationed here. Rügen is famous for its romantic seaside resorts and spas.

• *German Food*

Most of the German main dishes contain either meat, mainly pork, beef and veal or fish. Germans often eat potatoes, but pasta dishes are also very popular, especially with the younger generations.

Some typical German foods:

• **Sauerkraut** (德国泡菜): Probably the most famous vegetable associated with German food. It is eaten in Germany with potatoes and meat, but traditionally not eaten with fish as in many other parts in the world.

• **Knödel, either as Semmelknödel** (马铃薯麦团): Bread dumplings, eaten either with mushrooms in a creamy sauce or with meat dishes or Kartoffelknödel (potato dumplings).

• **Spargel** (德国芦笋): White asparagus is harvested in late April and until June 24. It has a very distinct flavor and is very healthy! Usually accompanied by ham and a white creamy sauce, this vegetable is really delicious.

• **Weisswurst** (白色小牛肉肠): Very pale veal sausage, cooked and eaten in Bavaria—usually in midmorning, before noon.

• **Stollen and Lebkuchen**: Delicious cakes, decorated biscuits and various gingerbread cookies are eaten at Christmas time in Germany.

• *Unique Germany*

Museums

Germany has a wide variety of museums, ranging from art museums, ethnological museums, historical museums, musical-oriented museums amongst other. In total, the country has about 6,000 museums and the number grows every year. The New National Gallery in Berlin is described by many people as the most beautiful museum in the world, being widely referred to as Temple of Glass. One of the most visited museums in the country is the haunting Jewish Museum in Berlin.

Art

From old masters to modern masterpieces, Germany is home to extraordinary treasures of the art world spanning every period and century. Guests marvel at fine art in all its forms of expression and discover architectural wonders that defined their eras.

Music

Music is the indispensable component in German's life. Germany made different period of the master of music, such as Mozart, Beethoven, Bach, Mendelssohn, Wagner, etc. Berlin philharmonic is famous in the world.

Car Producer

Germany is one of the world's states which is the largest producer of cars. The top-selling car brands were Volkswagen, Mercedes, Audi and BMW and around 6.1 million cars were sold in 2013.

Beer

Germany is a country that takes its beer seriously. Beer is an important part of Germany's culture. Beer includes water, carbohydrates, proteins, alcohol, carbon dioxide, vitamins and valuable minerals.

Oktoberfest

Oktoberfest is a 16-18 day festival held each year in Munich, Bavaria, running from middle or late September to the first Sunday in October. More than six million people from around the world attend this event every year. The Oktoberfest is an important part of Bavarian culture, having been held since 1810.

Nobel Prize Award

Germany ranks third in the world in terms of Nobel laureates, taking the credit for 106 awards and 24 of these awards have been in the fields of physics and chemistry.

Concept of Time

It is important to deal with the German punctuality, being late is unacceptable (unless there are special circumstances), but the advance is considered a violation of the other time.

Task: Draw your mind-map on the "Germany in My Eyes" page based on the facts of Germany and then introduce Germany to your peers by using your mind-map.

★ *5C Reading on Germany*

A. Read the following passage and underline the cooperation between China and Germany.

KUKA (Keller und Knappich Augsburg) is a German manufacturer of industrial robots and solutions for factory automation. It has been owned by the Chinese company Midea Group since 2016. The KUKA Robotics Corporation has 25 subsidiaries worldwide, mostly sales and service subsidiaries (子公司), including in China and other countries, like India, Russia, etc.

On June 8, 2016, SCETC (Sichuan Engineering Technical College) and KUKA AG signed the cooperation agreement on research and development of industrial robotic technology application and systematical cultivation of skilled personnel with an international vision, a good knowledge of international rules and adaptability to economic globalization. Yin Li, former governor of Sichuan Province, Shi Mingde, former Chinese Ambassador, Chen Xinyou, former director of Sichuan Provincial Economic and Information Commission, Eric Schweitzer, chairman of German Chambers of Commerce and Industry and Joschka Fischer, former vice chancellor and minister for Foreign Affairs of Germany attended the signature ceremony in Berlin, Germany.

The cooperation can support the enterprises in Deyang such as China National Erzhong Group Co., Dongfang Turbine Co. LTD, Dongfang Electric Machinery Co. LTD and so on to put their Going Out & Globalization strategy into reality.

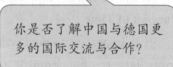

你是否了解中国与德国更多的国际交流与合作？

B. Discuss the following questions based on the above reading material.

1. Do you know what KUKA is?
2. If you were one of the students from SCETC, are you proud of the cooperation between SCETC and KUKA AG?
3. Can you give some reasons why KUKA AG signed cooperation agreement with SCETC?

PART III   Welcome Guests from the Land

★ *Project—Checking Out*

You are a clerk in Jinjiang Hotel. Please help your guest from Germany check out. Make sure you behave professionally, gracefully and impressively. Discuss with your partners how you would structure the dialogue.

Top 3 Questions I Need to Ask
1. _____
2. _____
3. _____

Hotel Desk Clerk Job Description

A hotel desk clerk is responsible for greeting and helping guests at the front desk of the hotel. The job duties include making reservations for hotel guests, coordinating the activities of cleaning staff and maintenance workers, checking guests in and out of the hotel, and collecting payment from guests.

• *Tasks*

A. Tell your partner the reason why you ask these questions.

B. Role-play: Make a dialogue to help the guest check out. You can use the sample dialogue as reference.

Sample Dialogue

Clerk (C)   Guest (G)

C: Good morning, sir. Can I help you?

G: Yes, we'd like to check out.

C: May I have your names and your room numbers, please?

G: I'm Mr. Black in Room 714 and another one is Mr. John in Room 715.

C: Hold on please. Okay, Mr. Black, it's 2,890 yuan in total. How would you like to pay?

G: On my visa card. Do you need the card?

C: No, we have your number on our computer. Let me print out the receipt for you. Here is your bill. Two single rooms for two nights at 2,890 yuan. If everything is okay, would you sign here, please?

G: Let me see. Oh, that's right. Here you are.

C: Thank you for staying at Jinjiang Hotel. I hope you'll come to our hotel again. Would you like me to call a taxi for you?

G: Yes, we'd appreciate it.

C: You have a nice day!

G: Thanks. You, too.

★ *The Land and the World*

Karl Marx—The Greatest Social Theorist

Karl Marx (1818-1883) was a philosopher, author, social theorist, and an economist. Marx's political and philosophical thought had enormous influence on subsequent intellectual, economic and political history. His name has been used as an adjective, a noun, and a school of social theory. He is famous for his theories about capitalism and communism.

Marx's ideas, such as Marxism, is the set of social, political, and economic theories created and espoused (拥护) by Karl Marx that became a prominent school of socialist thought. It has had a huge impact on societies, most prominently in communist projects such as those in China, the USSR, and Cuba. Among modern thinkers, Marx is still very influential among the fields of sociology, political economy.

Karl Marx's House in Germany, Trier　　**Karl Marx Portrait**　　**Marxism, Works of Karl Marx**

Mind-map: Germany in My Eyes

Name: _____   Date: _____

KWL Chart

Topic: _____   Name: _____   Date: _____

Know	Wonder	Learned
What do you think you already know about Germany?	What do you wonder about Germany? Write your questions below.	Write what you've learned about Germany.

Section 4   Italy

Learning Objectives

A flight to Rome is about 10 hours from Xi'an, 22 hours from Tokyo, 3 hours from London and 9 hours from New York.

After this section, you will be able to:

★ know the geographical features and uniqueness of Italy.

★ understand the colorful culture in Italy.

★ know the major attractions and landmarks in Italy.

★ apply Italian social norms, taboos and unique features to serving inbound Italian tourists, making them feel at home.

★ understand the Sino-Italian ties in various ways, such as the cooperation in the protection of cultural relics and tourism.

"意"味深长之意大利

意大利共和国，简称"意大利"，是一个欧洲国家，主要由南欧的亚平宁半岛及两个位于地中海中的岛屿西西里岛与萨丁岛所组成。国土面积为301333平方千米，人口6046万（2020年）。北方的阿尔卑斯山地区与法国、瑞士、奥地利以及斯洛文尼亚接壤，其领土还包围着两个微型国家——圣马力诺与梵蒂冈。此外，意大利在瑞士拥有坐落于卢加诺湖湖畔的意大利坎波内这个境外领土，它是意大利的外飞地与瑞士的内飞地，坎皮奥内与意大利本土仅相距1千米。全国行政上划分为20个大区（其中5个为自治区）、110个省与8100个城市。

意大利首都罗马，几个世纪一直都是西方文明的中心。14世纪，意大利成为欧洲文艺复兴的发源地。意大利是一个议会制民主共和国，也是一个发达的资本主义国家，欧洲四大经济体之一，是欧盟和北约的创始会员国，还是八国集团成员。意大利目前共拥有55项联合国教科文组织世界遗产，和中国同为全球拥有世界遗产最多的国家。意大利在艺术和时尚领域也处于世界领导地位，米兰是意大利经济及工业中心，也是世界时尚之都。

根据文化和旅游部发布的《2019年旅游市场基本情况》数据显示，2019年入境旅游人数1.45亿人次，其中欧洲占13.2%；意大利是我国主要国际客源市场前20位国家，位列欧洲客源国第五。根据中国旅游研究院发布的《中意旅游合作发展报告2020》，2009~2018年，意大利来华游客年均增长率为4.23%。2019年1~10月，意大利来华游客依然保持正增长，达到23.46万人次。

Italy Facts

• **Name**: Republic of Italy

• **Capital**: Rome

• **Government**: Democracy, Republic

• **Language**: Italian

• **Population**: 60.46 Million (2020)

• **Currency**: EUR 100 ≈ CNY 785.19 (2021)

• **National Symbols**: Italian Grey Wolf, Olive Tree, Oak Tree

• **National Day**: June 2

PART I   Let's Go

★ *First Glance*

Watch the video, and then answer the following questions.

1. What's your impression about Italy after watching the video?

2. What are the similarities between China and Italy?

★ *Viewing and Speaking*

A. Watch the video again and write down the corresponding aspects.

Italy Top 5	Tour Contents / Tour Activities
Eternal Rome	
Virtuoso Venice	
Tackling the Dolomites	
Amalfi Coast	
Touring Tuscany	

B. Answer the following questions according to what you have watched.

1. When is the best time to go to Italy?

2. How much does it cost to travel in Italy?

PART II *Explore the Land*

• *Geography*

Italy is a country in southern Europe. The country is located on a peninsula (半岛) in the Mediterranean Sea (地中海). Italy borders six countries: France, Austria, Switzerland, Slovenia (斯洛文尼亚), Vatican City and San Marino.

Italy is easy to recognize on any world map, as the country is shaped like a high-heeled boot. It looks like that the boot is kicking a ball, which is the island of Sicily (西西里岛). Italy has more than 7,600 kilometers of coastline as the peninsula is located for a large part in the Mediterranean Sea. Italy is popular for its many picturesque ports and sandy beaches. Italy has two bigger islands, Sicily and Sardegna (萨丁岛), and many smaller islands such as Capri, Ischia and Elba. The country is slightly larger in size than the three countries of the UK, the Netherlands and Belgium combined.

Italy surrounds two of the world's smallest countries. These are San Marino in Northern Italy, which is also the oldest republic in the world, and Vatican City in Rome, the smallest country in the world.

• *People*

Italy is quite densely populated, with most people living in the country's northern regions. Italians lead a modern lifestyle especially in the urban centers but they also celebrate century-old cultural traditions. Soccer, skiing, cycling, surfing or motor racing are just some of the sports Italians have very strong interest in.

The family is very important for Italians, where there are still many big families including grandparents, parents and children in the household. Italians love their food, which is usually prepared freshly by "la mama", the mother, or the "nonna", the grandmother. In the afternoon or evening it is common to meet up with family and friends on the piazza.

Some of the famous Italians are:

• **Marco Polo (1254-1324)**: The Italian explorer and merchant (商人) traveled as far as China, Mongolia and Japan and is known as one of the first European travelers along the famous Silk Road and the first to write down his experiences. His stories of encounters and adventures inspired Christopher Columbus to later search for the passage to the Orient.

• **Christopher Columbus (1451-1506)**: Worked as a cartographer in Italy before becoming a business man trading goods with many countries, Columbus visited England, Ireland, even Iceland, traveled to nearby Spain and Portugal and traded along the western African coast during his trips. Columbus completed four travels across the Atlantic Ocean and was the first European to reach the Americas in his search for a passage to the Orient. On his four voyages across the Atlantic Ocean he explored the Americas and reached as far as Nicaragua (尼加拉瓜) and Honduras.

• **Leonardo da Vinci (1452-1519)**: Leonardo da Vinci was a real genius. He studied and explored new ideas throughout his life. He was a painter, sculptor, architect, engineer and botanist. His famous painting of "Mona Lisa" can be seen in the Louvre Museum in Paris. Da Vinci also planned and invented many things and explored new concepts, like the calculator, a flight machine similar to a helicopter, a tank and even worked on findings about concentrated solar power. Many works were unfinished though as his interests were very broad. Da Vinci died in France after he left Italy as he did not feel acknowledged by his peers.

• *Language*

Italian language roots are in the Latin language. Italian is very close to French, as 89% of the vocabularies are shared, and 82% is shared with the Spanish vocabulary.

Italian is an official language not only in Italy but also in Switzerland, San Marino, and Vatican City. The Italian alphabet consists of 21 letters only. The letters j, k, w, x and y do not exist, except for loan words, Which means words that originate in another language.

The pronunciation is soft and very melodic (有旋律的) and so the language is used in opera and also popular by young pop music artists. Most young people in Italy learn to speak English, French or German in school. Some of the older people, however, do only speak a little Italian, but mainly use a regional language such as German or French or the unique Ladino (拉地诺语) language.

Here are some useful Italian words and terms:

Ciao (Hello).	Grazie (Thank you).	Prego (Please).
Bene (Good).	Come stai (How are you)?	Sì (Yes).
Scusami (Excuse me).		

· *Attractions*

Colosseum in Rome

The Colosseum (罗马圆形大剧场) is one of the landmarks most people can easily link to Italy. The huge oval amphitheater stands in the city center of Rome and construction was started in 70 AD. Built in Roman design borrowed from the Greeks, the amphitheater was built in the bad of a dried out lake. The Colosseum was the place in those days where the Romans held their popular fights and games. There were gladiator (角斗士) games, animal hunts and mock sea battles held in the Colosseum. About 50,000 people could be seated on the steps of this ancient amphitheater.

Roman Forum

The Roman Forum (古罗马广场) is next to the Colosseum. It is the original ancient town's central square with ruins of the temples, palaces and buildings of ancient Rome. The forum was built around 800 BC and was in use for some 1,400 years. The ruins of the buildings and temples however were only discovered during excavations in 1803.

Leaning Tower of Pisa

The famous Leaning Tower (比萨斜塔) is in fact the city cathedral's bell tower. The tower was constructed in 1173 but the structure was miscalculated (计算错误) and built on not so solid ground, so the tower began leaning early on. It is said that Italian scientist Galileo used the tower for various gravity experiments, such as dropping various objects from the top of the tower. The tower is only about 56 meters tall while the tower's tilt (倾斜) is actually more than 4.3 meters.

Grand Canal and the Rialto Bridge in Venice

Thousands of tourists come to Venice every year to see the houses built on wooden piles along the many canals and waterways of the city. There are about 500 wooden gondolas (贡多拉船) and many more water taxis ferrying people across the city. St. Mark's Square with the famous St. Mark's Cathedral and the bell tower are major attractions. The city's palaces and houses can either be reached by boat or foot, and there are no cars driving in this city.

· *Italian Food*

The Italian main dishes often contain pork and beef, seafood as well as potatoes, rice and pasta (wheat and egg noodles) products and of course, tomatoes.

Pizza is surely one of the most famous exports and in Italy it is usually baked in a wood-fired oven. Italian pizza is very thin, but loaded with fresh vegetables or thinly sliced ham, salami, artichokes or olives. The Italian pasta (variety of noodles) is renowned worldwide and there are more than 200 different shapes.

Italians love their food and many dishes are based on fresh vegetables and seafood too. There are delicious sweet cakes in Italy, such as panettone (a yeast cake with raisins), panforte (a hard and flat fruit cake) and almond pastries such as amaretti.

Here is some typical Italian foods:

Pizza: Probably the most famous Italian dish. It was invented in Napoli/Naples around 1860.

Calzone: Folded up pizza bread filled with tomatoes, ham, cheese and all kinds of filling.

Gelato: Gelato is a popular frozen dessert of Italian origin. Ice cream and gelato are both popular frozen desserts. Whereas ice cream is airier and has a higher fat content, gelato is softer and packed with flavor. Both contain a lot of sugar, but gelato is traditionally made with much less fat.

Mozzarella: Italian cheese balls, originally made from buffalo milk.

• *Unique Italy*

Football in Italy

Football is the most popular sport in Italy. The Italy national football team is considered to be one of the best national teams in the world. They have won the FIFA World Cup four times (1934, 1938, 1982, and 2006), trailing only Brazil (with 5), runners-up (亚军) in two finals (1970, 1994) and reaching a third place (1990) and a fourth place (1978). They have also won one European Championship (1968), also appearing in two finals (2000, 2012), finished third at the Confederations Cup (2013), won one Olympic football tournament (1936) and two Central European International Cups (1927 and 1933).

Italy's top domestic league, the Serie A (甲级联赛), is one of the most popular professional sports leagues in the world and it is often depicted as the most tactical national football league.

Milan Fashion Week

Milan Fashion Week is a clothing trade show held semi-annually in Milan, Italy. The autumn/winter event is held in February/March of each year, and the spring/summer event is held in September/October of each year.

It was established in 1958 and is part of the global "Big Four Fashion Weeks", the others being Paris Fashion Week, London Fashion Week and New York Fashion Week. The schedule begins with New York, followed by London, and then Milan, and ending with Paris.

Italian Car Brands

Italy has a tradition of building some of the most sought-after sports and luxury cars in motoring history. Although they sometimes fall short of the engineering quality of the German makes, or the affordability of the French market, the Italians have led the way in styling and character of their cars. The famous Italian car brands include Fiat, Alfa Romeo, Maserati, Ferrari, Lamborghini.

Task: Draw your mind-map on the "Italy in My Eyes" page based on the facts of Italy and then introduce Italy to your peers by using your mind-map.

★ *5C Reading on Italy*

A. *Read the following passage and know about the cooperation in culture and tourism between China and Italy.*

President Xi Jinping and his Italian counterpart Sergio Mattarella met with entrepreneurs (企业家) and representatives of cultural institutions from both countries and delivered keynote speeches during Xi's state visit last Friday (March 22, 2019).

Chinese Minister of Culture and Tourism Luo Shugang and Liu Yuzhu, Director of the National Cultural Heritage Administration of China exchanged ideas on future collaboration (合作) with Italian counterparts. Over 40 culture and tourism organizations and enterprises, including delegates from the Palace Museum, National Museum of China, and National Center for the Performing Arts, attended the conference.

In his keynote speech, the minister spoke highly of the Sino-Italian cultural cooperation system. He said fruitful results have been achieved with two countries working together on cultural heritage protection, tourism, creative design, film and TV industry.

The year 2020 marks the 50th anniversary of the establishment of diplomatic ties between China and Italy. Luo said both nations will further consolidate (巩固) comprehensive strategic partnership, and successfully run the "Year of Culture and Tourism" activities.

Alberto Bonisoli, the Italian Minister of Cultural Heritage and Activities, said China and Italy have set a great example of cultural exchange. Italy is willing to deepen mutual understanding and push Sino-Italian relations to the next level.

Minister Luo met and reached important consensus with Italian ministers Alberto Bonisoli in cultural heritage and activities, and Gian Marco Centinaio in tourism.

After the talks, national leaders from both countries witnessed the signing of multiple bilateral cooperation documents, including a memorandum of understanding on jointly advancing the construction of the Belt and Road, and the document on the return of Chinese relics confiscated by Italy.

中意双方将推动文化、旅游等领域更多合作，共筑"一带一路"。两国在文化旅游方面可以开展哪些合作？

B. *Discuss the following questions based on the above reading material.*

1. What are the favorable conditions for the two countries' cooperation in culture and tourism?

2. What can we learn from Italy in the protection of cultural relics?

3. Compared with Italy, what are China's strengths in culture and tourism?

PART III　Welcome Guests from the Land

★ Project—Room Service

An Italian guest wants to surprise his wife during the honeymoon stay in your hotel. Please discuss with your partners how you would offer the in-room dining. Make sure you behave professionally, gracefully and considerately.

• *Tasks*

　A. *Discuss the proper standard and procedure of in-room dining service to serve Italian guests.*

　B. *Discuss with your partners how to leave the couple unforgettable memory.*

Standard & Procedure of In-room Dining Service

1. Position yourself in front of the guestroom security viewer with their name tag visible to the guest.
2. Press doorbell or knock on the door and announce "Room Service".
3. If no answer, pause 10 seconds before knocking or ringing a second time.
4. If the "DND" sign is on or there is no response, use the nearest floor pantry phone to inform guest the order is ready.

Things Might Impress Guests

1. good service
2. pleasant surprise
3. small local specialty
4. a hearty card

★ *The Land and the World*

Marco Polo—Messenger of East and West

Marco Polo (1254-1324) was a famous merchant and explorer from Venice, Italy. In 1271, he embarked on a journey to the East with his father and uncle. He wrote *Il Milione*, known in English as *The Travels of Marco Polo* which describes his voyage to and experiences in Asia. Polo traveled extensively with his family, journeying from Europe to Asia from 1271 to 1295 and remaining in China for 17 of those years.

Marco Polo arrived in Yuan Shangdu (Upper Capital of Yuan Dynasty) in 1275 and traveled on to Dadu (Great Capital of Yuan Dynasty, present-day Beijing). During the following seventeen years in China, Marco Polo was trusted by Emperor Kublai Khan (忽必烈), and toured various places as an imperial inspector. Around 1292, he left China, acting as escort along the way to a Mongol princess who was being sent to Persia.

In his book, Marco Polo recalled his travel in Asia, and particularly in China, and he included accounts of his tours to the Western Regions and the South China Sea. The book covers his arrival in Dadu with his family, the Chinese emperor's hospitality, his appointment as an official, his tours in China and his various adventures. It ends with his return to Italy.

Marco Polo provided a comprehensive picture of China in the early Yuan Dynasty (1271-1368), including its politics, wars, court vignettes, traditional festivals, hunting, and so forth. He recounted Dadu's economy, culture, architecture, and local customs and practices, along with vivid depictions of thriving metropolises such as Xi'an, Kaifeng, Nanjing, Zhenjiang, Yangzhou, Hangzhou, Fuzhou, and Quanzhou. He wrote that China was a country where regal palaces shone with gilded walls and where even the common people were as wealthy as European monarchs.

Mind-map: Italy in My Eyes

Name: _____ Date: _____

KWL Chart

Topic: _____   Name: _____   Date: _____

Know	Wonder	Learned
What do you think you already know about Italy?	What do you wonder about Italy? Write your questions below.	Write what you've learned about Italy.

Section 5   Russia

Learning Objectives

A flight to Moscow is 10 hours from Shanghai, 12 hours from Singapore, 4 hours from London and 9.5 hours from New York.

After this section, you will be able to:

★ know the geographical features of Russia, especially how vast the land is.

★ list the typical landmarks and attractions in Russia.

★ develop an in-depth understanding of Russian history, culture and social norms.

★ learn the importance of strengthening China and Russia relationship in promoting tourism industry for both countries.

包"罗"万象之俄罗斯

俄罗斯横跨欧亚大陆，北临北冰洋，东临太平洋、西临波罗的海，东部隔白令海峡与美国相望，是世界上面积最大的国家。冬季长而寒冷，夏季短而温暖。它的亚洲部分面积大于欧洲部分面积，但是它的欧洲部分集中了全国四分之三的人口。全国人口约1.46亿（2020年），俄罗斯族占77.7%，另外有鞑靼、乌克兰、巴什基尔等190多个少数民族。俄语是俄罗斯联邦全境内的官方语言，各共和国有权规定自己的国语，并在该共和国境内与俄语一起使用。主要宗教为东正教，其次为伊斯兰教。首都莫斯科一直是俄罗斯的政治中心，而莫斯科的城市规划如同它在俄罗斯的地位一样——以中心为原点向四周辐射——以克里姆林来为原点向外，一个环线包着又一个环线。克里姆林宫一直是俄罗斯各个时期国家首脑的办公场所。

俄罗斯历史悠久、地域广阔、文化深厚、风俗各异，绚丽的自然风光和众多的名胜古迹展示了它独具魅力的异国情调。在文学、绘画、音乐、舞蹈等文化艺术领域都有着极大的世界影响力。俄罗斯和中国是陆路边境线最长的邻国，中俄双边关系密切，经贸和文化交流频繁。

俄罗斯人偏爱旅游，对旅游体验的质量要求较高，有接近半数的俄罗斯人有海外旅游经历。边境贸易旅游是中俄旅游的起源，近年来，俄罗斯旅华市场从以购物为主逐渐向以观光和休闲旅游为主的方向发展，俄罗斯游客的旅游目的地也在从中俄边境地区向内陆和沿海延伸。2000年中俄双方签署了团队旅游互免签证协议。2012年在中国举办"俄罗斯旅游年"，2013年在俄罗斯举办"中国旅游年"，为推广旅游打下了良好的基础。相比其他主要客源市场，俄罗斯来华旅游同比增速更快，是我国第三大旅游客源国。

Russia Facts

- **Name**: Russian Federation
- **Capital**: Moscow
- **Government**: Semi-presidential Federation
- **Language**: Russian
- **Population**: 146 Million (2020)
- **Life Expectancy**: 70.5 Years (2019)
- **Currency**: RUB 100 ≈ CNY 8.82 (2021)
- **National Symbols**: Bear, the Double-headed Eagle, Camomile
- **National Day**: June 12 (Russia Day)

PART I   Let's Go

★ *First Glance*

Watch the video, and then answer the following questions.

1. Which place attracts you most in the video?

2. Can you describe the vastness of Russia in one sentence?

3. What is Russia famous for?

★ *Viewing and Listening*

Watch the video again and match the locations to the descriptions.

Locations:

Kazan	Moscow	St. Petersburg	Baikal	Dagestan	Altai

Descriptions:

(   ) 1. I'm in the middle of religious crossroads for more than 1,000 years.

(   ) 2. I'm the third romantic place in the world, the northern mega place of the earth.

(   ) 3. I'm the land of gastronomic impression, the land of emerald rivers, miles of breathtaking roads, and colorful mountains.

(   ) 4. I'm the dynamic cosmopolitan (国际都市). Everything starts here.

(   ) 5. I'm the energy booster, amazing lake of crystal blue eyes.

(   ) 6. I have more than 6,000 years of cultural and historical treasures hidden in ancient cities.

PART II   Explore the Land

· *Geography*

Russia, the largest country in the world, occupies one tenth of all the land on the earth. It spans 11 time zones across two continents (Europe and Asia) and has coasts on three oceans (the Atlantic, Pacific, and Arctic). The Russian landscape varies from desert to frozen coastline, tall mountains to giant marshes. Much of Russia is made up of rolling, treeless plains called steppes (大草原). Siberia (西伯利亚), which occupies three quarters of Russia, is dominated by sprawling pine forests called taigas (针叶林). Almost half of Russia is covered in forests. Russia has about 100,000 rivers, including some of the longest and most powerful in the world. It also has many lakes, including Europe's two largest: Ladoga and Onega. Lake Baikal in Siberia contains about 20% of the world's fresh water and is the deepest lake in the world.

· *People*

About 78% of the population lives in the European part of Russia which is less than 25% of the total territory. Russia ranks ninth in the world in terms of population. People prefer to live in cities and towns. Russia is a multiethnic country. The greater part (about 75%) of the population refers to Orthodoxy (东正教). There are at least 190 ethnic groups in Russia who speak more than a hundred languages. Roughly 80% of Russians trace their ancestry to the Slavs (斯拉夫人) who settled in the country 1,500 years ago. Other major groups include Tatars (鞑靼人), who came with the Mongol invaders and Ukrainians.

· *Language*

Russian is a Slavic language. The language is the eighth most spoken language in the world but is the second most dominant language on the Internet. Russian is one of the six working languages spoken at the United Nations. Most young people in Russia also learn to speak English, French or German in school.

The most common ways to greet someone in Russian are:

Доброе утро. Dobroye utro (Good afternoon).

Добрый вечер. Dobryy vecher (Good evening).

Спасибо вам большое. Spasibo bol'shoye (Thank you).

· *Attractions*

Moscow

The city is located on the Moskva River in the center of European Russia. Moscow became the capital when Ivan the Terrible proclaimed himself the first tsar in the 16th century. Peter the Great moved his capital to St. Petersburg in 1712, but after the Bolshevik Revolution of 1917, Moscow was made the capital of the Soviet Union and the seat of the new Soviet government, with its center in the Kremlin.

Moscow has many of Russia's most famous sights including Red Square and St. Basil's Cathedral. With over 800 years of history there is also a wealth of architecture, museums and monuments to a colorful past. Perhaps the most surprising of these is its extraordinary metro system. It is the official residence to the president of Russia and is of utmost diplomatic significance. Today the city is the country's political, economical, and financial center. More than 10 million people live in its metropolitan area.

St. Petersburg

Founded in 1703 by Tsar Peter the Great, St. Petersburg was once the imperial capital of Russia. This port city on the Baltic Sea is the second largest city in the country. It is home to the fabulous Hermitage Museum (冬宫博物馆) and the Winter Palace.

Hermitage Museum is a museum dedicated to art and culture. Including the largest collection of paintings in the world, there are more than 3 million artworks, items and artifacts in display. The museum is actually a complex of 6 historic buildings including the famous and fabulous winter palace and theater.

Lake Baikal

Lake Baikal in the region of Siberia (西伯利亚) is the greatest freshwater lake in the world. Formed some 25 million years ago, this is believed to be the oldest lake in the world and the 7th largest lake in the world. With a surface area of 31,722 square kilometers, Lake Baikal is home to nearly 1,700 species of plants and countless animals and birds. With a charming scenic environment, this is one of the top notch tourist attractions in Russia.

More than 2,000 years ago, the great patriot Suwu tended his sheep beside this lake when he was banished by the Xiongnu chief as a shepherd.

Valley of Geysers

As the name suggests, Valley of Geysers is place full of geysers (间歇泉), hot spring and other geothermal (地热的) activities. Located in Kamchatka Peninsula (堪察加半岛), it is the second largest concentration of geysers in the world. Discovered in 1941, this place of great scientific importance produces some fascinating smoky sights. Included as a World Heritage Site, it is a part of Kronotsky Nature Reserve and one of the top tourist attractions in Russia.

Sochi

Sochi (索契) on the Black Sea is a great winter sports destination and, in fact, hosted the 2014 Winter Olympics. Despite winter snow, Sochi offers a subtropical climate and great beaches, making it a key part of the Russian Riviera. The resort city makes a great summer (and winter) getaway for Russians.

Vladivostok

Mountains and bays surround Vladivostok (海参崴), making it a stunning beautiful city in Russia's east. The last stop on the Trans-Siberian Railway, Vladivostok is the country's largest port on the Pacific Ocean; it is just a hop, skip and a jump away from the Democratic People's Republic of Korea and China.

Kazan

Kazan is sometimes referred to as the Istanbul of the Volga (伏尔加) because it is a city where European and Asian cultures meet. Also known as the third capital of Russia, after Moscow and St. Petersburg, Kazan residents enjoy one of the highest standards of living in Russia. Sights to see include the remains of the Kazan Kremlin that was destroyed by Ivan the Terrible; the Kul-Sharif Mosque, named after a man killed defending Kazan from Ivan; and Bauman Street, a pedestrian shopping street.

• *Russian Food*

The Russian main dishes contain pork and beef, lamb, chicken, fish, potatoes and root vegetables as well as porridge and bread. Sour cream accompanies many dishes. Russian food is full of flavor and the Russian cuisine is as diverse as the regions in the huge country.

Vodka is a popular alcoholic drink traditionally made from the distillation of fermented potatoes. Beer and tea are also widely consumed.

Here are some typical Russian foods:

• **Borscht or Red Beet Soup** (罗宋汤): Soup made with red beets and vegetables that are cut into small pieces. This red soup is often served cold and is then blended with yoghurt or sour cream from which the soup gets its pink color.

• **Blinis** (薄饼): Thin Russian pancakes often served with savory or sweet fillings.

• **Pirozhki** (俄式馅饼): Fried dough pockets or mini pies that are stuffed with meats or savory fillings sometimes come with apple or other sweet fillings.

• **Caviar** (鱼子酱): Salted or cured roe (fish eggs) from the wild sturgeon or other fish. However, black caviar is a delicacy and a costly treat which is only served on special occasions or eaten in small amounts.

• Unique Russia

Ballet

Among Russia's most striking cultural features is its ballet. Ballet may have originated in Italy and France, but in the intervening centuries the Russian style of ballet may be the most famous. *The Nutcracker, Swan Lake*, and *The Sleeping Beauty* of Tchaikovsky's classics are among the world's most popular performances. The Bolshoi Theater is one of the most famous performance halls in the entire world. The dancers themselves even enjoy more fame than their counterparts elsewhere. At the height of the Soviet Union, ballerina Maya Plisetskaya was a cultural ambassador to the rest of the world.

Matrioshka Dolls

Russian nesting dolls are well-known symbols of the country. These sets of dolls, known as matrioshka dolls (俄罗斯套娃), consist of a wooden figure that can be pulled apart to reveal another smaller version of the same image inside, and so on, often with six or more dolls nested inside one another. The painting of each doll usually symbolizes a Russian peasant girl in traditional costume.

Bread and Salt

"Khleb-sol" (bread-and-salt) is the most famous symbols of Russian hospitality and the oldest cultural tradition of welcoming a visitor with a round loaf with a salt cellar on top. Bread and salt represent the giver's wish that the recipient's pantry will always be full. Bread symbolizes key aspects of the national self-image. Treating the guest with bread-and-salt establishes relations of love and trust among guests and hosts, whereas the refusal to taste bread-and-salt is regarded as an insult.

Samovar

Samovars (俄式茶炊) appeared in Russia in the second quarter of the 18th century and became an integral part of every Russian household, restaurant or hotel. It is a unifying symbol for people when they gather to have tea parties and provides the right atmosphere for friendly conversation. Though samovars first appeared in the Urals, the production of samovars blossomed in Tula, an old city to the south of Moscow, also famous for its armories and spice-cakes. Today Russians still use the samovar, but mostly as an attribute of exotics and nostalgia. They remain a symbol of family's warmth and coziness, cordial get-togethers and traditional festivities.

Russian Literature

Russian literature has a worldwide impact, with writers such as Leo Tolstoy (*Anna Karenina* and *War and Peace*) and Fyodor Dostoevsky (*Crime and Punishment* and *The Brothers Karamazov*) still being read around the world.

Task: Draw your mind-map on the "Russia in My Eyes" page based on the facts of Russia and then introduce Russia to your peers by using your mind-map.

★ 5C Reading on Russia

A. Read the following passage and learn about the Trans-Siberian Railway.

The Trans-Siberian Railway is just one part of the massive Russian railway network, transporting passengers and freight safely at affordable prices. It connects the European rail network at one end with either Vladivostok or the Chinese rail network at the other. Currently, there are two pairs of weekly international trains.

The K3/K4 trains (called 003/004 in Russia and Mongolia), connecting Beijing and Moscow via Mongolia, using Chinese coaches, and the K19/K20 trains (called 019/020 in Russia), running between Beijing and Moscow via Manchuria using Russian coaches.

Traveling along this railway may be time-consuming, which takes about 7 days to finish the whole journey, but the scenery on the way is very impressive. Passengers can appreciate different scenery from three countries, such as grassland, the Gobi Desert, Lake Baikal, and views of the Russian countryside. Every day, passengers will see different scenery through the windows. They can also taste Russian flavors by appreciating cities and villages, meeting and talking with all kinds of passengers, and buying unique local souvenirs.

The railway connected Russia's wild but resourceful Siberia and Far East area with the populated European part. It brought great profits for Russia. Cities and towns sprang up along two sides of the railway; Siberian population grew rapidly as well as Russia's economic trade; those who were interested in primitive natural scenery and original Russian flavors of Siberia can finally reach the land, making it a new tourism zone.

你知道西伯利亚大铁路对中俄交流的意义吗？

B. Discuss the following questions based on the above reading material.

1. Where does the Trans-Siberian Railway go?

2. What kind of scenery can passengers enjoy along the Trans-Siberian Railway?

3. Do you know why the international trains will be fitted with different wheels before entering or leaving China?

PART III Welcome Guests from the Land

★ Project—Dining Service

You've tailor-made a 3-day Chengdu tour for a small group of Russian tourists. They want to try hot pot. You will take them to Hai Di Lao, a chain of hot pot restaurants founded in Sichuan Province in 1994, specializing in Sichuan hot pot. Please discuss with your peers and decide how to introduce Sichuan hot pot to them at the restaurant.

Features of Sichuan Hot Pot

1. _____

2. _____

3. _____

Your Goals

1. Make the tourists enjoy hot pot.

2. Make the tourists know more about Chinese food culture.

• Tasks

A. Tell your partner the major features of Sichuan hot pot.

B. Prepare a 3-minute introduction of Sichuan hot pot.

The Magic Words or Sentences You Might Need for the Presentation

Words:

split pot (spicy and bland sides) (鸳鸯锅)   spicy pot (全辣锅底)   dip (涮，蘸)

authentic flavor (正宗的味道)   sesame sauce (芝麻酱)   ingredient (食材)

mild flavor (清淡的口味)   dipping sauce (味碟)   seasoning (调味品)

Sentences:

1. The hot pot has a long history of over 1,000 years in China.

2. Sichuan hot pot is famous for its numbing and spicy flavor.

3. Generally, there are two types of soup base: spicy and bland.

4. There are various ingredients used in hot pots. The meat can be... and the vegetarian ingredients favored by many are…

5. When the broth is boiling, you may dip (quickly-cooked) ingredients in until cooked with your chopsticks.

★ *The Land and the World*

Galina Kulikova—A Long-term Friend of China

Galina Kulikova, first deputy chairperson of the Russia-China Friendship Association, was honored the Friendship Medal in 2019 by President Xi Jinping.

The award has special significance in the year marking the 70th anniversary of the founding of the PRC and the establishment of Russia-China diplomatic ties, Kulikova told Xinhua in an interview.

"I developed an interest in China at school in fifth or sixth grade when I started reading a lot about China. When I graduated from high school, I said I would go to places where they studied China," she said.

Kulikova studied at the Moscow State Institute of International Relations and then participated in the founding of the Soviet (Russia)-China Friendship Association in 1957, where she has been working for 62 years. The association is considered a leader of public diplomacy in bilateral relations and it does a lot to expand the social base of bilateral cooperation.

Kulikova is active year round in people-to-people diplomacy between China and Russia, and has been involved in China's tremendous changes. She has been invited to witness the military parade at the Tian'anmen Square on October 1, joining the Chinese people in the celebration of the

70th anniversary of the PRC. She also attended such celebrations on the 40th, 50th and 60th founding anniversaries of the PRC.

"While I am alive, I will continue my beloved work. I have dedicated myself to this and will devote the rest of my life to it," said the 84-year-old sinologist.

Mind-map: Russia in My Eyes

Name: _____   Date: _____

KWL Chart

Topic: _____   Name: _____   Date: _____

Know	Wonder	Learned
What do you think you already know about Russia?	What do you wonder about Russia? Write your questions below.	Write what you've learned about Russia.

裁　切　线

Chapter 7　The Middle East and Africa

Section 1　Egypt

Learning Objectives

A flight with transfer to Cairo is 10 hours from Beijing, 25 hours from Tokyo, 7 hours from London and 15 hours from New York.

After this section, you will be able to:

★ know the geographical features and importance of Egypt.

★ understand the multi-cultural modern Egypt found on a long and complicated history.

★ list the major ancient monuments of Egypt.

★ apply Egyptian social norms, taboos and unique features to serving inbound Egyptian tourists, making them feel at home.

★ know the China-Egypt ties in a wide range of economic and social development, as well as the influence of the Belt and Road Initiative.

"极"往知来之埃及

　　阿拉伯埃及共和国，简称"埃及"；地跨亚、非两洲，包括非洲东北部地区和亚洲西南端的西奈半岛，北濒地中海，东临红海；是大西洋与印度洋之间的海上航行捷径，也是欧亚非三大洲的交通要冲。国土面积100.1万平方千米，尼罗河纵贯全境，境内多为沙漠、半沙漠区。这片广袤的沙海上生活着1亿人，另有约600万海外侨民。伊斯兰教为国教，信徒主要是逊尼派，占总人口的84%；科普特基督徒和其他信徒约占16%。首都开罗是阿拉伯国家联盟总部所在地；卢克索为世界著名的古城；亚历山大和塞得港都是重要的港口城市。官方语言是阿拉伯语。

　　埃及是世界四大文明古国之一，历史悠久，名胜众多。主要旅游景点有金字塔、狮身人面像、卢克索神庙、阿斯旺高坝、沙姆沙伊赫等。旅游业是埃及经济支柱产业之一，产值占其国内生产总值（GDP）的比重达到13%至15%。2018年，埃及旅游收入98亿美元；2019年，上涨到130亿美元；2020年，受新冠肺炎疫情影响，下跌至40亿美元。目前，埃及政府实行旅游业振兴战略。

　　中埃两国友谊源远流长。作为连接世界几大古文明的重要纽带，丝绸之路自古便成为中埃两国友谊的桥梁；作为陆上丝绸之路和海上丝绸之路的交汇点，埃及至今仍具备天然的战略重要性。近年来，中埃共建"一带一路"，两国文明互鉴、文化交流和人文合作日益频繁。越来越多的埃及游客不远万里来到中国，正是"国之交在于民相亲"的真实写照。

Egypt Facts

- **Name**: The Arab Republic of Egypt
- **Capital**: Cairo
- **Government**: Presidential Republic
- **Language**: Arabic
- **Population**: 100 Million (2021)
- **Currency**: EGP 100 ≈ CNY 41 (2021)
- **National Symbols**: Golden Eagle, White Lotus
- **National Day**: July 23

PART I Let's Go

★ *First Glance*

Watch the video about some important Egyptian cultural sites, and then answer the following questions.

1. What's your impression of the scenery in the video?

2. Could you name some of the landmarks in the video and try to introduce them?

3. What do you want to know about Egypt after you watch the video? Write your thoughts in the KWL chart.

★ *Searching and Matching*

Search on the Internet and then match the English with its corresponding Chinese version.

• The Great Temple of Abu Simbel	• 底比斯
• The Pyramid of Khufu	• 帝王谷
• Thebes	• 卢克索神庙
• The Valley of the Kings	• 阿布辛贝神庙
• The Temple of Luxor	• 阶梯金字塔
• The Great Temple of Amon	• 阿蒙神庙
• The Step Pyramid	• 胡夫金字塔

PART II   Explore the Land

• *Geography*

Mainly located in the northeastern corner of Africa, Egypt is a transcontinental country in North Africa and the Middle East. The country extends into Asia by virtue of holding the Sinai Peninsula (西奈半岛)—it forms a land bridge between the African and the Asian continents. Egypt shares borders with Israel, Gaza Strip (加沙地带), Sudan and Libya. It also borders the Mediterranean Sea in the north and the Red Sea in the east. The Suez Canal, a man-made waterway, connects the Mediterranean Sea to the Indian Ocean via the Red Sea. The canal provides a more direct route between Europe and Asia. As a result, the waterway is vital for international trade and has been at the center of conflict since it opened in 1869.

Egypt's climate is mainly hot and dry. Rainfall occurs in the winter months when even snowfalls can be expected on the mountainsides of the Sinai Peninsula. Most of Egypt's landscape is dominated by deserts. A few oases are dotting the desert. Egypt and Sudan are the easternmost countries of the Sahara Desert.

• *People*

Egypt is home to the largest population in the Arab countries. Almost all people in Egypt (99%) live in areas around the coast of the Mediterranean Sea and along the Nile River. This includes the cities of Cairo, Alexandria, Aswan, and Port Said. Not many people live in the desert. In Egypt most of the people are Egyptians. Smaller ethnic groups include Turks, Greeks and the Berbers (柏柏尔人).

Famous Egyptans are:

• Muhammad Anwar el-Sadat, Laureate of the Nobel Peace Prize (1918-1981).

• Boutros Boutros-Ghali, the 6th Secretary-General of the United Nations (1922-2016).

- Naguib Mahfouz, Laureate of the Nobel Prize in Literature (1911-2006).
- Ahmed Zewail, Laureate of the Nobel Prize in Chemistry (1946-2016).

• *Language*

Arabic is the official language in Egypt, but the majority speak a distinct Egyptian Arabic dialect. People often refer to Egypt as the country with the most Arabic speaking population in the world. Some Egyptians still speak Coptic (克普特语). Today the main foreign languages taught at school are English and French.

Here are some basic words and useful expressions for tourists:

نهارك سعيد / nuharik saeid. / (Hello.)

اعفوا! /عذرا/ efwaan / edhraan. / (Excuse me.)

وداعًا / wdaeaan. / (Goodbye.)

• *Attractions*

Cairo

The largest city in Egypt is home to many famous Egyptian landmarks including the Cairo Tower, the Citadel and the Egyptian Museum. In the 10th century, Cairo was the center of the Islamic world. Thus many Islamic buildings such as mosques, madrassas or hammams can be explored. The Sultan Hassan Mosque is an iconic landmark of Cairo.

Alexandira

The second largest city in Egypt is home to more than 5 million people. The city was founded by Alexander the Great in 331 BC. The lighthouse of Alexandria was one of the Seven Wonders of the Ancient World. This is also the location where once the Great Library, the largest library in ancient times was standing. The ancient Pompey's pillar and the sphinx are among the best known ancient monuments of Alexandria.

Valley of the Kings

The site is located near Luxor on the western side of the Nile River. This is the location of 64 tombs and chambers that were once cut in the rocks. There the noble families and pharaohs (法老) of the New Kingdom were buried. Among the most famous tombs are those of Pharaoh Tutankhamen and Pharaoh Ramses Ⅵ.

Pyramid of Khufu

The Pyramid of Khufu (胡夫金字塔), or the Great Pyramid of Giza, is the highest and largest of all the pyramids of Egypt. It was the tallest building in the world until the Eiffel Tower was built in Paris, in 1889. Inside the pyramid, famous man-made objects have been found from ancient times. Many valuable items were buried with the dead Pharaoh, in the hope that they would take them to the afterlife.

Pyramid of Khafra

The Pyramid of Khafra or Khafre (哈夫拉金字塔) is the second largest of the pyramids of Giza. The pyramid was built by limestone blocks and fragments of its original casing are still visible at the top. There are two chambers contained within the pyramid, along with two entrances that lead to the burial chamber.

Pyramid of Menkaure

The Menkaure Pyramid (门卡乌拉金字塔) is the third largest pyramid on the plateau of Giza. Much smaller than the tombs of Khufu and Khafra, it marks the end of the era of giant pyramids.

Mount Sinai

The locals call Mountain Sinai (西奈山) "Jabal Musa". This mountain on the Sinai Peninsula is considered to be the place where Moses is said to have received the Ten Commandments (十诫).

Wadi Al-Hitan

Wadi Al-Hitan, also known as "Whale Valley", is a Natural World Heritage Site. The fossils found in the valley are evidence of the evolution of whales, showing the transition from land animals to ocean animals.

Sharm El Sheik Beach

Sharm El Sheik (沙姆沙伊赫) on the Sinai Peninsula is one of the most popular tourist resorts of Egypt. The resort borders the Red Sea and is famous for its magnificent diving sites and stunning sandy beaches.

• *Egyptian Food*

Kunafa

Kunafa (卡纳法) is a popular dessert in Egypt. It is made with thin noodle-like pastry, soaked in sweet, sugar-based syrup. As this is a famous Ramadan (斋月) dessert, the pastry's stuffings and toppings have developed to such an extent that shops compete with one another for the best kunafa during this month. Today, there are mango kunafa, chocolate kunafa and even cheesecake kunafa.

Qatayef

Commonly served during the Ramadan, qatayef (卡塔耶夫) is a dessert of Fatimid (法蒂玛时代) origin. It looks a bit like dumpling and is stuffed with cream and nuts. It is fried in hot oil and soaked in syrup afterwards, which leaves the pastry a shiny golden color and crispy taste.

Rice

Due to its lush agricultural land along the banks of the Nile, Egypt has formed the most important rice market in the North Africa region. Rice is considered the country's second most important export crop after cotton. Egyptian rice is normally a short grain, has a fluffy texture when cooked. As one of major staples in Egypt, papular rice dishes are Koshary (可沙利), Fattah

(法塔赫), Mahshi (埃及包饭) and rice pudding.

Torshi

While technically not a dish on its own, torshi (埃及泡菜) deserves its own mention as a staple of Egypt's cuisine because it is served with almost everything. In Egypt, almost any kind of vegetable can be turned into torshi: cucumbers, cauliflowers, carrots, peppers…

· *Unique Egypt*

Sun Festival

According to ancient Egyptian mythology, the Sun God is considered the most important deity for the ancient Egyptians. Commemorated at the biggest temple of the ancient world at Abu Simbel, the Sun Festival is celebrated in February and October when the sun rays reach the innermost sanctums of the temple and only the statue dedicated to the god of darkness remains in the dark. This statue has never seen sunlight in over 3,200 years.

The Great Sphinx

The Great Sphinx (狮身人面像) is a monumental statue located on the Giza plateau, 400 meters southeast of the Pyramid of Khafra. It represents a resting lion with a human head. The body and head are cut directly into the rock of a limestone promontory; the front legs are masonry; and the whole was once covered with a kind of painted plaster.

Mummy

The ancient Egyptians mummified (制成木乃伊) both human beings and animals as they believed it would allow the dead to pass safely into the afterlife. Over four million mummies with the shape of a stork-like bird have been unearthed by scientists in Egypt's Western Desert.

Entertainment

Cairo has the oldest and largest film and music industries in the Arab world. Since 1976, the capital has held the annual Cairo International Film Festival. There is also another festival held in Alexandria. Of the more than 4,000 short and feature-length films made in MENA region (中东和北非地区) since 1908, more than three quarters were Egyptian films.

Aswan High Dam

Aswan High Dam (阿斯旺高坝) is one of the world's largest artificial water reservoirs with an earthen dam wall. Prior to the building of the dam, the Nile flooded the area regularly and provided sufficient water to the communities living along the Nile. Today climate change and raising water levels are major challenges to the country.

where it all begins

Task: Draw your mind-map on the "Egypt in My Eyes" page based on the facts of Egypt and then introduce Egypt to your peers by using your mind-map.

★ 5C Reading on Egypt

A. Read the following passage about cultural exchange between China and Egypt.

Egypt and China signed on September 8, 2020 a cooperation protocol to teach the Chinese language in pre-university schools in Egypt as a second optional foreign language. The protocol was signed by the Egyptian Minister of Education and Technical Education, Tarek Shawki, and the Chinese Ambassador to Cairo, Liao Liqiang.

"Egypt is keen to benefit from the unique Chinese experience in economic development as well as other fields", Shawki said during the signing ceremony. "Today's agreement represents an illuminating image of the distinguished and fruitful relations between the two friendly countries, which we always strive to strengthen and support by all means to achieve the desired goals." He added that Egyptian-Chinese ties are deeply rooted as Egypt was the first Arab and African country to establish diplomatic relations with China in 1956.

According to the Chinese Embassy in Cairo, there are two Confucius Institutes in Egypt, one in Cairo University, the other in Suez Canal University, in addition to three independent Confucius classrooms in Egypt. A total of 16 universities in Egypt have either established Chinese language departments or teach the Chinese language within their curriculums. In March 2019, China's Tianjin Light Industry Vocational Technical College, Tianjin Transportation Vocational College, and Egypt's Ain Shams University signed a Memorandum of Understanding (MoU) for the Egypt Luban Workshop in Cairo. Luban workshop is the first project of international cooperation on vocational training supported by China's Tianjin municipality, which aims at improving academic education of top technical talents and serving the local economy and society via vocational training.

As lands of ancient civilizations that have left a rich heritage to the world, China and Egypt are striving to develop strategic partnership to the next level. Cooperation in education is a sure way to facilitate people-to-people exchanges between the two countries, and pave the way for building a China-Egypt community with a shared future.

你能说说中文在埃及的影响吗？

B. Discuss the following questions based on the above reading material.

1. Do you know that Chinese language has been taught in Egypt before you read the article? Do an online search for information about Egyptian oversea students and their stories in China.

2. Discuss the integration of Chinese teaching into the Egyptian education system?

3. Will such cultural exchange eventually benefit tourism in both countries? And why?

PART III   Welcome Guests from the Land

★ *Project—Tourist Guidance at Museum*

You are a tour guide for a group of Egyptian tourists to Sanxingdui Museum. You're supposed to help them explore Chinese culture. In order to make the visitors enjoy themselves, you need to take Egyptian culture into consideration.

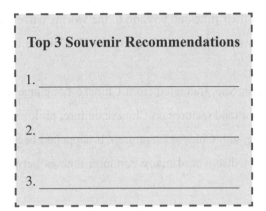

Top 3 Souvenir Recommendations

1. _____

2. _____

3. _____

· *Tasks*

A. *The guests want to buy souvenirs in the museum store after visiting. Discuss with partners and decide 3 things to recommend based on what you know about Egyptian people and culture.*

B. *Prepare a relevant tour commentary based on what you know about the museum.*

The Magic Words or Sentences You Might Need for the Presentation

Words:

ancient Shu culture (古蜀文明)   the Western Zhou Dynasty (西周)

bronze head with gold foil mask (金面铜人头像)   unearthed cultural relics (出土文物)

bronze mask with protruding eyes (铜纵目面具)   bronze standing statue (铜大立人像)

the bronze celestial tree (铜神树)   the Yangtze River Basin (长江流域)

bronze Fu (铜釜)   national treasure (国宝)   archaeology (考古)

the Bronze Age (青铜时代)   copper arts (青铜工艺)   bronze mask (铜面具)

jade tablet (玉璋)   jade dagger (玉戈)   ceramic figure (陶像)

Sentences:

1. The top 3 things / items that I want to recommend are…

2. … is located in… and originate from…

3. The Sanxingdui Museum, serving as… was built in…, and opened to the public in…

4. Sanxindui is recognized as… ancient sites because of…

5. … artifacts unearthed from… displayed in the Sanxingdui Museum show the achievements of… and supply important information about…

★ *The Land and the World*

Mai Ashour—Keen Observer of Chinese Culture

Sinologists are scholars who have long devoted their time and passion to the worlds woven by Chinese writers. They are the bridge between their own cultures and languages with Chinese ones, especially by the means of literature.

Mai Ashour is a young sinologist and translator. She graduated from Chinese Language and Literature Department, Cairo University. She used to attend lectures on Chinese culture, philosophy, history and literature, and subconsciously fell in love with Chinese literature. "It happened because it is very deep, unique and full of philosophy, and I discovered many common themes between China and Egypt," said Mai Ashour.

As a lover for Chinese literature, Mai Ashour translated a lot of Chinese short stories, poses and poems into Arabic and wrote a lot of articles about China and Chinese culture. She translated the book *Rang Hai Zi Ai Xue Xi* (*Make Study Enjoyable to Kids*) by Yang Xia right after her graduation. The book was published in 2012. In 2013, she decided to start translating literature as she felt it was about time to introduce a lot of Chinese literature, especially modern literature, to Arab readers, so she started translating Chinese short stories, poses and poems. Her translated works were published in different Arabic magazines, cultural newspapers and websites, reaching the largest number of Arab readers all over the world.

Mind-map: Egypt in My Eyes

Name: _____   Date: _____

KWL Chart

Topic: _____   Name: _____   Date: _____

Know	Wonder	Learned
What do you think you already know about Egypt?	What do you wonder about Egypt? Write your questions below.	Write what you've learned about Egypt.

Section 2   South Africa

A flight to Johannesburg is about 13 hours from Hong Kong, 18 hours from Tokyo, 12 hours from London and 17 hours from New York.

Learning Objectives

After this section, you will be able to:

★ know the geographical features and uniqueness of South Africa.

★ understand the vibrant culture in South Africa.

★ list the major attractions and landmarks in South Africa.

★ apply South African social norms, taboos and unique features to serving inbound South African tourists, making them feel at home.

★ understand the China-South Africa ties in various ways, such as the cooperation under the BRICS.

"非"比寻常之南非

南非共和国，简称"南非"，有"彩虹之国"之美誉，位于非洲大陆的最南端，陆地面积为122万平方千米。其东、南、西三面被印度洋和大西洋环抱，北邻纳米比亚、博茨瓦纳、津巴布韦、莫桑比克和斯威士兰，中部环抱莱索托，使其成为最大的国中国。西南端的好望角航线，历来是世界上最繁忙的海上通道之一，有"西方海上生命线"之称。东面隔印度洋和澳大利亚相望，西面隔大西洋和巴西、阿根廷相望。

南非全境大部分处于副热带高压带，属热带草原气候，气温比南半球同纬度其他国家相对低，年均温度一般在12~23℃。南非地处非洲高原的最南端，南、东、西三面之边缘地区为沿海低地，北面则有重山环抱。北部内陆区属喀拉哈里沙漠、多为灌丛草地或干旱沙漠、此区海拔650~1250米。周围的高地海拔则超过1200米。南非最高点为东部大陆崖的塔巴纳山，海拔3482米。南非旅游资源丰富，主要旅游景点有花园大道、法国小镇、太阳城、好望角、桌山等，南非也是户外探险的好去处，可以徒步、冲浪、鲨鱼潜水，可以去桌山徒手岩降，在原始森林高空滑翔，挑战世界最高的蹦极等。

根据文化和旅游部发布的《2019年旅游市场基本情况》数据显示，2019年入境旅游人数1.45亿人次，其中非洲占1.4%。南非作为非洲的第二大经济体，人均生活水平在非洲名列前茅，在整个非洲地区是中国重要的旅游客源国市场，具有巨大的旅游市场开发潜力。此外，南非工业体系是非洲最完善的，深井采矿技术位居世界前列，黄金、钻石生产量均占世界首位。中国和南非同为金砖国家成员，在金砖国家诸多领域合作中，旅游合作逐渐成为一大亮点。全球民宿预订平台爱彼迎（Airbnb）发布的金砖国家报告指出，2016年8月至2017年7月金砖国家之间互访的旅客人数同比增长134%。

South Africa Facts

• **Name**: Republic of South Africa
• **Capital**: Pretoria (administrative), Cape Town (legislative), Bloemfontein (judicial)
• **Government**: Multiparty Parliamentary Democracy
• **Languages**: 11 Official Languages (isiZulu, Afrikaans, Englis, etc.)
• **Population**: 59.62 Million (2020)
• **Life Expectancy**: 62.9 (2019)
• **Currency**: ZAR 100 ≈ CNY 44.37 (2021)
• **National Symbols**: Springbok, Protea
• **National Day**: April 27

PART I Let's Go

★ *First Glance*

Watch the video and then answer the following questions.

1. What's your impression about South Africa after watching the video?

2. What experiences or activities can you have in South Africa according to the video?

3. What is Cape Town famous for?

★ *Viewing and Listening*

Watch the video again and select the corresponding expression for each picture.

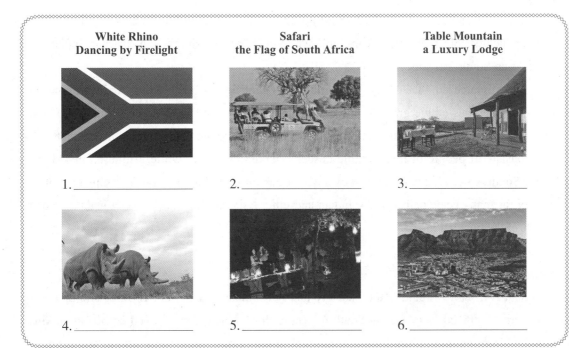

White Rhino
Dancing by Firelight

Safari
the Flag of South Africa

Table Mountain
a Luxury Lodge

1. _____

2. _____

3. _____

4. _____

5. _____

6. _____

PART II   Explore the Land

· *Geography*

South Africa occupies the most southern tip of Africa with a long coastline stretching more than 3,000 kilometers, which borders the Atlantic Ocean on the west and the Indian Ocean on the south and east. South Africa is bordered by Namibia to the northwest, Botswana and Zimbabwe to the north, Mozambique and Eswatini (斯瓦蒂尼) to the northeast and east. And Lesotho (莱索托), an independent country, is entirely surrounded by South African territory.

South Africa has more than 290 conservation parks. It is home to almost 300 mammal species, about 860 bird species and 8,000 plant species. The annual sardine run is the biggest migration on the planet. South Africa comprises eight World Heritage Sites and is divided into eight biomes.

· *People*

South Africa has quite a diverse group of people living within its borders. The ethnic makeup includes black South Africans, colored South Africans, white South Africans, Indian and other Asian South Africans.

An estimated 80.48% of the population self-identifies as black South African making it the most populous ethnic group in the country. The group itself is made up of many different indigenous African groups that speak Bantu languages. The colored ethnic group makes up 8.79% and consists of people of multi-ethnic descents including black, white, Chinese, and Malay. White South Africans account for just over 8% of the total population, but held complete political control for many years before 1994. Indian and other Asian South Africans only make up about 2.48% of the population.

· *Language*

South Africa is a multicultural society that is characterized by its rich linguistic diversity. There are 11 official languages in South Africa, each of which is guaranteed equal status. Most South Africans are multilingual and able to speak at least two or more of the official languages.

According to the survey of 2018, about 25.3% of the population spoke isiZulu at home and it is the most commonly spoken home language. English is only the home language for 1 out of 10 people living in South Africa. Even if English is not the first language for most people in South Africa, English is taught in most schools as first language and thus is understood and spoken by most people. English is used in offices, businesses, shops and as written language on street signs as well as in print magazines, newspapers and books.

Here are some useful expressions for tourists:

• Sawubona! Kunjani? (Hello. How are you?)

• Hoezit / Howzit? (How is it going? How are you?)

• Sharp. (OK.)

• Chow. (To eat.)

• *Attractions*

Kruger National Park

The Kruger National Park is world renowned for its spectacular wildlife. It is the largest nature reserve in South Africa and indeed one of the largest on the continent. The park boasts more species of mammals than any other African game reserve which includes the Big Five, cheetahs, giraffes and more. The density of wild animals found here is one of the highest on the planet, making for superb viewing opportunities no matter where the tourists are in the park. The southern and central regions of the Kruger are most frequented by visitors for the game viewing is most reliable here.

Unlike most other safari parks, Kruger is a self-drive destination with an excellent infrastructure and many places to stay inside the park, from tented camps to luxury lodges.

Table Mountain

With its peak reaching 1,086 meters above sea level, Table Mountain is so close to the sea and the city of Cape Town. It is the most iconic landmark of South Africa and the country's most photographed attraction. But it is much more than a scenic photograph background, or a place from where tourists can take a breathtaking photo of Cape Town for the mountain hides many surprises that wait to be discovered. There are about 2,200 species of plants found on Table Mountain and 1,470 floral species. Many of these plants and flowers are endemic to this mountain. The whole area has a biodiversity that is rare to find in other places on the earth. Therefore, Table Mountain was chosen as one of the new seven world wonders.

Durban Beaches

Tagged as one of South Africa's "Blue Flag" beaches, the Durban beaches are known for their individual charm and golden sandy shorelines. Here tourists can find beaches for windsurfing, long board surfing, diving, swimming, relaxing, or sunbathing. The water is warm and the weather is fine, which should make for an unforgettable holiday or getaway anytime of the year. The perfect time to visit is from December to February, when the beaches are also most ideal for sun-worshipers.

Victoria and Alfred Waterfront

The Victoria and Alfred Waterfront is an iconic mixed-use destination located in the oldest working harbor in the southern hemisphere. With Table Mountain as its backdrop, the Victoria and Alfred Waterfront sits within the beautiful city of Cape Town. It is a symbol of heritage and diversity, where people from all walks of life can play, live, shop, dine and work while immersed in the vibrant spirit and authentic local culture that exists in this bustling ecosystem.

Sun City Resort

Sun City Resort is known regionally as Africa's Kingdom of Pleasure. It is a luxury casino and resort, situated about two hours' drive from Johannesburg. The complex contains four hotels, two championship golf courses, two casinos, an atmospheric South African cultural village and more than 7,000 crocodiles within a sanctuary.

• *South African Food*

The food in South Africa is very diverse. The South African staple food for the locals is "mealies", which is corn, and seasonal vegetables, like potatoes, beans, carrots and peas.

South Africans love their meat and game meat such as kudu and springbok. However, most people eat beef, chicken, lamb and ostrich with their meals. The people in South Africa love a BBQ (here called "braai") and almost every house has got a fireplace which is called "braai-place".

Typical South African foods:

• **Bobotie**: Typical Cape Malay food containing rice, lamb and fragrant spices.

• **Koeksisters**: Taste like donuts (甜甜圈) soaked in sticky sweet sauce.

• **Mealie pap**: Corn porridge.

• **Biltong**: A cured and dried meat that is a typical South African snack and similar to beef jerky.

• **Boerewors**: Afrikaans for "farmers' sausage" which is often put on the grill, formed in a curl.

• *Unique South Africa*

National Arts Festival

The National Arts Festival is an important event on the South African cultural calendar, and the biggest annual celebration of the arts on the African continent. It has become the home for artists from different corners of the creative world, including dancers, musicians, painters, art lovers, etc. From theater to dance, opera to cabaret, fine art to craft art, classical music to jazz, poetry readings to lectures, every art form imaginable is represented in one of the most diverse festivals in the world. For 11 days every year from the last week of June to the first week of July, the eastern Cape Town of Grahamstown transforms from a sleepy haven of academics, students and entrepreneurs into the heart of South Africa's arts scene.

Seal Island

Located in False Bay just off the coast of Cape Town, Seal Island is swarmed with cape fur seals. The piles of seals use the island as their main breeding ground. Humans have tried to inhabit the island, but failed. However, the Great White Sharks also love the little island and at certain times of the year create a circle around it known as the Ring of Death. Any seal that swims too far is attacked by the sharks that actually leap from the water with the seals in their teeth before crashing down into the waves.

Afrikaans

Afrikaans is the youngest language in the world. By the early 20th century, it had developed from Dutch, French and other influences into a fully fledged language with its own dictionary. After a mere 90 years, Afrikaans is the second most spoken language and one of the 11 official languages of South Africa. There are about 7 million people speak Afrikaans in South Africa and Namibia, and around 23 million all over the world. It is said that Afrikaans is a very simple and easy language to learn.

Cape Town International Jazz Festival

The Cape Town International Jazz Festival is an annual music festival held in Cape Town. It started in 2000 as part of the North Sea Jazz Festival. From 2005 onwards, the festival was renamed to the Cape Town International Jazz Festival. Now it has developed to be the fourth largest jazz festival in the world and the largest jazz festival on the African continent. The festival was called the "Cape Town North Sea Jazz Festival" due to its association with the North Sea Jazz Festival in the Netherlands.

2010 FIFA World Cup

The 2010 FIFA World Cup was the 19th FIFA World Cup, the world championship for men's national association football teams. It took place in South Africa from June 11 to July 11, 2010. Actually, five African nations placed bids to host the 2010 World Cup: Egypt, Morocco, South Africa and a joint bid from Libya and Tunisia. In 2004, the international football federation, FIFA, selected South Africa over Egypt and Morocco to become the first African nation to host the finals.

Task: Draw your mind-map on the "South Africa in My Eyes" page based on the facts of South Africa and then introduce South Africa to your peers by using your mind-map.

★ 5C Reading on South Africa

A. Read the following passage and underline the parts related with China.

South African President Jacob Zuma says his country wants to join the informal group of major emerging economies that includes Brazil, Russia, India and China.

Speaking to reporters in Beijing Wednesday, Mr. Zuma said he has expressed a desire to be part of the group during visits to all four nations, which are collectively known as BRIC. The four nations have called for developing countries to play a bigger role in global financial institutions like the World Bank and International Monetary Fund.

Mr. Zuma is on a three-day visit to China aimed at increasing bilateral trade and investment. In a separate speech Wednesday, Mr. Zuma said South Africa aims to achieve annual economic growth of seven percent. He said the country hopes to reach that goal through heavy investments in electricity, education and transportation.

Mr. Zuma was accompanied to China by more than 200 South African business leaders, who are scheduled to meet with and sign deals with their Chinese counterparts. He met Tuesday with President Hu Jintao and was also scheduled to see other Chinese leaders including Premier Wen Jiabao during the visit.

Bilateral trade between South Africa and China topped $16 billion in 2009. However, South Africa recorded a $2.7 billion trade deficit with China last year, a gap Mr. Zuma said he will try to narrow. China has invested tens of billions of dollars across Africa over the past decade, as it seeks materials and markets for its growing economy.

为什么南非总统要带队访问中国？

B. Discuss the following questions based on the above reading material.

1. Why does South Africa want to join the informal group of major emerging economies?

2. What's the purpose of forming the BRIC countries?

3. How can South Africa and China cooperate within the framework of BRICS?

PART III Welcome Guests from the Land

★ *Project—Shopping*

You are the tour guide for a group of South African tourists who are interested in Chinese jade wares. Please discuss with your peers and prepare a brief introduction about Chinese jade. You need to take both Chinese and South African cultures into consideration.

> **Your Goals**
> 1. Make the tourists know more about Chinese jade culture.
> 2. Offer top quality services to the tourists.

- *Tasks*

   A. Match the English with the corresponding Chinese version.

• jade necklace	• 玉镯
• jade earring	• 玉坠
• jade ware	• 玉玺
• jade pendant	• 玉项链
• jade ring	• 玉戒指
• jade bracelet	• 玉耳环
• imperial jade seal	• 玉器

   B. Can you list some more items that South African tourists might like? List them in the following box and then discuss with your peers.

★ *The Land and the World*

Nelson Mandela—An Icon of Democracy and Social Justice

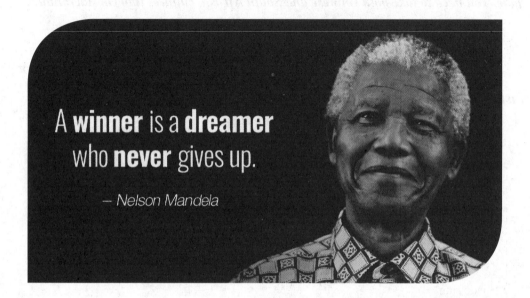

Nelson Mandela , in full Nelson Rolihlahla Mandela, byname Madiba, (born July 18, 1918, Mvezo, South Africa—died December 5, 2013, Johannesburg), black nationalist and the first black president of South Africa (1994-1999). His negotiations in the early 1990s with South African Pres. F.W. de Klerk helped end the country's apartheid system of racial segregation and ushered in a peaceful transition to majority rule. Mandela and de Klerk were jointly awarded the Nobel Prize for Peace in 1993 for their efforts.

The famous Chinese singer Huang Jiaju once composed a very popular song called *Glory Days*, which was a tribute to freedom and dedicated to Mandela, the spiritual leader of black human rights in South Africa.

Mind-map: South Africa in My Eyes

Name: _____   Date: _____

KWL Chart

Topic: _____   Name: _____   Date: _____

Know	Wonder	Learned
What do you think you already know about South Africa?	What do you wonder about South Africa? Write your questions below.	Write what you've learned about South Africa.

Section 3   The UAE

Learning Objectives

A direct flight to Abu Dhabi is 7 hours from Chengdu, 8 hours from London, 14.5 hours from New York, and 6 hours from Bangkok.

After this section, you will be able to:

★ know the geographical and demographical features of the UAE.

★ list the typical landmarks and attractions in the UAE.

★ apply the social norms, taboos and unique features to serving inbound tourists from the UAE, making them feel at home.

★ know the influence of Chinese technologies, commodities and services on the life of the people in the UAE.

浮想"联"翩之阿联酋

　　阿拉伯联合酋长国（简称"阿联酋"）位于阿拉伯半岛东部，有"沙漠珍珠""海湾之畔的沙漠之花""骑在骆驼背上的民族"等称号。由阿布扎比、迪拜、沙迦、富查伊拉、阿治曼、哈伊马角和乌姆盖万7个酋长国组成，国土总面积8.36万平方千米。人口约950万（2019年）。居民大多信奉伊斯兰教，多数属逊尼派。阿拉伯语为官方语言，通用英语。阿布扎比既是阿联酋首都，也是阿布扎比酋长国首府。

　　阿联酋石油资源非常丰富，石油储备量居世界第七，但经历了几次石油危机后，开始实施经济发展多元化战略，发展旅游业是重中之重。为吸引游客，阿联酋不惜斥巨资打造了多个号称"世界第一"的现代城市旅游景观。比如，坐落在首都阿布扎比耗资30亿美元修建的酋长皇宫酒店是世界上造价最高的酒店，享有"八星级酒店"的美誉。世界第一高楼——迪拜哈利法塔耗资100亿美元。世界第一大人工岛——迪拜棕榈岛被誉为"世界第八大奇迹"。把现代与传统完美结合的阿联酋每年都吸引无数来自世界各地的富商名流和观光客们。

　　中国与阿联酋自1984年建交以来，两国友好合作关系发展顺利。近年来，两国高层互访和各级别往来不断，在国际和地区事务中相互支持。2018年，中阿实施互免签证政策，阿联酋来华游客人数增长快速。2019年阿联酋来华人数为1.18万人次，同比增长22.3%。2020年7月16日，由中国文化和旅游部与阿联酋经济部共同主办的中国—阿联酋旅游合作论坛以视频连线方式成功举办。论坛提出中阿都需要对彼此的客源市场做更为深入而系统的研究，加强数字化建设和当代科技的应用，让游客有更高的获得感和满意度。

UAE Facts

- **Name**: The United Arab Emirates
- **Capital**: Abu Dhabi
- **Languages**: Arabic, English
- **Population**: 9.50 Million (2019)
- **Currency**: AED 100 ≈ CNY 177.02 (2021)
- **Government**: Federation of Monarchies
- **National Anthem**: Ishy Bilady (Long Live My Nation)
- **National Symbol**: Golden Falcon
- **National Day**: December 2

PART I Let's Go

★ *First Glance*

Watch the video on MOOC, and then answer the following questions.

1. Can you use three words or phrases to describe your impressions of the UAE after watching the video? Please give your reasons.
2. What do you want to know more about the UAE after learning the online course? Write your thoughts in the KWL chart.

★ *Viewing and Speaking*

Watch the video again. Match the names with the corresponding pictures below and then describe each picture briefly.

| **Burj Khalifa Tower** **Sheikh Zayed Grand Mosque** | **Ferrari World Abu Dhabi** **Burj Al Arab** | **Palm Jumeirah** **the Louvre Abu Dhabi** |

1._____

2._____

3._____

4._____

5._____

6._____

PART II   Explore the Land

· *Geography*

The UAE is a small, mostly desert-like country which covers 83,600 square kilometers. It borders the Persian Gulf to the north, Saudi Arabia to the south and west, and Oman to the east. The country has mountains in the eastern part and a dry desert with rolling sand-dunes in the center. The main cities and urban centers are located mainly along its coasts. It does not have a freshwater lake, but there are several oases in the emirate of Abu Dhabi. Its temperatures can easily reach more than 40℃ in summer. Natural hazards include sand storms, dust storms and haze.

· *People*

The UAE has a population of about 9.99 million people, including foreigners. The male population is twice as large as the female. Most people in the UAE (85%) live in the three largest emirates Abu Dhabi, Dubai and Sharjah (沙迦). People of many different cultures and backgrounds have found their new home in the UAE. Only about 12% of all people in the UAE are Emirati. The majority of the people living here are foreigners and expatriates, i.e. people from around the world who come to the UAE for work. Indians are the largest foreign group, followed by foreigners from Pakistan and Bangladesh (孟加拉国). 76% of Emiratis are Muslims and follow Islam which is not only the largest religion, but also the state religion in the UAE. However, the government is tolerant towards people practicing other faiths although it strongly resists the spreading of other religions.

· *Language*

Arabic is the predominant language in the UAE. Arabic is one of the oldest, greatest and sacred languages in the world. The Arabic alphabet has 28 letters and is written from right to left. There are 18 distinct letter shapes, which vary slightly depending on whether they are connected to another letter before or after them. There are no capital letters. The full alphabet of 28 letters is created by placing various combinations of dots above or below some of these shapes.

The most common ways to greet someone in the UAE are:

واهلان أهلا Ahlan wa sahlan / Ahlan (Hello).

الخير صباح Sabah al khayr (Good morning).

الخير ميسى Misa al khayr (Good evening).

• *Attractions*

Abu Dhabi

Oil-rich Abu Dhabi, the UAE's capital, is positioning itself as a culture and leisure hub.

Cultural Capital

Opened on November 11, 2017, the Louvre Abu Dhabi (阿布扎比卢浮宫) is the first universal museum in the Arab world. Designed by French architect Jean Nouvel, its layout resembles an Arab medina, and the dome casts an enchanting "rain of light" inspired by the shadows of overlapping palm trees in the UAE's oases. The museum brings the Louvre name to Abu Dhabi and presents both ancient and contemporary works of historic, cultural, and sociological interest from around the world.

Islamic Architecture

Built in honor of the UAE's founder Sheikh Zayed bin Sultan Al Nahyan, Sheikh Zayed Grand Mosque (谢赫扎耶德清真寺) is a true reflection of Arabian splendor. With the capacity for an astonishing 40,000 worshippers, it is the largest mosque in the UAE and the third largest in the world. 82 domes and more than 1,000 columns decorate the structure, and reflective pools amplify its beauty. As the sun sets, a unique lighting system reflecting the phases of the moon transforms the mosque's white and gold colors.

Exciting Recreation Center

Covering over 83,613 square meters, Ferrari World (法拉利世界) is the largest indoor theme park in the world, shaped like a massive three-pointed star when viewed from above, with a 65-meter Ferrari's yellow prancing horse logo on the curved red roof. Inside the theme park, visitors have the opportunity to visit an operating Ferrari factory, drive a real Ferrari, and wander through a gallery of 70 years of Ferrari models. The "Bell Italia" trip takes visitors on a Ferrari ride through a mini-diorama of the Italian marvels, including Venice, the Roman Colosseum (罗马斗兽场), the Amalfi Coast (阿玛尔菲海岸), and Ferrari's hometown of Maranello (马拉内罗). Meanwhile, the park is also home to the world's tallest and fastest roller coaster.

Dubai

Once a small fishing village, Dubai is today one of the most international cities in the world. Dubai offers a truly memorable experience to all visitors. Whether it is by the banks of the Creek, or at the top of the highest building, Dubai breathes a sense of possibility and innovation. And with an unparalleled coastline, beautiful desert and magnificent cityscapes, memories are just waiting to be made here.

Ambitions & Innovations

It's hard not to admire Dubai for its untiring verve, ambition and ability to dream up and realize projects. This is an ultimate-pursuit society that has birthed high buildings and palm-shaped islands. Sci-fi concepts such as flying taxis, a lightning-fast hyper-loop (超级高铁) train and an army of robot cops (机器人战警) are all reflections of a mindset that fearlessly embraces the future.

Shopping Paradise

The Dubai Mall is the world's largest destination for shopping, entertainment and leisure. Featuring over 1,200 retail stores, two major department stores and hundreds of food and beverage outlets, the Dubai Mall covers more than 1 million square meters—an area equivalent to 200 football pitches. It is also the ultimate family entertainment destination with the Dubai Aquariumand Underwater Zoo, the Olympic-sized Dubai Ice Rink, children's 'edutainment' concept Kidzania and a massive indoor cinema complex—just some of the ways to keep everyone busy.

Desert Safari

A desert safari is one of the best ways to experience Emirati culture. From quad biking over sand dunes to camping under the stars to taking a sunrise hot air balloon tour, guests may experience life as a Bedouin (贝都因人). All-terrain vehicles carry passengers out into the dunes for sand boarding, camel treks, picnics, balloon rides, and starlit barbecues without any other signs of human habitation in sight.

Sharjah

While Dubai is all about flashy tall buildings and shop-till-you-drop malls, neighboring Sharjah concentrates on culture and history. It is home to some of the best museums and art galleries in the country: the restored Sharjah Heritage Area and the amazing Mleiha Archaeological Site (考古遗址). This emirate is doing more than anywhere else in the UAE to preserve its heritage and becomes Capital of Islamic Culture.

• *Arabic Food*

In the UAE, rice, fish and lamb or chicken meat are considered the main staple food. Pork is not permitted for Muslims so it is not commonly found or eaten. Spices such as cardamon, coriander, caraway seeds, cloves, saffron and cinnamon give the Middle Eastern dishes a distinctive taste.

Popular dishes in the UAE:

• **Machboos** (大锅饭): Lunch dish made with slow cooked lamb or chicken, rice, dried lemon and spices.

• **Kabab** (烤肉串): Skewers of chicken or goat meat, marinated and grilled and served with rice or flatbread.

• **Baba Ganoush** (茄子蘸酱): Mashed grilled eggplants with garlic, lemon juice and sesame paste, usually eaten with flat bread.

264

• **Fareed** (乱炖): Typically made during Ramadan, this meat and vegetable stew is usually cooked with potatoes, marrows, carrots, lamb or chicken.

• **Lukaimat** (点心): Deep-fried light dough balls which are served with date syrup.

• *Unique UAE*

Burj Kahlifa Tower

Soaring 828 meters into the sky, the Burj Khalifa (哈利法塔) is the tallest building in the world, twice the height of New York's Empire State Building and three times as tall as the Eiffel Tower in Paris. Completed in 2010, the mighty tower represents the beating heart of Dubai and its brave ambitions.

Burj Al Arab

The distinctive sail-shaped silhouette (剪影) of Burj Al Arab Jumeirah is more than just a stunning hotel, it is a symbol of modern Dubai. Rising on a man-made island, 280 meters from the shores of the renowned Jumeirah beach and designed to resemble the graceful sail of an Arabian dhow, it soars to a height of 321 metres, dominating Dubai's coastline.

Palm Jumeirah

Billed as the Eighth Wonder of the World, Palm Jumeirah (棕榈岛) is Dubai's most amazing offshore destination due to its unique palm tree-inspired form, consisting of a trunk with 17 fronds all crowned by a circular crescent. Located off the coastal area of Jumeirah beach, it is part of the three Palm Islands—Palm Jebel Ali and Palm Deira.

Abu Dhabi Falcon Hospital

The Abu Dhabi Falcon Hospital (阿布扎比猎鹰医院) is the world's first and largest hospital dedicated to the falcon, the UAE's national bird. Since opening its doors in 1999, the unique hospital sees about 6,000 birds each year, occupying 200 air-conditioned treatment rooms. Falcons and falconry have been connected to Emirati culture for centuries, with this bird of prey playing a vital part in Bedouins' lives, with falcons hunting bustards, curlews and other animals for food.

Al Sadu

Al Sadu (萨杜) is a traditional technique of weaving the hair of camels and the wool of goats and sheep into fabric for blankets, carpets, pillows, tents and the decoration of camel saddles and belts. It represents one of the most valuable economic contributions that women made to their society and was placed in 2011 on the UNESCO List of Intangible Cultural Heritage in Need of Urgent Safeguarding.

Task: Draw your mind-map on "The UAE in My Eyes" page based on the facts of the UAE and then introduce the UAE to your peers by using your mind-map.

★ *5C Reading on the UAE*

A. Read the following news about the injection of Chinese-developed COVID-19 vaccines by world leaders.

World Leaders Receive COVID-19 Vaccine Shots Developed by China

On November 3, 2020, Prime Minister and Vice-President of the UAE and ruler of Dubai Sheikh Mohammed bin Rashid Al Maktoum tweeted a picture of him receiving a shot of a COVID-19 vaccine.

The UAE announced on December 9, 2020, the official registration of a COVID-19 vaccine developed by the China National Pharmaceutical Group, or Sinopharm, the official WAM news agency reported.

The UAE became the first country to offer Chinese-developed COVID-19 vaccines to all citizens and residents for free, on December 23. The trials in UAE shows the Chinese vaccine provides 86 percent efficacy against COVID-19 infection.

The vaccine was granted Emergency Use Authorization in September by the health ministry to protect frontline workers most at risk of COVID-19.

The phase Ⅲ trials in the UAE have included 31,000 volunteers from 125 countries and regions.

你还能说说中阿互信体现在哪些方面吗?

B. Discuss the following questions based on the above news.

1. What do you think of the injection of Chinese-developed COVID-19 vaccines by world leaders?

2. Why did the UAE offer Chinese-developed COVID-19 vaccines to its citizens and residents for free?

3. Could you use several words to describe the relationships between China and the UAE?

PART III　Welcome Guests from the Land

★ Project—A Farewell Speech

You are a tour guide for a business tour group from the UAE. You are going to see off your guests at the airport and you need to make an informal farewell speech to them. Please discuss with your peers, write down the farewell speech and show your speech to your peers. Also, you need to take the UAE culture into consideration.

A Farewell Speech

_____

_____

_____

_____

_____

_____

The Sentences You Might Need for Your Preparation

Sentences:

1. Your visit to our... city of... has come to a close.

2. It has been a great pleasure for me to have served as your local guide.

3. I'd like to say thanks for your cooperation which has made my job a lot easier.

4. I'm glad you have enjoyed your stay here.

5. I hope to offer you better service when you visit next time.

6. I look forward to meeting you again soon in the future.

★ *The Land and the World*

Sun Jiansheng Builds Green Path on the Belt and Road

Sun Jiansheng came to the UAE in 2007 and started his business from a small supermarket. After years of hard work, the business of the supermarket has been extended into e-commerce, food imports and exports. Although getting a foothold in the local business sector, Sun still felt unsatisfied. Later, he found an opportunity in vegetable growing. The local cuisine of the UAE mainly consists of barbecued and fried dishes, with a very limited choice of vegetables. The imported vegetables are very expensive and not very fresh. Sun decided in 2012 to invest heavily to build an organic vegetable farm in the Nazwa Desert. The climate is hot and dry and growing vegetables in the desert requires large investment and is very difficult.

When Sun Jiansheng began building his farm, he upheld the green concept of environment-friendliness, fine cultivation and sustainable development. In order to grow fruits and vegetables not suitable for hot climate, Sun got a special license from the Dubai government to dig six deep wells with an average depth of over 100 meters, to draw underground water for irrigation. The drip irrigation technology has guaranteed every drop of water would be used to its maximum effect. He also set up transformers to draw electricity to construct water-cooling greenhouses with carefully controlled temperature, which is economical and energy saving. The dung of cows and camels in local livestock farms was also utilized as fertilizers.

After years of hard work, Sun's farm has a total area of 87,000 square meters, with 20 water-cooling greenhouses, and more than 100 square meters of storehouses that keep the produce fresh. Every day, the green farm produces several tons of more than 30 kinds of vegetables and fruits, which are sold to supermarkets as well as canteens of Chinese companies in the UAE.

Mind-map: The UAE in My Eyes

Name: _____   Date: _____

KWL Chart

Topic: _____   Name: _____   Date: _____

Know What do you think you already know about the UAE?	**Wonder** What do you wonder about the UAE? Write your questions below.	**Learned** Write what you've learned about the UAE.

参考文献

［1］李光耀.李光耀观天下［M］.北京：北京大学出版社，2017.

［2］李志勇.客源国概论［M］.成都：四川大学出版社，2020.

［3］藤布尔 C M.崛起之路：新加坡史［M］.欧阳敏,译.3版.上海：东方出版中心，2020.

［4］唐玲萍.旅游客源国概况［M］.昆明：云南大学出版社，2012.

［5］王佩良.主要旅游客源国概况［M］.北京：高等教育出版社，2017.

［6］王兴斌.中国旅游客源国概况［M］.北京：旅游教育出版社，2020.

［7］Butler S. New Zealand［M］∥王守仁，仲伟和.体验世界文化之旅阅读文库.北京：高等教育出版社，2017.

［8］Saunders G. Indonesia［M］∥王守仁，仲伟和.体验世界文化之旅阅读文库.北京：高等教育出版社，2017.

后　记

既然名为"后记"，那么就应该是本书使用完毕才看到的吧。

同学们，你们是否在这本书的带领下，看到了不一样的世界，感受到了世界和中国的联系以及文化因多样而交流，因交流而互鉴，因互鉴而发展，悟到了旅游是架起不同文化之间沟通交流的桥梁呢？我们真诚地希望你们能从国家内容（Content）知识入手，分析文化（Culture）异同，认识到不同文化因交流（Communication）而互鉴发展，对待不同的文化需要有思辨能力（Critical Thinking），在思辨过程中树立对中国道路、理论、制度、文化的自信（Confidence），特别是最基础最广泛最深厚的文化自信，并将这种自信内化为行为，展现到今后的工作中去。

各位同仁，感谢您选择本书。编写团队在参加四川省职业院校教师教学能力比赛获得一等奖的基础上，借鉴其他同类优秀教材的长处，同时邀请专家研讨论证，并经多次商榷形成了本书的编写思路，参与编写的人员均付出了艰辛的努力，同时校企合作企业提供了大量专业任务设计真实案例。我们希望这本书能够在您的教学中发挥更大作用，助力您的职业发展，同时也请您把在使用过程中的宝贵意见反馈给我们，以便我们进一步改进和提升。

本书中部分语言素材和图片来源于国内外图书、报纸杂志、广播电视和网站等，由于无法确认并联系到著作权人，未能一一注明出处，如有侵权，恳请相关作者看到后与我们联系。

《客源国概况》编写团队